Tra

7/98

the Lewis
& Clark Trail

by

Julie Fanselow

"The best pure travel guide to the route."

--USA Today

"The information about the primary historic sites and trail segments appears to me to be very accurate and useful. To my knowledge, there is no other publication which provides such a comprehensive list of lodging, camping and dining facilities. In my opinion, this is one of the best, certainly one of the most practical, guide books to the Lewis and Clark Trail."

--Richard Williams, Coordinator
National Park Service
Lewis and Clark National
Historic Trail

FALCON®

HELENA, MONTANA

To the memories of:
Meriwether Lewis (1774-1809)
William Clark (1770-1838)
and Ruth Fanselow (1925-1987)

Falcon® is continually expanding its list of recreational guidebooks. All books include detailed descriptions, accurate maps, and all the information necessary for enjoyable trips. You can order extra copies of this book and get information and prices for other Falcon books by writing to Falcon Publishing, Inc., P.O. Box 1718, Helena, MT 59624 or calling our toll-free number, 1-800-582-2665. Also, please ask for a free copy of our current catalog listing all Falcon books.

Falcon® Publishing, Inc.
P.O. Box 1718, Helena, MT 59624

Text pages printed on recycled paper.

CONTENTS

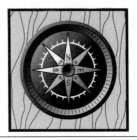

ACKNOWLEDGMENTS

I spent the better part of 1993 researching and writing *Traveling the Lewis & Clark Trail*. Soon after I started, I realized I could have easily made this book a lifetime project—a heady and somewhat terrifying thought when faced with a deadline. So I relied heavily on the knowledge of others who have made Lewis and Clark their passion, along with people who know intimately the regions described in this guide. Among them: Chan Biggs, Victor Bjornberg, Butch Bouvier, Larry Cook, Bonnie Cook, Bob Doerk, George Harbaugh, Robin Harbaugh, Lynn Hoffman, Terry Korpela, Craig Madsen, Chuck Mead, Mark Selvik, Bob Singer, Kathy Warnock, Jane Schmoyer Weber, Wilbur Werner, Mark Wetmore, and Richard Williams. Dozens of other people at local museums, historical sites, visitor centers, and travel bureaus also provided valuable information. Thanks to you all.

Here in Idaho, I have dear friends and colleagues who have given me the personal and professional support to pursue my free-lance career. I'd particularly like to thank Pat and Jerry Marcantonio, Helen Anderson, Karen Fothergill, Bobbi Hall, Drew DeSilver, Trudy Young (and everyone at The Monthly), and Sam and Kelly Yost. Thanks also go to everyone at Falcon Press who had faith that this series of historical trail guides would work, and to my editors, Randall Green and Will Harmon.

Thanks to my father, Byron Fanselow; my brother, Jeff Fanselow; my father- and mother-in-law, Ray and Carrol Whiting; and all my other relatives for their love, encouragement, and support. Finally, thanks to Bruce Whiting...husband, friend, steadying influence, and co-author of my next enterprise. I couldn't have done it without you, Bruce.

PREFACE

These days, travelers think little of crossing a continent in a matter of hours. But less than 200 years ago, a small group of Americans undertook a journey so complex and so potentially dangerous that their president and benefactor, Thomas Jefferson, and their fellow citizens half expected they would never return. In less capable hands, the mission surely would have failed. But Meriwether Lewis and William Clark had the intelligence, the bravery, and the generous spirit to see it through.

The trip was the Lewis and Clark Expedition of 1804-1806, and it ranks among the world's greatest journeys of discovery. This guidebook aims to help travelers—both actual and armchair—relive the expedition's excitement and drama. In these pages, you will find details about the major historic sites all along the Lewis and Clark Trail, along with information on modern recreational and scenic attractions and visitor amenities along the way. In short, this is a guide for people who want to retrace Lewis and Clark's route while finding some adventures of their own.

It's true we can whip across our nation in mere hours or days. But these are journeys of expedience, not experience. Today, we must give ourselves the luxury of taking time to linger and learn, even dawdle and drift.

Few artifacts of the Lewis and Clark journey remain, and in many areas, interpretation is minimal. A trip along the trail today is very much a journey of imagination. But there are many places visitors can well imagine what it was like to be Lewis and Clark, and this book aims to guide you to the best of those places.

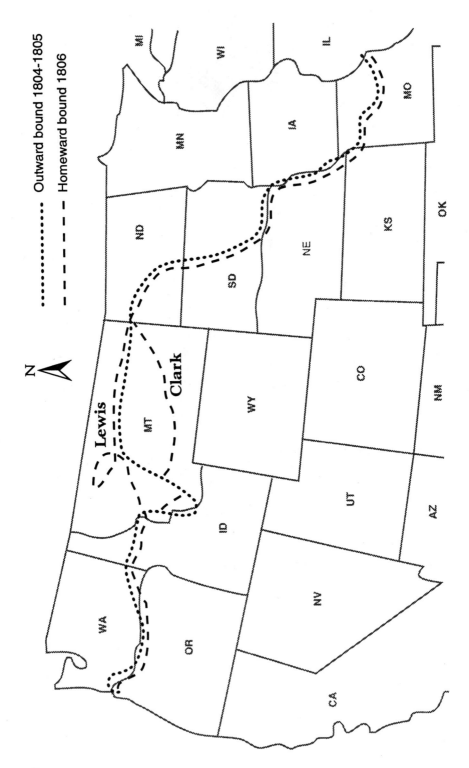

CHAPTER ONE

THE CORPS OF DISCOVERY: A BRIEF HISTORY AND OVERVIEW

From his youth, Thomas Jefferson was fascinated with the West. Not so much the West as he understood it, for even as president he never traveled far from his Virginia home, but the West as he imagined it: a land of mystery and revelation, a land where the United States could stretch its boundaries and grow into a pre-eminent world power.

In his inaugural address of 1801, Jefferson described America as "kindly separated by nature and a wide ocean from the exterminating havoc of one quarter of the globe, possessing a chosen country with room enough for our descendants to the thousandth and thousandth generation." With these blessings, he asked, "what more is necessary to make us a happy and prosperous people?" Yet Jefferson expected it would take the passing of a full forty generations just to explore the whole of the United States. Remarkably, it took only four years to chart a large measure of the territory.

For years, Europeans and Americans believed that by following the Missouri River to its headwaters, they would discover a Northwest Passage to the Pacific Ocean. French, British, and Spanish explorers had long tried to prove this theory, and when the United States was born in 1776, the contest for domination of the Western frontier became a four-way race.

The power struggle continued for another quarter-century, with the young American nation siding first with one European power, then another. Ultimately, France's desire to limit English influence in North America made possible the U.S. acquisition of the Northwest via the Louisiana Purchase. For $15 million—less than four cents an acre—the United States bought more than 800,000 square miles of land.

The Louisiana Purchase had an incalculable effect on the future of the United States. With its boundaries set by the Missouri and Missis-

Keelboat replicas.

sippi river drainages, the deal doubled the country's area, giving the young nation access to a wealth of valuable natural resources. Assessing the agreement's impact, noted historian Bernard DeVoto wrote: "There is no aspect of national life, no part of our social and political structure, and no subsequent event in the course of our history that it has not affected." And what a bargain it proved to be: even by the time the interest was paid, the Louisiana Purchase cost America a total of just $23 million.

The Louisiana Purchase is often viewed as the event that precipitated the Lewis and Clark Expedition, but plans for the trek were already well under way by the time the deal was signed. In fact, Jefferson had long wished for an expedition and started laying groundwork for the mission in the fall of 1802. At that time, he asked the Spanish minister, the Marques de Casa Yrujo, whether Spain would object if the United States sent a small party to explore the Missouri River to seek the Northwest Passage. (Spain was to transfer the land in question to France under an 1800 treaty, but the move hadn't yet taken place.) Yrujo wrote back that he saw no need for the exploration since the European powers had already sought and disproved the notion of a Northwest Passage. Yrujo also warned Jefferson that Spanish authorities would be notified if he proceeded with the idea.

Undaunted, Jefferson sent a secret message to Congress in January 1803. He asked for an appropriation of $2,500 for an expedition to seek the source of the Missouri River and, upon finding it, follow the best course westward to the Pacific Ocean, "for the purpose of extending the external commerce of the United States."

Jefferson had hired Meriwether Lewis as his private secretary, at least in part with an eye to the possible expedition. As DeVoto wrote in his edition of the Lewis and Clark journals, "Lewis was a family friend, but Jefferson had many friends better qualified by background and education to be secretary to the President. He was however, uniquely qualified for a project which Jefferson had cherished for many years, the exploration of the Missouri River and the lands west of its source." In his letter offering employment to Lewis, Jefferson wrote, "Your knowledge of the Western country, of the army and all its interests and relations have rendered it desirable for public as well as private purposes that you should be engaged in that office."

Lewis was born August 18, 1774, just a few miles from Jefferson's home in Virginia, the second of three children of plantation owners William and Lucy Meriwether Lewis. His father died when Meriwether was just five years old. Lucy soon married again, and the family moved to Georgia. Early on, Meriwether showed great intellect, but much moodiness, too.

By age thirteen, Meriwether was sent back to Virginia to continue his education and learn how to run the plantation, which was still in his family. After his stepfather, John Marks, died in the early 1790s, young

Bronze relief depicting signing of the Louisiana Purchase, Missouri State Capitol grounds, Jefferson City.

Meriwether traveled to Georgia to bring the rest of his family back to Virginia. Soon after, he joined the Army. He had served six years and risen to the rank of captain by the time Jefferson sought his help in Washington, D.C. Lewis, just twenty-six years old when he received the job offer of secretary in March 1801, readily agreed. A year and a half later, he was working at Jefferson's behest to draw up plans for the Western expedition.

Congress approved the appropriation in February 1803. Secretary of War Henry Dearborn officially authorized the mission in July 1803. Preparations for the journey went into high gear as Lewis gathered supplies and ordered a keelboat built. He traveled to Philadelphia for a crash course in all kinds of scientific disciplines. He learned from Andrew Ellicott how to take celestial observations. Dr. Benjamin Rush, along with helping plan the expedition's scientific and cultural goals, instructed Lewis in rudimentary medicine.

Originally, Lewis was to select a second-in-command from the party's ranks after the expedition had gotten under way. But as preparations progressed, Jefferson and Lewis—aware of the trip's significance—decided it might be best to select Lewis' right-hand man before the journey started. The man they chose was William Clark, under whose command Lewis had served seven years earlier.

Clark was born August 1, 1770, in Virginia, the younger brother of George Rogers Clark (who became a hero in the Revolutionary War). William followed in his family's military footsteps, and by 1795 was put in command of an elite company of riflemen at Fort Greenville, Ohio. It was there he met Meriwether Lewis, and the men quickly became friends. William soon left the Army to take care of his older brother, George Rogers, who was battling alcoholism and debt in Indiana. But he and Lewis stayed in touch by mail and visits.

On June 19, 1803, Lewis wrote to Clark, told him of the mission, and said, "If therefore there is anything...in this enterprise, which would induce you to participate with me in its fatigues, its dangers, and its honors, believe me there is no man on earth with whom I should feel equal pleasure in sharing them with as yourself." He further noted that Jefferson would promise Clark—who had resigned as a lieutenant—a full captain's commission and all the attendant benefits. "Your situation will in all respects be precisely such as my own," Lewis concluded.

Weeks went by with no word from Clark. Jefferson and Lewis prepared to ask Lt. Moses Hooke, their second choice, if he would accept the role. But Clark's reply finally came on July 29. "My friend I do assure you no man lives with whom I would prefer to undertake such a trip as yourself," Clark wrote to Lewis, thus ending any thoughts of what history might have come to call the "Lewis and Hooke Expedition."

The co-leaders set about the task of choosing the men to accompany them. In Lewis' words, they looked for "good hunters, stout, healthy, unmarried, accustomed to the woods and capable of bearing bodily fatigue in a pretty considerable degree." Some members of the expedition were recruited for special skills they possessed: Lewis wanted Patrick Gass along as a carpenter and boatbuilder, for example. Gass had grown up in western Pennsylvania and into manhood with the young nation, ever moving west with the frontier, and he turned out to be one of the most interesting members of the expedition.

George Drouillard was selected as an interpreter and hunter, and the importance of his latter task couldn't be underestimated: It took four deer and an elk or one deer and a buffalo to feed the entire group for twenty-four hours. John Shields, a relative of Daniel Boone, hired on as gunsmith, and Clark later wrote: "The party owes much to the ingenuity of this man by whom their guns are repaired when they get out of order, which is very often."

One recruit had no say in the matter. Ben York, a Clark family slave, had been William Clark's constant companion since early childhood and there was no question he would accompany Clark on the trip west. York became the first black man to join a military expedition, cross the Continental Divide, and reach the Pacific Ocean. He was a large, strong, and good-natured man. The Indians considered York "great medicine," and would travel long distances to see and touch him.

The recruits sensed they were embarking on a journey of great importance. On April 8, 1804, John Ordway wrote: "Honored parents: I am now on an expedition to the westward with Captain Lewis and Captain Clark to the western ocean. This party consists of twenty-five picked men, and I am so happy as to be one of them." Even Seaman, Lewis' Newfoundland dog, proved a valuable member of the expedition. He retrieved game and, with his barking, alerted the party to the presence of grizzly bears and buffalo.

Many of us spend untold hours agonizing over what belongings to take on a two-week vacation, so it is hard to imagine what it might be like trying to pack for a trip of undetermined length. The food alone weighed seven tons. Other items selected included a blacksmith's forge, mill for grinding corn, carpenters' tools and axes, surveying and navigational instruments, medical supplies, cooking utensils, an iron boat frame, fifty-two lead canisters weighing 420 pounds for sealing 175 pounds of gunpowder, six kegs—or thirty gallons—of brandy, and canvas for tarpaulins.

Congress' $2,500 appropriation purchased the following: mathematical instruments, $217; provisions, $224; materials for portable packs, $55; pay for hunters, guides, and interpreters, $300; pay for members' moving expenses, $100; weapons, $81; camp equipment, $255; medical supplies, $55; boats, $430; and $87 for contingencies. The largest single budget item, $696, paid for Indian presents. That amount purchased

47.5 yards of red flannel, 12 dozen pocket mirrors, 73 bunches of beads, 2,800 fishhooks, and 4,600 needles.

Even back then, the federal government had a tough time living within its means. Although only $2,500 was originally allocated, the corps carried a letter of credit from Jefferson, and actual expenditures wound up totaling about $38,000. Still, few people would dispute the investment was worth it. Aside from strengthening American claims to the West, the expedition had an immeasurable impact on scientific, anthropological, and geographic knowledge.

The Corps of Discovery--a nickname given to the expedition by Jefferson--finally left Camp Wood, Illinois, on May 14, 1804. The men returned on September 23, 1806, two years, four months, and ten days after they had departed. In the interim, they lived one of the greatest examples of exploration and cooperation the United States—or the world, for that matter—has ever seen...a trip we shall examine in much greater detail as we follow the corps' progress west.

Stepping back in time with a visit to the Lewis and Clark Center at St. Charles, Missouri.

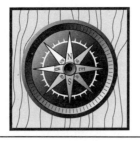

CHAPTER TWO

HOW TO USE THIS BOOK

By the time its travels were completed, the Lewis and Clark Expedition had logged more than 7,500 miles paddling, hiking, and riding across the continent and back.

Obviously, it would be difficult to duplicate such a journey today. But it is possible to take a great two-week Western vacation focusing on the Lewis and Clark Trail. What's more, the historical aspects of a Lewis and Clark vacation can easily be combined with your favorite leisure activities, be they camping, boating, sightseeing, fishing, golf, hiking, or just plain taking it easy.

SUGGESTED TRIP

The following is a suggested Lewis and Clark trip designed to fit within a two-week vacation period:

Day One: The St. Louis/St. Charles Area, Missouri. Start the tour with a visit to the **Lewis and Clark State Memorial** on the banks of the Mississippi River in Illinois (just off Illinois Highway 3 south of Alton). Next, visit the **Museum of Westward Expansion and Gateway Arch**; **William Clark's grave** in St. Louis' Bellefontaine Cemetery; and the **Lewis and Clark Center** in St. Charles. Overnight in St. Charles.

Approximate driving time/distance: Not applicable; all sites in St. Louis metropolitan area.

Day Two: St. Charles, to Kansas City, Missouri. Drive west along the Missouri River. Possible stops include the Daniel Boone Home; the German-style town of Hermann; **Jefferson City**, where a relief on the Capitol Grounds depicts the signing of the Louisiana Purchase; **Arrow Rock**; and **Fort Osage**, a trading post Clark helped build after the expedition. Missouri highways 94 and 100 parallel the river from St. Charles to Jefferson City. From there, follow U.S. Highway 63 to Columbia; Interstate 70 to Boonville; Missouri 41 through Arrow Rock to

Marshall; and US 65 and US 24 to Fort Osage and the Kansas City area. Overnight in Kansas City.

Approximate driving time/distance: six hours, 275 miles.

Day Three: Kansas City, Missouri, to Sioux City, Iowa. Visit **Lewis and Clark State Park** (northwest of Kansas City on Missouri 45) and nearby **Atchison, Kansas**, where the expedition spent July 4, 1804. Travel north on I-29 to **Meriwether Lewis Museum of Missouri River History** at Brownville, Nebraska (along US 136), then follow US 136 and US 75 to the **Omaha/Council Bluffs** area. Cross the river and have lunch at the Council Bluffs **river overlook** commemorating Lewis and Clark. Return to US 75 and visit **Fort Atkinson State Park** (Nebraska). Take either US 75 or I-29 to Onawa, Iowa, where a replica of the Corps of Discovery's keelboat is on display at Iowa's **Lewis and Clark State Park**. Continue north to Sioux City and see the **Sergeant Floyd Monument**. Overnight in Sioux City.

Approximate driving time/distance: seven hours, 340 miles.

Day Four: Sioux City, Iowa, to Pierre, South Dakota. Take I-29 north to Vermillion, South Dakota, and visit **Spirit Mound**. (Mound may be seen from South Dakota 19; ask permission to hike to its top.) Next, visit the **Gavins Point Dam Visitor Center** west of Yankton, South Dakota. Have lunch in one of the many nearby park areas. Take South Dakota 46 and South Dakota 50 to Platte, then South Dakota 45 to I-90. Follow the interstate to Chamberlain, then take South Dakota 50 and 34 north and west to Pierre. Visit **Farm Island State Recreation Area** and the **Teton Council Site**. Overnight in Pierre.

Approximate driving time/distance: seven hours, 325 miles.

Day Five: Pierre, South Dakota, to Bismarck/Mandan, North Dakota. Drive north to Mobridge on US 83 and US 12. Visit the **Sacagawea and Sitting Bull monuments** west of town, and continue north on South Dakota 1806, which changes to North Dakota 24 at the border. Follow North Dakota 24 and 6 north to **Fort Abraham Lincoln State Park** and visit its On-A-Slant Indian Village. If time permits, take a cruise on the Lewis and Clark riverboat. Overnight in Bismarck or Mandan.

Approximate driving time/distance: 4.5 hours, 225 miles.

Day Six: Bismarck/Mandan, North Dakota, to Williston, North Dakota. Take US 83 north to Washburn. Visit the **North Dakota Lewis and Clark Interpretive Center and Fort Mandan** replica, then take North Dakota 200 to the **Knife River Indian Village National Historic Site**. North Dakota 200 loops back to US 83. Drive north to North Dakota 37. Follow North Dakota 37 and 1804 north of **Lake Sakakawea**, stopping for a picnic lunch at one of the parks en route. Overnight at Williston.

Approximate driving time/distance: 5.5 hours, 260 miles.

Day Seven: Williston, North Dakota, to Fort Benton, Montana. Start the day with a visit to the **Missouri-Yellowstone confluence** and nearby **Fort Union National Historic Site**. Take US 2 across northern Montana to Havre then follow US 87 south to **Fort Benton**. (Consider breaking the trip for one to three days here for a riverboat ride down the **Wild and Scenic Missouri River**, the stretch of waterway most like that seen by Lewis and Clark.) Explore Fort Benton's riverfront. Overnight in Fort Benton or Great Falls.

Approximate driving time/distance: Seven hours, 385 miles (to Fort Benton); 420 miles (to Great Falls).

Day Eight: Fort Benton, Montana, to Dillon, Montana. Take US 87 from Fort Benton to Great Falls. Visit the **Great Falls of the Missouri** and the Lewis and Clark National Historic Trail Interpretive Center. Drive south on I-15 to Exit 209, and take the **Gates of the Mountains** boat tour. If time permits, visit the Montana Historical Society in Helena, then drive southeast on US 287 to Three Forks and **Missouri Headwaters State Park**. From Three Forks, take Montana 2, 55, and 41 to Dillon, watching for **Beaverhead Rock** en route. Overnight in Dillon.

Approximate driving time/distance: Five hours, 250 miles (from Great Falls).

Day Nine: Dillon, Montana, to Missoula, Montana. Visit Clark Canyon Dam and the **Camp Fortunate Overlook** southwest of Dillon. Continue on over **Lemhi Pass**, following the directions given in Chapter Seven. (This road may not be suitable for large RVs or vehicles; check locally for current road conditions.) Pick up Idaho 28 at Tendoy, Idaho, and continue north to Salmon. Follow US 93 over **Lost Trail Pass** and down to **Ross' Hole** and the Bitterroot Valley. Stop in Lolo, site of **Traveler's Rest**. Overnight in Missoula.

Approximate driving time/distance: Five hours, 200 miles.

Day Ten: Missoula, Montana, to Lewiston, Idaho. Retrace US 93 south to Lolo and take US 12 west to Lewiston, Idaho, allowing plenty of time for the 108-mile stretch between Lolo Pass and Kamiah, Idaho. Possible stops include the **Lolo Pass Visitor Center**, Powell Ranger Station (the site of **"Colt Killed Creek"**) and the rugged **Lolo Motorway**, which traces the Lewis and Clark route much more closely than US 12. (See directions in Chapter Seven and inquire locally for road conditions.) If time permits, also visit the Nez Perce National Historic Park sites at Kamiah, Weippe, Orofino, and Spalding. Overnight in Lewiston.

Approximate driving time/distance: Five hours, 225 miles (Allow more time for exploration of the Lolo Motorway).

Day Eleven: Lewiston, Idaho, to The Dalles, Oregon. Drive west of Lewiston/Clarkston on US 12, stopping briefly at the **Lewis and Clark Trail State Park** near Dayton. Pick up Washington 124 at Waitsburg, and continue west to **Sacajawea State Park** near Pasco. Reconnect with US 12 and follow it to US 730 across the Oregon border. Visit **Hat Rock**, named by Captain Clark. From Umatilla, Oregon, take either Washington 14 or I-84 (via I-82) west to The Dalles, Oregon, gateway to the Columbia Gorge. Overnight in The Dalles.

Approximate driving time/distance: 5.5 hours, 270 miles.

Day Twelve: The Dalles, Oregon, to the Pacific Ocean. Cross the Columbia River and continue west on Washington 14. Stop at **Beacon Rock**, named by the expedition. Hike to the top or drive to the state park lookout/picnic area. Other activities might include a visit to Bonneville Dam or the Lewis and Clark cruise on the Sternwheeler *Columbia Gorge* at Cascade Locks. From the Portland/Vancouver area, proceed west to the ocean via one of the routes described in Chapter Eight. (US 26 from Portland is fastest.) Overnight on the coast.

Approximate driving time/distance: 3.5 hours, 180 miles (using US 26 to coast).

Day Thirteen: On the Pacific Coast, Oregon/Washington. Visit **Fort Canby State Park** and its Lewis and Clark Interpretive Center on Washington's Cape Disappointment. Return to Oregon and visit **Fort Clatsop National Memorial**, the **Salt Works**, and **Ecola State Park**.

Approximate driving time/distance: About 35 miles; sites all located on the Pacific Coast.

This thirteen-day trip is tailored to fit into a two-week vacation, which, including weekends, typically encompasses sixteen days. But most people will need to factor in several travel days at each end of the trip to drive from home to St. Louis, and from Astoria back home. Add a few more days to your vacation, if possible, or see a part of the trail this time, saving the remainder for another year. Another option might be flying to St. Louis, renting a vehicle, driving the trail to Oregon, and flying home from there.

Several shorter variations on this trip are possible. Some travelers may want to focus their explorations on the heart of the Lewis and Clark Trail, including sites from the first winter camp at Fort Mandan (in what is now North Dakota) to the Bitterroot Mountain crossing on the Montana/Idaho border. Such a journey is roughly outlined in Days Five through Ten above, but explorations along this part of the route could easily be expanded to fill two or more weeks.

Others may want to look more closely at Montana, the state with more miles of Lewis and Clark Trail than any other. The separate, homeward routes taken by the co-captains on their way east in 1806 are both well worth exploring. A side trip northwest from Great Falls (described in Chapter Seven) traces Lewis' trek to Camp Disappointment and the Two Medicine Fight Site, an area within easy reach of Glacier National Park. Meanwhile, Clark's eastward route wound through the Big Hole basin of western Montana, past the old camp at Three Forks, and on down the Yellowstone River, closely paralleling I-90. A major landmark along the way, Pompey's Pillar, is the only place along the trail where actual physical evidence of the expedition's visit remains to this day.

WHEN TO GO

Much of the Lewis and Clark Trail lies in the High Plains and mountains of the West, where weather is typically unpredictable and often extreme. The best period for travel is probably mid-July through mid-September. Fortunately, the trail has plenty of indoor interpretive centers and attractions to help travelers pass the time should inclement weather strike.

Modern explorers may want to plan their trip to coincide with one of the annual Lewis and Clark festivals held along the trail. St. Charles, Missouri, stages an annual Lewis and Clark encampment the third weekend of May. Lewis and Clark State Park near Onawa, Iowa, holds its event the second weekend each June. Great Falls, Montana, celebrates its Lewis and Clark heritage later in June, and Cut Bank, Montana, holds its Lewis and Clark Days festival toward the end of each July.

Gavins Point Visitor Center on Lewis and Clark Lake, Nebraska.

HOW TO TRAVEL

There are two schools of thought on how to drive across America. Some folks like to take the major, limited-access highways and get where they are going as fast and as soon as possible. Others prefer the scenery and slower pace of secondary roads.

After thousands of miles spent researching American historic trails, I've come to the conclusion that it's best to mix secondary roads and major highways. I take secondary highways and backroads most of the time, but every once in a while—when I get tired of dodging farm machinery and watching for dogs and children by the roadside, or if I need to make a little time, having dawdled a little too long—I get on an interstate.

But remember: the joy of discovery most often comes far from the interstates and large cities, and that is what a modern-day journey along the Lewis and Clark Trail is all about. You won't see many chic boutiques, trendy restaurants, or tourist traps along this route. What you will find is land, water, wind, mountains—and people who stubbornly find ways to live where life isn't too easy.

Of the 7,500 miles traveled by Lewis and Clark, nearly 6,000 miles were traveled on water. For that reason, modern explorers should attempt to include at least one (and preferably more) river trips on their own journey. Many scheduled boat rides—such as those at Bismarck, North Dakota; the Gates of the Mountains near Helena, Montana; and the sternwheeler *Columbia Gorge* at Cascade Locks, Washington—last just a few hours and are easily worked into most travel itineraries. Others, notably excursions on Montana's Wild and Scenic Missouri River, require at least a full day and can take up to a week. However much time you can give to river exploration will be time well spent.

In many cases, two or more roads parallel the waterways followed by Lewis and Clark. When planning a trip, write in advance to the state transportation departments and request free highway maps and state visitors guides (see addresses near the end of this chapter.) Use a highlighter pen and, with the help of this book and the visitors guides, map out the route that looks most interesting.

Most of the areas described in this book are easily accessible with any passenger car or truck in good working condition. In a few locations, however, it is wise to inquire locally before setting out. Roads can be closed part of the year, and some roads, notably Lemhi Pass and the Lolo Motorway, are not suitable for RVs or vehicles towing large trailers. It's also smart to outfit your vehicle with the following: dashboard compass, working odometer, full-size spare tire and jack, gasoline can, shovel, axe, and a basic emergency kit including flashers. Once on the road, pay attention to the gas gauge: It's a long way between filling stations in many parts of the West.

WHERE TO STAY; WHAT TO EAT

The Lewis and Clark Trail primarily runs through small-town and rural America. Lodging options are limited along a few stretches, so it pays to do some advance planning. The trip outlined above recommends overnight stops in places where motels and campgrounds are fairly plentiful.

Because of its distance from urban America, a Lewis and Clark Trail vacation is quite affordable. Larger cities along the route typically offer a mixture of chain motels and mom-and-pop inns. Smaller towns usually have at least one locally owned motel. These can be a great bargain, often less than thirty dollars a night for a double. Reservations are a good idea in some areas, especially the Oregon/Washington coast and Montana's larger towns. In general, however, finding a room before 6 p.m. or 7 p.m. shouldn't pose much trouble.

Consider camping along at least part of the trail. Aside from being economical, camping affords a better taste of what it was like for the Corps of Discovery—after all, Lewis and Clark and company sure didn't have their choice of motels in 1804. Camping options range from RV parks to primitive, pick-your-own sites in the national forests. You might even choose to sleep in a tepee or fire lookout.

Quite a few small towns along the Lewis and Clark route have municipal parks that offer free or very low-cost camping to tourists passing through. Many are well posted at the entrances to town. As much as possible, I've noted the presence of these parks throughout the text of this book.

Travelers can save money by packing a cooler full of sandwiches, drinks, and snacks. But part of the fun of traveling is eating in restaurants at least once in a while. When the time comes, consider sampling some regional cuisine: catfish in Missouri, buffalo burgers on the Great Plains, huckleberry pie in western Montana and Idaho, and seafood in the Northwest.

Each of the travel chapters ends with a list of lodging options, campgrounds, and restaurants for areas along the trail. The chapters and the listings follow Lewis and Clark's route generally from east to west (with a few variations for the homeward bound trips). In most cases, establishments mentioned are simply representative of those available in each town; listing in this book does not imply endorsement of any kind. Hotel, motel, and bed-and-breakfast rates listed are generally for double occupancy during the summer travel season and were accurate as of 1993.

More complete lists of hotels, motels, campgrounds, and restaurants are available from state and local tourism bureaus, many of which have toll-free phone numbers for information. State tourism offices are listed later in this chapter, and many local offices are noted throughout the book.

WHAT TO PACK

Bearing in mind that Western weather can be unpredictable and fast-changing, even in mid-summer, it's best to be prepared with a variety of clothing. On hot days, lightweight, light-colored clothing will be most comfortable. But pack a sweater, jacket, and rain gear for when the weather turns cold or wet. Sneakers or walking shoes are best for touring historic sites, but toss in a pair of lightweight hiking boots and sport sandals. Casual clothing is appropriate everywhere along the trail. Don't forget a swimsuit, sun block, and wide-brimmed hat.

Campers should make sure their gear is waterproof and able to stand up to high winds. A ground cloth and extra tent stakes are good ideas. Other camp essentials include a simple tool kit with a hammer, axe, and pocket knife; a reliable camp stove and fuel (wood campfires are prohibited in some locations); cooking and eating utensils; a can opener; insect repellent; a bucket for hauling water and washing dishes; biodegradable dish soap; rope (for clothesline and other uses); first-aid and snake-bit kits; a camp lantern and flashlight; matches; trash bags (along with separate space for recyclables); and a bag for dirty laundry.

Travelers hoping to preserve their trip in pictures should include a wide-angle lens and polarizing filter for the high, wide horizons and beautiful skies. Binoculars might come in handy, as will books and travel games. And don't forget a good atlas or state highway maps—the maps in this book are general and should always be used in conjunction with a more detailed local highway map.

TRAVELING WITH KIDS

To children, all of life is an adventure, with new discoveries made every day. Seen from this perspective, a trip along the Lewis and Clark Trail makes an ideal family vacation. It's interesting, educational, informal, and can easily be combined with a more traditional Western vacation, say, to Yellowstone National Park or the Oregon coast. Moreover, it is an economical vacation choice, since most historic sites are free or cheap, and since nearly all of Lewis and Clark's route lies far from expensive big cities and traditional tourist attractions.

Still, it's always a challenge to keep kids happy and occupied. Here are a few ideas on how to do it. Have them keep a journal like Lewis and Clark did, describing their trip in words and pictures. (Journaling is a great way to develop writing skills, and this is a grand time to start.) Plan a Lewis and Clark scavenger hunt, making a list of items the kids can look for along the way. Such "treasures" might include a keelboat, dugout canoe, Indian earth lodge, river, animals, and statues of Lewis, Clark, Sacagawea, York, and Lewis' dog, Seaman. You might want to provide an inexpensive camera so your child can take photos as the discoveries are made.

If you're camping, consider packing along a separate tent for the children (if they're old enough). Most kids love having a tent of their own, and it will give the grown-ups some rest and privacy, too. Kids also enjoy having a bit of their own money to spend on vacation. Help them learn financial responsibility and decision-making by giving each child a special trip allowance. Make sure they know this money should cover any souvenirs or extras they want to buy, and that it should last the whole trip.

WHAT TO READ

Many travelers will want to read more about Lewis and Clark before, during, or after tracing the captains' route of discovery. For maximum enjoyment, get a copy of the Lewis and Clark journals and read along with what the voyagers found as they crossed the continent. The complete journals are published in several multi-volume editions (with Gary E. Moulton of the University of Nebraska the editor of the most recent, definitive set), but a one-volume abridgement will suit the vacation traveler's purposes just fine. Many people believe Bernard DeVoto's American Heritage Library edition is the best.

One of my favorite books about Lewis and Clark is Dayton Duncan's *Out West: An American Journey*. I first read this wonderful book upon its publication in 1987, and it accompanied me on my own explorations of the route while researching this guidebook. Duncan traced the explorers' route on his own in a camper van. In clean and thoughtful prose, his book weaves history with modern-day observations about life in the western United States. It is a gem.

Other books that might be of interest include *Undaunted Courage* by Stephen Ambrose; *Lewis and Clark: Historic Places Associated with Their Transcontinental Exploration*, compiled by Roy E. Appleman and recently reprinted by the Lewis and Clark Trail Heritage Foundation and the Jefferson National Expansion Historical Association; Gerald Olmsted's *Fielding's Lewis & Clark Trail*; *The Way to the Western Sea*, by David Lavender; *Lewis & Clark: Pioneering Naturalists*, by Paul Cutright; *Lewis and Clark: Partners in Discovery*, by John Bakeless; and *Lewis and Clark: Voyage of Discovery*, by Dan Murphy and David Muench.

There are many others. In fact, don't be surprised if, during the course of your Lewis and Clark explorations, you find yourself wanting to read everything you can about the captains and the expedition. "Once you get interested, you become a buff, and there's constant controversy about why they did this, how they did this, what did that look like, what were they wearing," says Butch Bouvier, a Lewis and Clark aficionado from western Iowa. "It's constant. It's exciting."

Finally, there are a wealth of other good travel guides about the regions covered in this book. Among those I would recommend are *Mon-*

tana Handbook, by W.C. McRae and Judy Jewell; *Idaho Handbook*, by Don Root; *Idaho for the Hungry*, by Jenna Gaston; *Trail of the Great Bear*, by Bruce Weide; and *Oregon Handbook*, by Stuart Warren and Ted Long Ishikawa.

TENDING THE TRAIL

The Lewis and Clark National Historic Trail is one of eleven routes so designated by the federal government. It was established in 1978 and spans 3,700 miles. The trail is administered by the National Park Service in cooperation with many federal, state, and local agencies; the Lewis and Clark Trail Heritage Foundation Inc. and other private organizations; and private landowners along the route. Together, they work to preserve and interpret sites of historical significance and areas where the trail can still be retraced.

The National Park Service has published a brochure showing its designated water, land, and motor route segments. The map also lists and briefly describes key historic and recreational sites along the way. Copies may be obtained at many locations along the trail by writing the National Park Service, 700 Rayovac Drive, Suite 100, Madison, WI 53711; or by calling (608) 264-5610.

People interested in learning more about the Corps of Discovery may want to join the Lewis and Clark Trail Heritage Foundation. This not-for-profit organization formed in 1969 to continue the work started by the Lewis and Clark Trail Commission, which Congress established in 1964. The organization holds an annual convention each August, and participants take part in a variety of activities including field trips and seminars. The foundation publishes *We Proceeded On*, a scholarly yet entertaining quarterly journal dedicated to the Lewis and Clark expedition and related topics. Many foundation members also take part in local and state chapter activities. For information, write the Lewis and Clark Trail Heritage Foundation, P.O. Box 3434, Great Falls, MT 59403. You can also access the foundation's website at http://www.lewisand clark.org

Both the National Park Service and the Trail Foundation seek to encourage and assist public and private interests to identify, preserve, and interpret sites important to the Lewis and Clark expedition. Information is available from the Park Service office in Madison.

STATE TOURISM OFFICES

Illinois Bureau of Tourism
State of Illinois Center
100 West Randolph St.
Chicago, IL 60601
(800) 223-0121

Missouri Division of Tourism
Truman Office Building
P.O. Box 1055
Jefferson City, MO 65102
(800) 877-1234

Kansas Travel & Tourism Division
700 SW Harrison, Suite 1300
Topeka, KS 66603
(800) 2KANSAS

Iowa Division of Tourism
200 East Grand Avenue
Des Moines, IA 50309
(800) 345-IOWA

Nebraska Travel & Tourism Division
P.O. Box 94666
Lincoln, NE 68509
(800) 228-4307

South Dakota Department of Tourism
711 East Wells Avenue
Pierre, SD 57501
(605) 773-3301

North Dakota Parks & Tourism
604 East Boulevard
Bismarck, ND 58505
(800) 437-2077

Travel Montana
Department of Commerce
Helena, MT 59620
(800) 541-1447

Idaho Travel Council
700 W. State St., 2nd Floor
Boise, ID 83720
(800) 635-7820

Washington State Tourism Division
P.O. Box 42500
Olympia, WA 98504
(800) 544-1800

Oregon Tourism Division
775 Summer St. N.E.
Salem, OR 97310
(800) 547-7842

A NOTE ON SPELLING

Modern readers always wonder how Lewis and Clark, who were certainly among the smartest people of their day, could be such terrible spellers. Their journals contained, for example, twenty-seven different spellings of Sioux and twenty-four different versions of Charbonneau, the French interpreter who joined the party during its 1804-1805 winter stay in North Dakota. And proper names weren't the only object of such mangling; Lewis, Clark, and their men had a way of garbling even simple words.

The reality was that in the early nineteenth century, even the most learned Americans used wildly irregular spellings. Even Noah Webster, who published his pioneering dictionaries in the late 1700s and early 1800s, advocated such variants as "wimmen," "groop," and "bilt." Many historians insist on preserving the captains' misspellings in journal quotes. The author appreciates the argument behind such preservation, but for the sake of readability, I have rendered all journal quotes into modern, standard English. In the case of the Indian woman who accompanied the expedition, I use the spelling "Sacagawea," generally considered to be most accurate, unless a different spelling is used in a proper

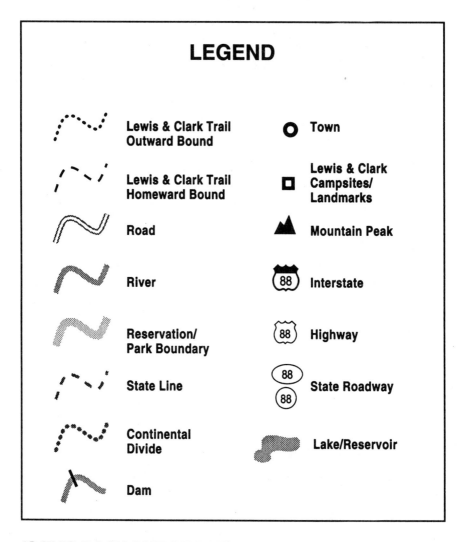

LEGEND

Lewis & Clark Trail Outward Bound	○ Town
Lewis & Clark Trail Homeward Bound	☐ Lewis & Clark Campsites/ Landmarks
Road	▲ Mountain Peak
River	(88) Interstate
Reservation/ Park Boundary	(88) Highway
State Line	88 / 88 State Roadway
Continental Divide	Lake/Reservoir
Dam	

IS THIS BOOK OUT OF DATE?

In a few years, the United States will celebrate the bicentennial of the Lewis and Clark Expedition. All along the route, communities and organizations are making plans for new visitor facilities and programs celebrating the Lewis and Clark legacy. Some may be in place by the time you read this book.

Other things may change, too. Restaurants and motels may open, close, or take new names, and visitor attractions may alter operating schedules.

If you find an error, omission, or change, please write me in care of Falcon Press, P.O. Box 1718, Helena, MT 59624. We will use your input in future editions of *The Traveler's Guide to the Lewis & Clark Trail*. Until then, may you have many wonderful voyages of discovery!

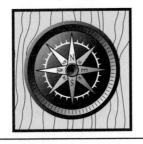

Chapter Three

Illinois, Missouri, and Kansas

I set out at 4 o'clock p.m., in the presence of many of the neighboring inhabitants, and proceeded on under a gentle breeze up the Missouri.

- William Clark, May 14, 1804,
upon leaving Camp Wood

CAMP WOOD

Our journey begins at a monument on the banks of the Mississippi River. There, surrounded by a gauntlet of rocks, sits a ring of substantial stone pillars commemorating the start of the Lewis and Clark Expedition.

The actual site of Camp Wood has long since disappeared, swallowed up by urban development, industrialization, and the shifting channels of the Mississippi, Missouri, and Wood rivers. Historians believe the camp sat about three miles north of the monument, an area dredged by oil companies operating in the vicinity.

But it was in this general area that the expedition planned and trained for its mission. The party camped here from December 12, 1803, through May 14, 1804, mostly under the command of Clark, who whipped the corps into a disciplined band while Lewis gathered supplies and information in St. Louis.

Lewis and Clark weren't the first white visitors in the vicinity. Jacques Marquette and Louis Joliet discovered the confluence in 1673, and other early European explorers followed. Their impressions of the site blended horror and delight. Describing a thicket of dead trees clogging the river, Marquette wrote he "had seen nothing more dreadful."

The Corps of Discovery.

But Father Pierre Francois de Charlevoix called it "the finest confluence in the world. The two rivers are much the same breadth, each about half a league; but the Missouri is by far the most rapid, and seems to enter the Mississippi like a conqueror."

Strictly speaking, the Lewis and Clark expedition didn't begin at Camp Wood at all, but in Pittsburgh, Pennsylvania, where Lewis picked up the keelboat he had ordered built for the voyage. The boat was supposed to be ready July 20, 1803, but when Lewis arrived, he found it nowhere near completion. The boatbuilder hired for the task had a penchant for drink, and it was all Lewis could do to keep the man at his task. The boat was finally finished August 31. It measured fifty-five feet in length, was eight feet wide at its center, and could carry about ten tons of cargo. Lewis set out down the Ohio River with at least eleven other men, including several expedition recruits, and a single pirogue, or dugout canoe.

It wasn't easy going. The Ohio was unusually low that year, and the crew frequently had to unload the keelboat cargo to get the craft past shallows, riffles, and other obstructions in the channel. The party stopped in Wheeling, West Virginia, to get additional supplies and a second pirogue.

After more stops in Marietta and Cincinnati, Ohio, and Big Bone Lick, Kentucky, Lewis reached the Falls of the Ohio near Louisville, Ken-

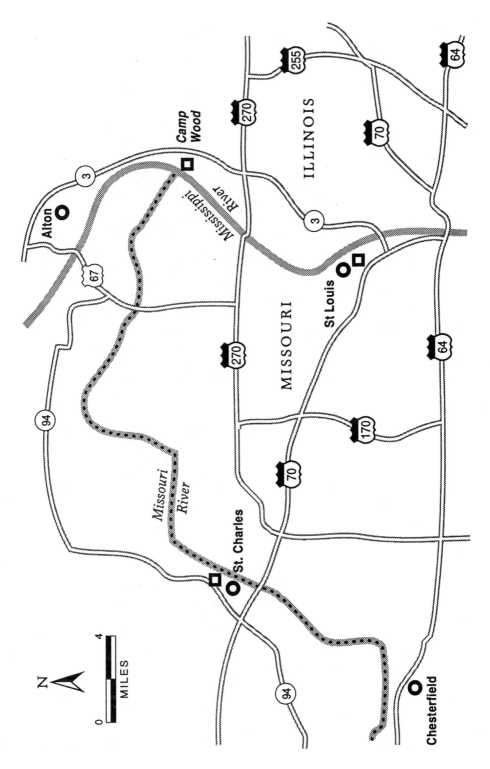

tucky, in early October 1803. Here, he was finally reunited face to face with his friend Clark. The party spent nearly two weeks in the area, during which Lewis and Clark had long conversations with Clark's older brother, George Rogers Clark, who knew much about the personalities and places on the frontier. When the corps left Clarksville, as the family settlement near Louisville was called, it included the two leaders; Clark's slave, York; and several of the men who would make up the permanent party: William Bratton, John Colter, Joseph and Reuben Field, Charles Floyd, George Gibson, Nathaniel Pryor, George Shannon, and John Shields. Colter of Virginia and Shannon of Ohio had come downriver with Lewis; the rest joined up near the Falls of the Ohio.

From Clarksville, the expedition made good time. At Fort Massac in Illinois, the captains recruited George Drouillard, Joseph Whitehouse, and John Newman. Moving up the Mississippi River at last, the corps passed Fort Kaskaskia and Cahokia, Illinois. The expedition reached the Camp Wood site on December 12. Originally, Lewis had hoped to be two hundred or three hundred miles up the Missouri River before making the first winter camp. But the lateness of the season, combined with the fact the territory up the Missouri had not yet been transferred to the United States, meant the journey's official start would have to wait until spring.

With winter camp established, Lewis and Clark wasted little time starting final preparations for their mission. Lewis had initially thought the expedition would include ten to twelve men, but the Ohio River cruise had convinced the leaders that at least twice that many would be needed to propel the boats, hunt, interpret, manage supplies, and ward off any Indian attacks. So throughout the winter, Clark continued to recruit.

Once enlisted, the high-spirited young soldiers had to be trained. At first, discipline was quite a problem. Drinking and fighting were rampant, and there also were instances of insubordination, refusal to stand guard, theft of government property, and men going AWOL. Roy E. Appleman, author of the National Park Service's account of the expedition, wrote, "At one time or another, practically all the men in camp engaged in some wrongdoing. Yet some of the rowdiest and most undisciplined, such as (John) Colter and Reuben Field, were later to number among the most reliable in the command." Clark used a mixture of punishment and incentive to handle the men, and discipline had improved greatly by the time the corps left Camp Wood.

Over the winter, the party also made numerous refinements to the keelboat to promote more efficient loading. Lockers were built to protect supplies, with lids that could be lifted to serve as defensive breastworks in the event of attack. Clark also outfitted both the keelboats and the pirogues with weapons including a small cannon (for the keelboat) and swivel guns.

Amid the busy preparations, Clark faced some bitter disappointments during the days at Camp Wood. For one thing, he was frequently sick. Worse, he learned shortly before the corps' departure that his commission as captain in the Corps of Engineers had been denied by the War Department. In a letter including Clark's commission as a second lieutenant in the Corps of Artillerists, Lewis explained to his friend that in the peacetime Army, officer vacancies were scarce, and the Corps of Artillerists position was all that was available. But as he had promised earlier, Lewis swore to Clark that—in his mind, if not that of the government—Clark was his co-captain. It was a secret kept safely between the friends for the duration of the 2.5-year mission.

While Clark ran Camp Wood, Lewis was in St. Louis performing tasks we shall examine in the next section. Clark and the corps left Camp Wood May 14 and arrived in St. Charles two days later.

To get to the Illinois Lewis and Clark monument, drive Illinois Highway 3 three miles north of its intersection with Interstate 270 (the major beltway around St. Louis), and watch for signs pointing the way.

A road leads west from busy Illinois 3, past a diversion-canal bayou where fathers teach their children to fish. The road dead ends in view of the monument. Here, the state of Illinois erected eleven stone pillars, one for each of the states Lewis and Clark passed through on their journey. A plaque on each pillar details a key incident in the expedition's travels.

The monument site is quiet aside from the waves that sometimes break as a boat chugs by. There are no visitor amenities, nothing to do but stand and contemplate. But if you're in the area, the monument is worth a visit, as are the nearby attractions of St. Louis and St. Charles, if for no other reason than to help place the expedition, its duties, and its goals in perspective.

Illinois 3 is also known as The Great River Road. A few miles upriver from the monument sits Alton, Illinois, a city well known for riverboat gambling and an antiques district. Both are located near the riverfront area. The seventh and final Lincoln-Douglas presidential debate was held at the intersection of Broadway and Market streets here in 1858.

Alton's Spencer T. Olin Community Golf Course, designed by Arnold Palmer, is considered the best public course in the metropolitan St. Louis area. The Piasa Bird, located on a limestone bluff along Illinois 100, re-creates the flying-monster pictograph discovered in 1673 by Pere Marquette. Illinois 100 also parallels a twenty-mile bike trail between Alton and Pere Marquette State Park, one of Illinois' largest and most popular. Call (800) 258-6645 or stop by the Alton visitor center (kitty-corner to the Alton Belle Casino parking lot) for more information on activities and events in southwestern Illinois.

The Gateway Arch in St. Louis, Missouri.

ST. LOUIS

At the time of the Lewis and Clark Expedition, St. Louis was a mere forty years old but already on its way to becoming one of the most important cities in the United States. Here, keelboats and flatboats carrying passengers from the East and South met river boats that served the frontier ports on the upper Mississippi and Missouri rivers. Its location made St. Louis the ideal hub of transportation, exploration, mercantile activity, and culture. Consequently, the city attracted everyone from fur traders to scientists, military agents to missionaries. It was here Captain Lewis gathered much of the intelligence essential to the expedition's success, as well as where both Lewis and Clark witnessed the ceremonies marking the transfer of Upper Louisiana from France to the United States.

Any visit to St. Louis should begin at the Jefferson National Expansion Memorial, best known for its graceful stainless-steel centerpiece, the 630-foot Gateway Arch. The Arch is America's tallest monument, topping the 555-foot Washington Monument and the 305-foot Statue of Liberty. It is a marvel of engineering and design.

The Museum of Westward Expansion beneath the Arch celebrates the vision of Thomas Jefferson and offers one of the nation's best overviews of why the Lewis and Clark Expedition took place. Exhibits are arranged in a wagon-wheel fashion, with each decade radiating off a hub. In the center stands a life-size statue of Jefferson, who stood six-foot-three. He is seen gazing out toward an ocean mural on the far wall, and strategic lighting ensures Jefferson's shadow is cast in all directions, just as his influence looms formidably even today.

Central to the museum's Lewis and Clark interpretation are the large, floor-to-ceiling photographs of sites along the expedition route. These beautiful images serve as a backdrop for everything else on display. Smaller photos show plants and animals seen by the corps, and a map of the Louisiana Purchase illustrates how that event nearly doubled the size of the United States.

Other exhibits pay tribute to later great American explorers, from the Oregon Trail pioneers to Charles Lindbergh and the Apollo astronauts. The museum also offers fine interpretive programs, including talks by rangers who act the part of frontier figures. And no visit would be complete without a ride to the top of the Arch. After a four-minute ride up the monument's innards in a pod-like tram car, the visitor is treated to outstanding views reaching thirty miles both east and west on a clear day.

The museum is open from 8 a.m. to 10 p.m. Memorial Day through Labor Day and 9 a.m. to 6 p.m. the rest of the year. Admission is $2 per person or a maximum of $4 per family. The Arch tram runs from 8:30 a.m. to 9:30 p.m. during the summer and 9:30 a.m. to 5:30 p.m. in the off-season and costs $2.50 for adults and teens and .50 cents for children ages three through twelve. All facilities are closed Thanksgiving, Christmas, and New Year's Day. For more information, call (314) 425-4465.

Although Lewis spent the most time in St. Louis the winter before the expedition, it was Clark who eventually made the city his home. After the expedition, Clark owned several buildings—none still standing—in the general vicinity of what is now the Gateway Arch. These included various Clark residences; his museum of Indian curiosities (an early St. Louis tourist attraction); and storehouses and offices he used in dealing with the Indians. Late in life, Clark lived mainly at his farm on Bellefontaine Road about 3.5 miles north of the city, but he died at the downtown home of his son, Meriwether Lewis Clark.

Clark is buried at the mammoth Bellefontaine Cemetery, five miles north of downtown on Florissant Avenue. The grave is situated on an elaborate stone plaza featuring an obelisk and bust of the explorer, along with a buffalo's head and gargoyle. Clark is described here as a "soldier, explorer, statesman and patriot. His life is written in the history of his country." No one would dispute that. Some may, however, question the Biblical quote also prominently displayed: "Behold, the Lord thy God hath set the land before thee. Go up and possess it." Certainly, that was what Lewis and Clark did. But these captains, along with their boss the president, envisioned a United States where the Native Americans and the more recently arrived whites could exist in harmony. The notion that the continent was somehow ours to plunder with no thought given to consequence came largely after the time of Jefferson, Lewis, and Clark.

To find the grave from the Florissant entrance, take Willow Avenue to Vine Avenue, bear left then right onto Althea Avenue, then left onto Aspen Avenue. Aspen runs into Meadow Avenue, where the Clark family plot is located. Better yet, stop at the office for a map to Clark's grave and a look at a chart of the Clark family tree, with branches hailing from St. Louis, Louisville, and Michigan. Guided tours are available by appointment. The cemetery is open to visitors from 8 a.m. to 5 p.m. daily.

SIDETRIP: ST. LOUIS ATTRACTIONS

St. Louis is the largest city along the Lewis and Clark route, and it offers an abundance of attractions. The riverfront area bustles with activity: visitors can choose from a riverboat cruise, Cardinals game at Busch Stadium, or explorations of the shops, restaurants, and nightlife of Laclede's Landing, the restored historic area just north of the Arch.

South of the Arch, the Soulard area thrives on live musical entertainment, with more than thirty restaurants and pubs, many offering jazz and blues. Soulard is also home to the Anheuser-Busch Brewery, where free tours (complete with product samples) are offered Monday through Saturday.

St. Louis has an abundance of unusual museums, including the National Bowling Hall of Fame (west of Busch Stadium), the National Video

William Clark's grave at Bellefontaine Cemetery, St. Louis, Missouri.

Game and Coin-Op Museum (at 801 N. 2nd St.), the Dog Museum (1721 S. Mason Road), the Magic House/St. Louis Children's Museum (516 S. Kirkwood Road), and the Dental Health Theater, with its three-foot-high fiberglass teeth (727 N. 1st St.).

Forest Park boasts a wealth of attractions including the St. Louis Zoo, with more than 3,400 animals; the St. Louis Science Center, with its Omnimax Theater and McDonnell Planetarium; the Muny, an outdoor performing arts center; and the St. Louis Art Museum. The park also offers bicycle rentals, bike/jog/walk paths, fishing, boating, skating, golf courses, and tennis courts.

Six Flags Over Mid-America, one of the nation's biggest amusement parks, is located about thirty miles southwest of downtown, near the Allenton exit off I-44. Raging Rivers, a water park, is at the opposite end of the metro area in Grafton, Illinois. For more information about St. Louis-area attractions, call the convention and visitors commission at (800) 247-9791 or write to 10 S. Broadway, Suite 1000, St. Louis, MO 63102.

ST. CHARLES

Although Camp Wood can rightfully be called the expedition's starting point, St. Charles was where final preparations were made, last-minute supplies obtained, and the boat load readjusted. Moreover, as we have seen, the expedition was shy one captain upon its arrival in St. Charles May 16, 1804. Lewis caught up to the corps May 20, and they formally got under way the next day.

In his journal, Clark described St. Charles in this way: "This village is about one mile in length, contains about 100 houses and about 450 inhabitants, chiefly French. Those people appear poor, polite, and harmonious." Founded in 1769 as a fur-trading post by Louis Blanchette, a French-Canadian hunter, St. Charles was the first permanent white settlement on the Missouri River. Early white inhabitants called the area Les Petites Cotes ("The Little Hills") because of the surrounding terrain.

After the United States took over the Louisiana Territory, St. Charles's influence grew. Its location near the confluence of the Mississippi and Missouri rivers made it an ideal outfitting port for land and water routes to the West. The city also was the eastern terminus of the Boonslick Road, which led to the Boone brothers' salt works in Howard County. St. Charles served as Missouri's first state capital from 1821 to 1826.

The Lewis and Clark Center at 701 Riverside Drive has exhibits on the expedition. Its centerpiece is a second-floor diorama by artist Evangeline Groth that traces the corps' journey to the Pacific Ocean. Other displays tell why some of the expedition's supporting characters— Sacagawea, Patrick Gass, Ben York, and Lewis's dog, Seaman—were so important to the venture's success. Reproductions of items used by the expedition are also on view. Another display notes that the last-minute purchases made in St. Charles included tin cups, knives, "and all the tobacco in town."

The center has a trading post and also offers a variety of classes and programs for school and youth groups. It is open daily (except major holidays) from 10:30 a.m. to 4:30 p.m. Admission is one dollar for adults and fifty cents for children ages three through seventeen. For more information, call (314) 947-3199.

After visiting the center, take some time to explore St. Charles. Its historic district is filled with charming shops and restaurants, some tucked back off Main Street, and guided walking tours are available. The Goldenrod Showboat, a stationary vessel, presents Broadway fare along the banks of the Missouri.

The Lewis and Clark Rendevous, staged the third weekend each May, includes a re-enactment of the corps's 1804 encampment. Other activities include a parade, crafts and foods of the period, a fife and drum corps muster, and military re-enactment groups demonstrating 18th and 19th century drill tactics. Full-size replicas of the expedition's boats also are on view. St. Charles's other major annual event is the Festival of the Little Hills, held the third weekend of each August.

St. Charles serves as a major access point to the Katy Trail, one of America's most unusual state parks. See the side trip later in this chapter for more information. And for more on things to see and do in St. Charles, stop by the Visitors Bureau at 230 South Main Street, or call (800) 366-2427.

THE SHAKEDOWN CRUISE

I-70 cuts a wide, straight swath across Missouri, allowing motorists to traverse the state in about four hours. But travelers who succumb to I-70 miss some of the most beautiful hill country and the quaintest small towns in the Midwest...reason enough to consider following the meandering Missouri River and the route of Lewis and Clark across at least part of the Show-Me State. Good roads parallel the river on both sides to Jefferson City. Farther west, the river's path becomes more difficult and time-consuming to follow, and a bit of short-cutting makes more sense.

From St. Charles, take Missouri 94 southwest. This is Daniel Boone country, where the famous American frontiersman spent the last two decades of his life from about 1799 through 1820. In other words, the aging pioneer was living here when Lewis and Clark trekked through the area in 1804 and again in 1806, but no record exists of an encounter between the parties.

For an in-depth look at Boone's life, visit the Daniel Boone Home on Highway F near Defiance. One of Missouri's most popular attractions, the dwelling was completed in 1810 and still houses many Boone family heirlooms. The grounds also include "The Judgment Tree," a large elm under which Boone settled disputes between white men and local Indians. Other important Boone-family sites in eastern Missouri include Daniel's grave at Marthasville.

More important for our explorations, this country also served as the shakedown cruise section for the Lewis and Clark Expedition, the area where the men became intimate with the river on which they would do most of their traveling over the next two and one-half years. Of the 7,500-plus miles covered by Lewis and Clark, roughly three-quarters of them were on the Missouri River. Rising in southwest Montana where the Madison, Gallatin, and Jefferson rivers join, the river drains one-sixth of the land in the contiguous United States. Hundreds of rivers and creeks join the Missouri over its 2,315-mile course to the Mississippi.

For tens of thousands of years, the Missouri was free and wild. But as the nation expanded, the need for hydroelectric power and flood control resulted in one of world's largest public works projects. Today, a series of dams stretching from Fort Peck (in Montana) to Gavins Point on the Nebraska-South Dakota border has changed the Missouri into a river far different from the one Lewis and Clark saw.

Indeed, the Missouri of 1804 was considered to be the most unruly river in America, and it didn't take the corps long to find out why. Keelboats were pulled along by hand with a one thousand-foot line called a cordelle tied to the mast. The keelboat often had to be towed against a strong current, and it typically took at least twenty men to cordelle a keelboat along most sections of the Missouri. At times, sandbars made cordeling impossible. In those instances, the boat would be poled or even rowed upstream. A small mast sail was sometimes used if winds were favorable, yet snags were another constant hazard. Blistering summer heat, thundering rainstorms, mosquitoes, gnats, and ticks made matters still more difficult all across Missouri and onto the Plains.

The expedition had other matters to address as well. Jefferson had compiled a long list of duties and objectives, chief among them keeping journals. Along with noting latitude, longitude, and landmarks, the captains were to record extensive details of any Indian nations encountered; "the soil and face of the country, its growth and vegetable productions, especially those not of the U.S."; animals; minerals, "volcanic appearances"; and climate.

Both Lewis and Clark kept journals, and their versions of the trip are the most well known today. But other expedition members contributed written accounts, too. Whitehouse's was one of the most detailed; Clark frequently fed him information in the hope that if the captains' journals were lost, another comprehensive account might survive. Others who kept journals were Patrick Gass, Nathaniel Pryor, Charles Floyd, and John Ordway. Gass, perhaps the most unlikely journal writer, was the first to hit print. He'd had only nineteen days of schooling, but he wrote faithfully during the expedition, and his work, edited afterward by a schoolteacher, came out in 1807—the first book to be published about the expedition.

Mapmaking was another of the expedition's primary duties. In an 1805 letter, Jefferson wrote, "The work we are now doing is, I trust, done for posterity in such a way that they need not repeat it. We shall delineate with correctness the great arteries of this great country. Those who come after us will extend the ramifications as they become acquainted with them and fill up the canvas we begin."

Clark did most of the mapmaking. Using simple navigational instruments and his own estimates, he measured the length and direction of each bend of the rivers and the distance they had traveled, scribbling these courses and distances next to his sketch maps. In most instances, his "guesstimates" were remarkably accurate. Clark's maps recorded a wealth of other information, too, including campsites, creeks and rivers, Indian villages, and bad rapids.

And as instructed, the captains made note of the plants and animals they encountered. More than 120 animals and 170 plant species, many new to science, were described in the journals. Consequently, two entire plant categories—Lewisia and Clarkia—were named after the explorers, and their names also were freely assigned to landmarks and natural features across the land. When the corps members published their work, readers were fascinated to hear for the first time of such beasts as grizzly bears, bighorn sheep, and pronghorn antelope.

With all these duties, it would seem Lewis and Clark had scant time for adventure. But barely under way, Lewis had a close brush with death on May 23, 1804. On that day, the captains stopped to explore an area known as Tavern Cave, located east of present-day Washington, Missouri. "The challenge was too much for Lewis," David Lavender wrote in his book, *The Way to the Western Sea*. "While Clark was adding his name to the register inside the cavern, Meriwether found a break in the precipice, ascended it, and began working his way along the edge. A foothold crumbled. He slid and bounced downward about twenty feet. Just short of disaster, Clark wrote in his journal, 'He saved himself by the assistance of his knife,' driving it wildly one assumes, into some crevice that held. Just how he extricated himself from the dizzy perch does not appear." In fact, Lewis didn't even mention the incident in the version of his journals he was finally preparing for publication at the time of his death in 1809. Perhaps he was somewhat embarrassed by his dangerous behavior in the face of such an important assignment.

Tavern Cave can still be found, but there is no interpretation at the site, which is now on private land. Moreover, it has largely been filled in by brush, dirt, and railroad construction since the days of Lewis and Clark, and the signatures of early visitors have long since disappeared. What is left is located north of the settlement of St. Albans, north of Missouri 100 via County Road T. (Unlike most states, Missouri marks many of its secondary roads with letters, not numerals—a system started in 1932.) Inquire locally for further directions and permission to visit.

Washington, accessed by crossing the Missouri River on Missouri 47 at Dutzow, is a town of about 10,000 people with a good selection of interesting shops and restaurants and a marina and boat ramp on the Missouri River. Lewis and Clark camped in the vicinity two days after the episode at Tavern Cave. From Washington, continue west on Missouri 100, through Missouri's scenic and hilly wine country. New Haven and Hermann are two other communities worth exploring in this area.

First settled around 1805, New Haven was originally called Miller's Landing for pioneer Philip Miller. The Missouri-Pacific Railroad reached here in 1855, and the present town was laid out and renamed the next year. Today's New Haven begins up on Missouri 100 and tumbles down the river bluffs to a pleasant landing district. A stairclimb from the downtown district leads to a viewpoint. The downtown area also has a movie theater, an antiques mall, and a year-round Christmas store, in addition to a restaurant—Meriwether's New Haven—named in honor of Captain Lewis.

John Colter, one of the most famous members of the Lewis and Clark Expedition, settled a few miles east of New Haven in 1810. After the expedition, Colter went on to great fame as the first white man to discover what is now Yellowstone Park. He was probably buried in the New Haven area, although the location is uncertain. His grave was likely never marked and may have disappeared when the local river bluffs were reshaped to construct a levee—one of a handful that was able to withstand the floods that wracked the Midwest during the summer of 1993.

Hermann, sometimes called Little Germany, is reminiscent of Rhine Valley towns with its distinctive architecture. White settlers had arrived in the area by the early 1800s, and a town historical marker notes how the returning Lewis and Clark Expedition "joyfully hailed the sight of cows along the riverbank here."

Hermann was founded by the German Settlement Society of Philadelphia in 1836 as a place where German customs and language could be preserved "amid the benefits of America." The town was laid out on part of an 11,300-acre parcel purchased by Society agent George F. Bayer for $15,612. The society disbanded in 1839, but a steady stream of Germans continued to arrive for years afterward.

The year 1843 was a momentous one in Hermann history. That year, many newly arriving German emigrants died when a steamboat exploded. In 1843, Hermann also became the fourth town to serve as seat of Gasconade County—a title it retains today. The present courthouse was built in 1898. At one point, the town also boasted a German-language newspaper known for its anti-slavery views and a German school. River shipping and winemaking became big industries.

Hermann is a fairly touristy place, but one can understand why city slickers from St. Louis and Kansas City might want to head here for a weekend. Wine and beer tasting are big activities; fortunately, there are also plenty of accommodations available for anyone who samples a bit too much. The hill country of central Missouri is definitely no place to drink and drive.

Hermann has a nice campground in its city park, with spots designed for tenters as well as RVs. In addition to restrooms with showers, the park also has plenty of picnic tables, tennis courts, great playground equipment, and a pool. Check the weather report before pitching a tent here, however: Signs warn visitors the area is subject to flash flooding.

Cross the Missouri again at Hermann and proceed west on Missouri 94 to Jefferson City. The highlight here is a bronze relief depicting the signing of the Louisiana Purchase. Robert R. Livingston (seated) and James Monroe are seen witnessing French Marquis Francois de Barbois Marbois signing the purchase agreement, one of the greatest events in American history. With their pen strokes, these men nearly doubled the size of the United States.

Other sights on the Capitol grounds include several lovely fountains and an imposing statue of President Jefferson. The Capitol itself hasn't had the greatest luck. First built in 1826, it was destroyed by fire in 1837.

Missouri River near Hermann, Missouri.

The second building, started that year, burned in 1911 after being struck by lightning. The present Capitol was built in 1918.

Inside, the Missouri Museum features historical and contemporary displays. Thomas Hart Benton's mural, "A Social History of the State of Missouri," is painted on all four walls of the House Lounge, located on the west wing of the third floor. The statehouse is open and free tours are available daily except Easter, Thanksgiving, Christmas, and New Year's Day.

Jefferson City's other attractions include the Jefferson Landing State Historic Site, with several buildings dating from the 1830s-1850s; the Governor's Garden, where outdoor drama is sometimes held; and the Runge Nature Center at 2901 W. Truman Boulevard, featuring a large aquarium and hands-on nature exhibits. July is a big month for celebrations: a large Fourth of July party featuring fireworks shot off from a Missouri River barge; the annual Old Car Roundup set each mid-July downtown; and the Cole County Fair, held the last week of the month.

From Jefferson City, the traveler once again has a choice of routes. U.S. Highway 63 provides speedy access to Columbia and I-70 to the north, while Missouri 179 takes a more leisurely approach, reaching the interstate west of Columbia. Missouri 179 stays somewhat closer to the river; a popular attraction en route is River Hills Farm at Marion. Lewis and Clark camped nearby on June 4, 1804, and the farm now features a zoo, trail, gift and snack shops, and pick-your-own produce.

Columbia sits several miles from the Missouri, but what it may lack in location, it more than makes up in culture and recreation. Columbia is home to the main University of Missouri campus, Columbia College, and Stephens College, which together add some 27,000 students to Columbia's population of about 70,000. Campus highlights include the Francis Quadrangle at MU, where six ionic columns are all that remain of Academic Hall, destroyed by fire in 1892; Stephens College's Firestone Baars Chapel, designed by Eero Saarinen, the same architect responsible for the Arch in St. Louis; and the Chinese Pavilion at Columbia College.

Cultural attractions include the Shelter Insurance Gardens, where concerts are staged at 7 p.m. each Sunday during June and July; Maplewood Barn Theatre, where outdoor dramas are presented in a converted barn Memorial Day through Labor Day; and a variety of art galleries. (Columbia College is considered one of the nation's top fine and commercial art schools; its gallery is located on North 10th Street.) Recreational possibilities range from swimming, golf, and tennis to cycling on the nearby Katy Trail. Columbia Mall at Stadium and Bernadette streets is the city's largest, but Columbia also has a thriving downtown district centered near Providence Road and East Broadway. For more information on area attractions, call (314) 875-1321.

SIDETRIP: THE KATY TRAIL

In 1986, the Missouri-Kansas-Texas (MKT) Railroad decided to end operations on a trans-Missouri route from near St. Charles to Sedalia. The decision paved the way for creation of the Katy Trail, a two hundred-mile biking, hiking, and handicapped-use trail made possible under the National Trail Systems Act. ("Katy" is the popular abbreviation for MKT.) The trail is being developed in thirty- to forty-mile stretches, with most slated for completion in 1994.

The Katy Trail parallels the Missouri River across much of Eastern Missouri, affording Lewis and Clark buffs an opportunity to see the river "trail" up close. Scenic wonders abound, too. Lewis and Clark noted the limestone bluffs south of Rocheport (on US 40 west of Columbia), known as the Manitou (or Moniteau) Bluffs for the Indian word for Great Spirit. These bluffs once had many pictographs, and one may still be seen over a landmark known as Lewis and Clark Cave. Clark noted the artwork in his journal entry of June 7, 1804: "A short distance above the mouth of a creek is several curious paintings and carving on the projecting rock of limestone inlaid with white, red and blue flint of a very good quality...." Katy Trail users wheel or walk past an array of wildflowers, and the trail's location along the Missouri River flyway means migrating bird and waterfowl sightings are common.

Katy Trail State Park was designed for bicyclists and hikers. Wheelchairs are welcome, too, but other motorized vehicles (except official and emergency vehicles) are prohibited. Users should stay on the trail, as the areas immediately outside trail boundaries are often on private property. Pets should be kept on a leash.

Businesses catering to trail users are springing up all along the Katy Trail. For example, Scenic Cycles in Marthasville rents traditional bikes as well as tandems and side-by-side, surrey-like "honeymooner" cycles. Special trailside parking areas are also found in many towns along the way. For more information on the Katy Trail, contact the Missouri Department of Natural Resources, P.O. Box 176, Jefferson City, MO, 65102, or call (800) 334-6946.

ARROW ROCK AND FORT OSAGE

Boonville, located near I-70 and Missouri 87, is one of the oldest towns in central Missouri and has more than four hundred buildings on the National Register of Historic Places. The town has a good selection of food and lodging, along with brown-bag concerts in the summer, the Missouri River Festival of the Arts in August, and daily tours of the historic districts.

From Boonville, the river flows west then north to Arrow Rock, long a major stopping point for people headed west. Lewis and Clark reached the area June 9, 1804, and Clark noted "several small channels running

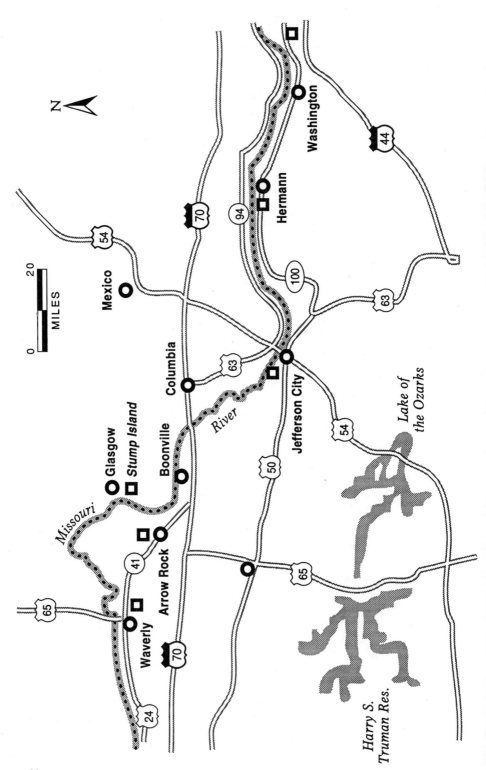

out of the river below a bluff and prairie (called the Prairie of Arrows)."
Even at that time, the area had already received its name.

In the mid-19th century, many emigrants passed through the area on their way to the western trailheads leading to Santa Fe, Oregon, and California. The town's population peaked around 1860 but dropped off after the Civil War and the decline of traffic on the nearby Missouri River.

Today, Arrow Rock looks much like it did in the mid-1800s. A new state interpretive center (open 10 a.m. to 4 p.m. Monday through Saturday and noon to 6 p.m. Sunday) explains the town's history, and visitors can see the past up close by walking through town. Historic buildings include the Old Tavern (dating to 1834) and a home occupied by famed frontier artist George Caleb Bingham from 1837 to 1845.

About two dozen merchants and innkeepers are doing their best to keep Arrow Rock alive, and the town enjoys thriving tourism, especially in the summer and fall. Major events include an arts festival the third weekend of May and crafts festival the second weekend each October. The Lyceum Theatre presents a half-dozen different dramas each summer, with performances usually set Wednesday through Sunday evenings. The town has several bed-and-breakfasts, and camping is available at Arrow Rock State Park.

Arrow Rock, Missouri.

Fort Osage, Missouri.

Arrow Rock State Historic Site is located seventeen miles from Boonville and fifteen miles from Marshall. To get there, take I-70 Exit 98 to Missouri 41. For more information, call (816) 837-3330.

Glasgow, Missouri, is home to another site noted in the expedition's journals. Lewis and Clark named "Stump Island" during the corps' camp of June 10-11, 1804, and the occasion is now remembered with an interpretive sign at Glasgow's city park. The town is located nineteen miles north of Boonville via Missouri 87.

From Arrow Rock, continue northwest on Missouri 41 to Marshall, the seat of Saline County and gateway to Van Meter State Park, an area featuring ancient Indian burial sites and ceremonial mounds (twelve miles northwest on Missouri 41 and 122). At Marshall, pick up US 65 going west; it turns into US 24 at the small crossroads of Waverly.

US 24 proceeds west through an area filled with orchards offering everything from asparagus to blackberries to Christmas trees, depending on the season. The rural vistas blend with picturesque small-town scenes: young men working on a souped-up yellow car, complete with painted red flames streaking across its side, and older folks porch-sitting into the twilight. Sweetly scented fruit blossoms replace diesel fumes, and a hawk may be spotted soaring above the trees. Best of all: almost no billboards. These roads have character.

Many small towns along the Lewis and Clark route have annual summer festivals or community picnics, usually advertised with signs posted near the village limits. If you happen to be in the right place at the right time, by all means stop and investigate. Anticipate a good meal, friendly conversation, and maybe some sightseeing tips, too.

Lexington, Missouri, was settled in 1822 by former residents of Lexington, Kentucky. The town became a busy river port and was the site of a three-day Civil War battle won by the Confederates. The battlefield is now a state historic site, and a cannonball fired during the September 1861 event may still be seen lodged in a column at the courthouse.

Lewis and Clark reached the present site of Fort Osage in late June 1804 and named it Fort Point, noting its suitability for a military installation. In 1808, Clark returned to supervise the construction of a fortified trading post to sway the Indians from Spanish and British influence. Fort Osage was operated by the government until 1822 and played an active and important part in the earliest development of the Louisiana Territory.

Interest in Fort Osage was revitalized during Missouri's statehood centennial in the 1920s. Restoration started in 1941 and was completed in 1962. To get to the site, take US 24 to Buckner, then turn north on Sibley Street (Highway BB). Directional signs point the rest of the way to the park.

Fort Osage was run by George Sibley, and he seemed to enjoy his post, noting in his diary: "I am very comfortably fixed." A household inventory done in 1813 included a cherry dining table, ten Windsor chairs, a walnut cupboard, and brass candlesticks. In his diary, Sibley noted his typical daily meals: coffee and unbuttered toast for breakfast; beef, pork, or venison and potatoes for mid-day dinner; and a dish of tea and milk and hominy for supper. "Frequently, we are honored with an Osage chief or war captain to dine or sup with us," he added, "and very often are favored with the company of the princesses and young ladies of rank, decked out in all the finery of beads, red ribbons and vermillion, silver ornaments and scarlet blankets."

Start your visit with a walk through the museum, which outlines the post's operations. A showcase displays items recovered during archaeological excavations at the site, including building materials, tools, household furnishings, and personal items. There's also an exhibit detailing the history of the U.S. Army at Fort Osage.

Next, stroll the grounds and visit some of the restored buildings. Authentically attired living history interpreters are frequently on hand to describe what life was like during Fort Osage's heyday. Reproductions of trade-era goods including tin wear, beads, buttons, tin whistles, lanterns, and more are available for purchase in the factory.

Fort Osage stages several special events each year, including the Spring Flint Knap-In (held in mid-May), Independence Day festivities on the Fourth of July, Children's Day in early August, and a Christmas

Frontier Open House in early December. An annual calendar of events is published each March. To request a copy, call (816) 795-8200 ext. 260.

The Jackson County Parks and Recreation Department also offers 19th century sit-down dinners of roast turkey or braised lamb stew and side dishes prepared as they were during the early 1800s. Meals are served in the Factor's Dining Room on authentic reproduction Spode dinnerware. Cost is $30 per person, with a minimum of eight people. For more information, contact the Parks and Recreation Department at (816) 795-8200 ext. 264.

The Fort Osage admission fee is $3 for teens and adults and $2 for children ages five through thirteen; children under five are admitted free. The site is open from 9 a.m. to 5 p.m. Wednesday through Sunday mid-April through mid-November and weekends only the rest of the year. Stop at the visitor center to buy tickets before proceeding onto the actual fort reconstruction.

Picnic grounds are available both at Fort Osage and at nearby Hayes Park, which also has a playground. A honey farm and several orchards in the vicinity welcome visitors.

Fort Osage, Missouri.

SIDETRIP: KANSAS CITY-AREA ATTRACTIONS

With its fine architecture, broad boulevards, and European-style gardens and fountains, Kansas City often surprises visitors who expect little more than an overgrown cow town. In fact, Kansas City is one of the Midwest's largest and most progressive metropolitan areas.

Get oriented at Kansas City's visitor center, among the best and most helpful in the United States. It is located at Exit 9 just off I-70 in view of the massive Harry S. Truman Sports Complex, where baseball's Royals and football's Chiefs enjoy separate stadiums capable of seating a total of 118,000 fans.

Sports-crazy Kansas City doesn't limit itself to spectator events. The city hosts an abundance of recreational activities, including golf, swimming, horseback riding, boating, hiking, and tennis. Much of the activity centers around 1,772-acre Swope Park. Worlds of Fun and Oceans of Fun, two popular theme parks, are located thirteen miles north of Kansas City on I-435.

Culture plays an equally strong role in Kansas City. The Nelson-Atkins Museum of Art (45th and Oak streets) includes fifty-eight galleries and the largest collection of Henry Moore sculptures in the United States. Kansas City was home to artist Thomas Hart Benton, whose home may be toured at 3616 Belleview Avenue.

Top shopping areas include Westport, where Kansas City began and where westward-bound emigrants frequently outfitted themselves for their trips, and Country Club Plaza, the first planned shopping center in the United States. Antiques fans flock to 45th Street and State Line Road, a district with more than fifty antique, arts, and crafts dealers. The open-air City Market at 5th and Walnut streets near the river is a good place to stock up on fresh fruit.

Crown Center just south of downtown is yet another place to shop, eat, and party—free concerts take place every Friday evening during the summer.

Kansas City's tribute to the Corps of Discovery rests high atop a bluff at 8th and Jefferson, overlooking the confluence of the Missouri and Kansas Rivers. The small park, known as Lewis and Clark Point, has a plaque marking the expedition's September 15, 1806, visit on its homeward journey. The captains stood on this point and noted its "perfect command of the river" before proceeding to shoot an elk and gather custard apples, or paw-paws, for that day's respite.

History buffs may also want to pay a visit to Kansas City's suburban neighbor to the east, Independence. The town served as a primary jumping-off spot for the Oregon Trail, the California Trail, and the Santa Fe Trail. All are described in detail at the National Frontier Trails Center, 318 W. Pacific Ave. Every Labor Day Weekend, Independence stages

Santa-Cali-Gon Days, a festival marking the city's role as "Queen City of the Trails." Independence was also the hometown of President Harry S. Truman, and tours are available at several important sites, including the Truman Library and the home at 219 N. Delaware St., where Harry and Bess lived from their marriage in 1919 to his death in 1972.

For more information on Kansas City, write the Convention and Visitors Bureau of Greater Kansas City at 1100 Main St., Suite 2550, Kansas City, MO 64105, or call (800) 767-7700.

LEWIS AND CLARK STATE PARK (MISSOURI)

From Kansas City, take I-71 north to Missouri 45 (Exit 5), the route closest to the Missouri River. Lewis and Clark camped in the vicinity of Leavenworth, Kansas, on July 1, 1804, and September 13, 1806. Leavenworth is also known as the first incorporated town in the Kansas Territory and as site of Fort Leavenworth, an outpost traversed by branches of the Oregon and Santa Fe trails in the mid-1800s.

A short ways upriver, the town of Weston was a thriving port town from its founding in 1837 until a flood moved the Missouri River a mile away in the late nineteenth century. Weston went through some tough times, its 1853 population of five thousand dropping to one thousand by

Lewis and Clark Point. The confluence of the Missouri and Kansas rivers in Kansas City, Missouri.

Lewis and Clark State Park, Missouri.

1890. But in recent years, Weston has made a new name for itself through historic preservation and a charming little downtown shopping district.

Weston is also noted for its excellent limestone springs. Lewis and Clark paused to enjoy the water in 1804, and by the 1830s, the springs were a popular stopping place for wagons heading west. One of those who stopped was Benjamin J. Holladay, who settled in the area in 1838. Realizing that the limestone water, free of acid and iron, was perfect for making whisky, Holladay opened a distillery in 1856. The McCormick Distilling Company, as it is known today, is still in operation and offers free tours daily March through November.

Continue north on Missouri 45 to Lewis and Clark State Park, twelve miles northwest of Weston. Interpretive panels here tell the story of Lewis and Clark, who passed through the area July 4, 1804. Although this is one of Missouri's smaller state parks, it is blessed with the presence of a 365-acre lake popular for fishing, swimming, boating, and water skiing.

Sugar Lake—called Gosling Lake by Lewis and Clark—is a good example of an oxbow lake, a phenomenon seen up and down the banks of the Missouri River. Oxbow lakes are formed by abandoned flood plain meanders. A thousand or more years ago, the river meandered over a wide valley creating vast wetlands. Constant river bed erosion during flooding deepened the main channel, gradually isolating bends or oxbows. Eventually, the oxbows lost all but flood-level contact with the river, creating shallow lakes. Modern-day flood-control measures continue to isolate these oxbow lakes.

Lewis and Clark State Park has a seventy-site campground, with facilities that include hot showers, a laundry room, dump station, and playground. Sugar Lake is known for its bass, bluegill, channel catfish, carp, and buffalo fish. The park is also home to a fish hatchery. For more information, call (816) 579-5564.

INDEPENDENCE CREEK (KANSAS)

From Lewis and Clark State Park, it's just a short drive to Atchison, Kansas, where the Corps of Discovery spent the first of three Fourth of Julys on their two-and-one-half-year trip. The town of Atchison marks the occasion at Independence Park, down on the city's riverfront. A sign there reads: "The Lewis and Clark Expedition passed this area on July 4, 1804. They camped north of here at the mouth of a creek which they named Independence Creek, in honor of the day. They celebrated 'by an evening gun and an additional gill of whisky to the men.'" Clark, in his journal, remarked that "as we approached this place the prairie had a most beautiful appearance, hills and valleys interspersed with copses of timber gave a pleasing diversity of the scenery."

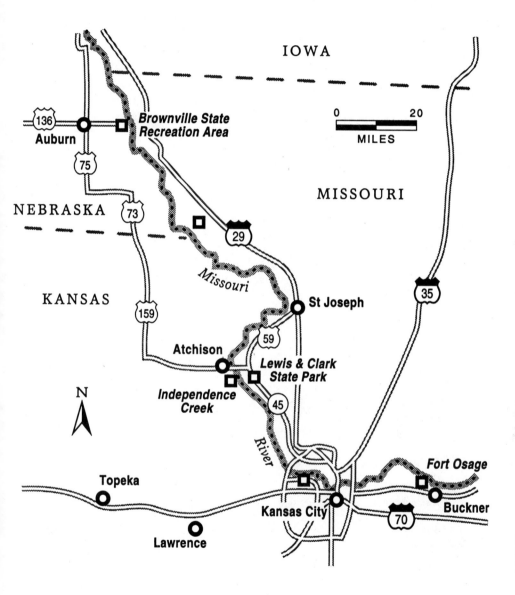

IOWA

Brownville State
Recreation Area

136
Auburn

75

NEBRASKA

73

KANSAS

159

MISSOURI

Missouri

29

St Joseph

59

Atchison

Lewis & Clark
State Park

Independence
Creek

45

River

N

Topeka

Fort Osage

Kansas City

70

Buckner

Lawrence

35

0   20
MILES

Atchison is also noted for its Victorian-era architecture. Eighteen structures built during the late 1800s (including the birthplace of pioneering aviatrix Amelia Earhart) are featured in a 2.4-mile walking/driving tour. Stop by the Santa Fe Depot Visitor Center and Museum, 200 S. 10th St., for a brochure.

The International Forest of Friendship is another popular attraction, honoring people from all over the world who have contributed to aviation and space travel. The park's centerpiece is a tree grown from a sycamore seed taken to the moon on Apollo 14. Atchison has a community theater, outdoor downtown shopping mall, hiking trails, and more than twenty-five city lakes. For more information, call (800) 234-1854.

From Atchison, cross the Missouri River back to Missouri and follow US 59 to St. Joseph, where the Pony Express was headquartered during its brief existence in 1860-1861. Two main sites interpret the "lightning mail" system: the Patee House Museum at 12th and Penn and the Pony Express Museum at 914 Penn St. Other popular museums include the St. Joseph Museum at 11th and Charles and the Albrecht-Kemper Museum of Art at 2818 Frederick Blvd.

The northwest corner of Missouri offers a good opportunity to return to the interstate and make some time. Get on I-29 (via I-229 out of St. Joseph) and drive north to Rock Port, Missouri. From there, take US 136 west to Brownville, our first Nebraska stop.

Riverfront at Atchison, Kansas. Photo by Lynn Hoffman.

LODGING

ALTON, ILLINOIS

Holiday Inn, (800) HOLIDAY, IL 3 at IL 140.

Lewis and Clark Motor Lodge, (618) 254-3831, IL 3 (East Alton).

Stratford Motor Hotel, (618) 465-8821, 3rd Street at Market St.

Super 8 Motel, (800) 800-8000, 1800 Homer Adams Pkwy. $42.

GREATER ST. LOUIS, MISSOURI

Best Inns of America, (618) 397-3300, I-64 and IL 157 (Caseyville, Illinois). $43.

Hampton Inn, (800) HAMPTON, I-270 Exit 26B (Florissant). $51-$59.

Holiday Inn-West Airport, (800) HOLIDAY, I-270 and St. Charles Rock Rd. (Bridgeton). $75.

Knights Inn, (314) 291-8545, 12433 St. Charles Rock Rd. (Bridgeton). $38-$48.

Motel 6 (Airport), (314) 427-1313, 4576 Woodson Rd. $36.

Ramada Inn, (800) 228-2828, 333 Washington Ave. $59-$99.

Super 8 Motel, (800) 843-1991, 12705 St. Charles Rock Rd. (Bridgeton). $44.

ST. CHARLES, MISSOURI

Boone's Lick Trail Inn Bed and Breakfast, (314) 947-7000, 1000 S. Main St. $65-$105.

Budgetel Inn, (800) 4-BUDGET, I-70 at Fifth St. $49-$61.

Country Inn by Carlson, (800) 456-4000, 2750 Plaza Way. $50.

Econo Lodge, (800) 446-6900, I-70 Exit 227. $39.

Loccoco House II of St. Charles Bed & Breakfast, (314) 946-0619, 1309 N. Fifth. $55-$65.

Red Roof Inn, (800) 843-7663, I-70 Exit 227. $44.

WASHINGTON, MISSOURI

Lewis and Clark Inn, (314) 239-0111, 500 Hwy. 100 East. $41-$45.

Super 8 Motel, (800) 800-8000, MO 47 and 100. $39.

Washington House Bed and Breakfast, (314) 239-2417, 3 Lafayette St. $51-$75.

HERMANN, MISSOURI

Captain Wohlt Inn Bed & Breakfast, (573) 486-3357, 123 E. Third St.

Hermann Motel, (573) 486-3131, 112 E. 10th St. $32.

JEFFERSON CITY, MISSOURI

Best Western Inn, (800) 528-1234, 1937 Christy Dr. $46.

Comfort Inn, (800) 221-2222, 1926 Jefferson St. $42-$48.

Hotel DeVille, (573) 636-5231, 319 W. Miller St. $50-$68.

Ramada Inn, (800) 228-2828, 1510 Jefferson St. $59.

ROCHEPORT, MISSOURI

School House Bed & Breakfast, (314) 698-2022, Third and Clark St. $50-$100.

COLUMBIA, MISSOURI

Best Western Columbia Inn, (800) 528-1234, 3100 I-70 Drive S.E. $44-$54.

Budget Host Crossways Inn, (800) 456-1065, I-70 Exit 127. $27-$36.

Budget Host Crossways Inn, (800) 456-1065, I-70 Exit 127. $27-$36.

Guesthouse Inn, (314) 474-1408, I-70 Exit 128A. $47.

Drury Inn, (800) 325-8300, 1000 Knipp St. $61.

Eastwood Motel, (800) 274-3278, 2518 Business Loop 70E. $34-$44.

Red Roof Inn, (314) 442-0145, 201 E. Texas Ave. $37.

BOONVILLE, MISSOURI

Comfort Inn, (800) 4CHOICE, I-70 and MO 5. $43-$53.

The Homestead Motel, (816) 882-6568, MO 5.

Morgan Street Repost Bed & Breakfast, (816) 882-7195, 607 E. Morgan St. $50-$100.

ARROW ROCK, MISSOURI

Airy Hill Inn, (816) 837-3458.

Borgman's Bed & Breakfast, (816) 837-3350. $40-$45.

Cedar Grove Bed & Breakfast, (816) 837-3441. $50-$60.

DownOver Bed & Breakfast Inn, (816) 837-3268. $40-$60.

Miss Nelle's Bed & Breakfast, (816) 837-3280. $45.

LEXINGTON, MISSOURI

Lexington Inn, (816) 259-4641, US 24 and MO 13. $38.

GREATER KANSAS CITY, MISSOURI/KANSAS

American Inn, (816) 373-8300, 4141 S. Noland Rd. (Independence). $29-$36.

Best Western Country Inn-North, (800) 528-1234, 2633 N.E. 43rd St. $60.

Comfort Inn Northeast, (800) 221-2222, 1051 N. Cambridge (I-435 and Front St. Exit 57). $42-$48.

Drury Inn-Stadium, (800) 325-8300, I-70 Exit 9. $65.

Howard Johnson Convention Center (800) IGO-HOJO, 610 Washington St. $55.

Motel 6, (816) 228-9133, I-70 Exit 20 (Blue Springs). $34.

Ramada Inn South, (800) 228-2828, 6701 Longview Rd. $45.

Super 8, (800) 843-1991, I-70 and Noland Rd. (Independence). $44.

Westport Inn, (800) 932-3201, 801 Westport Rd. $61-$69.

Woodstock Inn Bed & Breakfast (816) 833-2233, 1212 W. Lexington Ave. (Independence). $45-$50.

WESTON, MISSOURI

Apple Creek Bed & Breakfast, (816) 386-5724, 908 Washington. $50-$75.

Benner House Bed & Breakfast, (816) 386-2616, 645 Main St.

The Hatchery Bed & Breakfast, (816) 386-5700, 618 Short St. $50-$75.

Inn at Weston Landing, (816) 386-5788, Short St. and Welt. $75-$90.

ATCHISON, KANSAS

Allen House Bed & Breakfast, (913) 367-6380, 623 N. 5th. $47-$52.

Atchison Motor Inn, (913) 367-7000, US 73 and US 59. $36.

Comfort Inn, (800) 221-2222, 409 S. 9th St. $40-$48.

Williams House Bed & Breakfast, (913) 367-1757, 526 N. 5th. $45-$50.

ST. JOSEPH, MISSOURI

Days Inn, (800) 325-2525, 4312 Frederick Ave. $40-$45.

Drury Inn, (800) 325-8300, 4213 Frederick Ave. $50.

Holiday Inn, (800) HOLIDAY, 102 S. Third St. $53-$64.

Pony Express Motor Inn, (816) 233-3194, I-29 Exit 47. $30-$50.

ROCK PORT, MISSOURI

Rock Port Inn, (816) 744-6282, I-29 Exit 110. $36.

CAMPING

GREATER ST. LOUIS, MISSOURI/ILLINOIS

Babler Memorial State Park, (314) 458-3813, twenty minutes west on MO 109.

North Greater St. Louis KOA, (618) 931-5160, 3157 West Chain of Rocks Rd. (Granite City, IL).

St. Louis RV Park, (800) 878-3330, 900 N. Jerfferson Ave. (downtown).

St. Louis West KOA, (314) 257-3018, I-44 bus loop (Allenton, MO).

ST. CHARLES, MISSOURI

Sundermeier RV Park, (314) 724-8686, 111 Transit St.

Twin Island Lake Campground, (314) 447-0011, 7375 Twin Island Lake (eight miles east of I-70 via US 40/61).

HERMANN, MISSOURI

Hermann City Park, (573) 486-5953, junction of MO 19 and 100.

COLUMBIA, MISSOURI

KOA-Columbia, (314) 474-2911, I-70 Exit 128A.

BOONVILLE, MISSOURI

Bobber Campground, (816) 882-7135, I-70 and Hwy. B.

ARROW ROCK, MISSOURI

Arrow Rock State Historic Site, (816) 837-3330, MO 41.

GREATER KANSAS CITY, MISSOURI/KANSAS

Basswood Country RV Resort, (800) 242-2775, 15880 Interurban Rd. (Platte City).

Kansas City East KOA, (816) 625-7515, I-70 Exit 28 (Oak Grove).

Lake Jacomo Campground, (816) 229-8980, Colbern Rd. (Blue Springs).

Longview Reservoir, (816) 229-8980, View High Dr. (Lees Summit).

Miller's Kampark, (816) 781-7724, I-35 Exit 16 (Liberty).

Trailside Campers Inn of K.C., (816) 229-2267, I-70 Exit 24 (Grain Valley).

WESTON, MISSOURI

Weston Bend State Park, (816) 386-5443, MO 45.

RUSHVILLE, MISSOURI

Lewis and Clark State Park, (816) 579-5564, MO 45.

ATCHISON, KANSAS

Atchison County Lake, (913) 367-1653, Atchison County.

Atchison State Fishing Lake, (913) 367-7811, north on KS 7.

Warnock Lake, (913) 367-4179, City of Atchison.

ST. JOSEPH, MISSOURI

AOK Campground, (816) 324-4263, I-29 Exit 53.

Walnut Grove Campground, (816) 233-1974, I-29 Exit 53.

ROCK PORT, MISSOURI

KOA-Rock Port, (816) 744-5485, I-29 Exit 110.

RESTAURANTS

ALTON, ILLINOIS

Alton Belle Casino, (800) 722-3625. Restaurant and lounge aboard riverboat.

Cafe La Rose, (618) 463-2711, 300 Alby (in the Old Post Office Mall). Soups, sandwiches, and desserts at lunch.

Stratford Motor Hotel, (618) 465-8821, 3rd and Market. Sunday brunch buffet.

Tony's Restaurant and Lounge, (618) 462-8384, 312 Piasa. Steaks, chops, and Italian specialties.

GREATER ST. LOUIS, MISSOURI

The Border Grill, (314) 997-3700, 9119 Olive Blvd. Southwestern food.

Bogie's, (314) 241-9380, 809 N. 2nd. Specialties include prime rib.

Charlie Gitto's Pasta House, (314) 436-2828, 207 N. 6th. Popular with the sports crowd.

Hacienda Mexican Restaurant, (314) 962-7100, 9748 Manchester Rd. Mexican food, happy hour tapas buffet.

Jake's Steaks, (314) 621-8184, 707 Clamorgan Alley. Steaks with a Southwestern flair.

Lt. Robert E. Lee Restaurant, (314) 241-1282, St. Louis riverfront. Riverboat restaurant with view of Arch and St. Louis skyline.

Muddy Waters, (314) 421-5335, 724 N. 1st St. Charbroiled catfish and homemade soups.

The Old Spaghetti Factory, (314) 621-0276, 727 N. 1st St. Italian food amid antiques and a trolley car.

ST. CHARLES, MISSOURI

Gingham's Homestyle Restaurant, (314) 946-0266, 1881 Sherman. Open 24 hours.

Lewis and Clark's, (314) 947-3334, 217 S. Main. Contemporary menu in historic building.

The Miller's Daughter, (314) 946-4262, 329 S. Main St. British cuisine.

River Star Cafe, (314) 949-2525, 117 S. Main. Lunch and dinner at indoor-outdoor cafe.

Riverside Restaurant and Bar, (314) 949-2656, 204 N. Main. Dining on deck overlooking the Missouri River.

WASHINGTON, MISSOURI

The Basket Case Import and Deli, (314) 239-7127, 5th and Cedar. Thick sandwiches and exotic beverages.

Little Sicily, (314) 239-0099, 602 W. 5th. Family-style Italian dining.

Old Dutch Restaurant, (314) 239-0030, 3rd and Elm. Country breakfasts, casual luncheons, and candlelight dinners.

HERMANN, MISSOURI

Vintage 1847 Restaurant, (573) 486-3479, at Stone Hill Winery. Casual dining with scenic hilltop view.

JEFFERSON CITY, MISSOURI

Carnegie's at the Plaza, (573) 635-1234, in the Capitol Plaza Hotel and Convention Center. Elegant dining.

Das Stein Haus, (573) 634-3869, 1436 Southridge Dr. German food.

Madison's Cafe, (573) 634-2988, 216 Madison. Casual dining featuring homemade pastas.

COLUMBIA, MISSOURI

Carlos Garcia's, (314) 442-1184, 909 Business Loop 70E. Northern Mexican food.

Heritage House Smorgasbord, (314) 443-4567, 1010 I-70 Drive S.W.

Jack's Gourmet Restaurant, (314) 449-3927, 1903 I-70 Business Loop 70E. Dinner club featuring steak and seafood.

Katy Station, (314) 449-0835, 402 E. Broadway. Dine in converted boxcars and train station.

The Original Bobby Buford Restaurant, (314) 445-8647, I-70 and Stadium Blvd. Steak and seafood.

BOONVILLE, MISSOURI

Bobber Restaurant, (816) 882-6334, I-70 and Hwy. B. Open 24 hours.

ARROW ROCK, MISSOURI

Arrow Rock Ice Cream Emporium, (816) 837-3337. Sandwiches, desserts.

The Evergreen Restaurant, (816) 837-3251, MO 41. Fine dining in restored 1840s home. Call for reservations.

The Old Schoolhouse Cafe, (816) 837-3331. Breakfast and lunch.

The Old Tavern, (816) 837-3200, Main St. Country-style cooking.

GREATER KANSAS CTY, MISSOURI/KANSAS

Chappell's Restaurant and Lounge, (816) 421-0002, 323 Armour Rd. Steaks and burgers amid big sports memorabilia collection.

City Seen Restaurant, (816) 472-8833, Town Pavilion Mall (12th and Main). Contemporary American cuisine.

Corner Restaurant, (816) 931-6630, 4059 Broadway. Westport's favorite breakfast spot.

Dick Clark's American Bandstand Grill, (913) 451-1600, 10975 Metcalf Ave. (Overland Park, Kansas). American food amid rock music memorabilia.

Gates Barbecue, (816) 923-0900, 4707 Paseo and five other locations. Often voted KC's best.

Milano, (816) 426-1130, 2450 Grand Ave. (Crown Center). Casual Italian dining.

Stanford & Sons, (816) 561-7454, 504 Westport Rd. Fun dining in one of KC's oldest buildings.

Winstead's, (816) 252-9363, 1428 S. Noland Rd. (Independence). Steakburgers, fountain specialties.

WESTON, MISSOURI

America Bowman Restaurant, (816) 386-5235, Short and Welt St. Traditional Irish dishes in pub-style dining room.

Don's Market and Deli, (816) 386-5625, 420 Main St. Daily specials and famous cheeseburgers.

Weston Pizzeria, (816) 386-5233, 414 Main St. Pizza and sandwiches.

ATCHISON, KANSAS

The Great Wall, (913) 367-3350, 806 Commercial. Chinese-American food.

Paulucci Restaurant and Lounge, (913) 367-6105. Italian-American cuisine.

ST. JOSEPH, MISSOURI

Boathouse Restaurant, (913) 364-0544, 4012 River Rd. Riverfront dining specializing in fish and Cajun cuisine.

The Bucket Shop, (913) 238-8888, 5225 Lake Ave. Steak, seafood, sandwiches.

Frederick Inn Steak House, (913) 364-5151, 1627 Frederick Ave. Steak, seafood, prime rib, children's menu.

Old Hoof & Horn Restaurant, (913) 238-0742, 429 Illinois Ave. Steak, prime rib, lunch specials.

ROCK PORT, MISSOURI

Trail's End Restaurant, (816) 744-6389. I-29 Exit 110. Open 24 hours.

CHAPTER FOUR

NEBRASKA, IOWA, AND SOUTH DAKOTA

This scenery already rich pleasing and beautiful was still far-ther heightened by immense herds of buffalo, deer, elk, and antelopes which we saw in every direction feeding on the hills and plains. I do not think I exaggerate when I estimate the number of buffalo which could be (comprehended) at one view to amount to 3,000.
—Meriwether Lewis, September 17, 1804,
near present-day Chamberlain, South Dakota.

BROWNVILLE STATE RECREATION AREA

Summer on the Missouri River can be an unpredictable time, as the Corps of Discovery learned in July 1804. One day, the men would be in danger of sunstroke. The next, they'd be shivering through a thunderstorm. Clark described a typically atypical summer day, July 14, like this: "Some hard showers of rain this morning prevented our starting out until 7 o'clock. At half past seven, the atmosphere became suddenly darkened by a black and dismal-looking cloud...in this situation the storm which passed over an open plain from the northeast struck the (our) boat on the starboard quarter, and would have thrown her up on the sand island dashed to pieces in an instant, had not the party leaped out on the leeward side and kept her off with the assistance of the anchor and cable until the storm was over.... In this situation we continued about forty minutes when the storm suddenly ceased and the river became instantaneously as smooth as glass."

Meriwether Lewis Museum of Missouri River History at Brownville, Nebraska.

The episode Clark described took place near present-day Indian Cave State Park in southeast Nebraska. The next night, the corps camped near Brownville, Nebraska. Settled in 1854, Brownville is among Nebraska's oldest towns. Brownville has a population of only about 150 people, but it frequently has several times that many visitors. Many come to trace the past at Brownville State Recreation Area.

Brownville is best reached via U.S. Highway 136, west from Rock Port, Missouri, or east from Auburn, Nebraska. A historical marker at the recreation area notes that on July 15, 1804, Lewis and Clark camped south of here on the northeast side of the river after traveling about ten miles. The next morning, the keelboat caught on a snag in the river; despite the delay, the corps made twenty miles that day. Clearly, the men of the expedition were becoming expert boatmen.

The recreation area's centerpiece is the Meriwether Lewis Museum of Missouri River History, the *Meriwether Lewis,* a steam-powered U.S. Army Corps of Engineers vessel that is drydocked within sight of the river. In its heyday, the *Meriwether Lewis* helped stabilize the Missouri for navigation starting in the 1930s. The boat remains pretty much as it was during its active career, and anyone who served on a similar craft would find it especially interesting. Tours are available, and there are plenty of exhibits including a Missouri River Rat Hall of Fame and a former cabin filled with Lewis and Clark lore. Admission is one dollar for adults and fifty cents for kids ages six through twelve. (Younger children are admitted free.) Hours are 10 a.m. to 5 p.m. daily June through August, with the same hours, but on weekends only May and September.

Brownville State Recreation Area has a pleasant primitive campground in a grove of trees not far from the steamboat. (Some sites even command views of the old vessel through the trees). There is no fee for camping, but there are only fourteen sites, and they tend to go quickly. *The Spirit of Brownville* paddlewheeler offers two-hour cruises from the park at 3 p.m. Thursday through Sunday in July and August. Call (402) 825-6441 for rates and information.

Brownville is an interesting little town with its own concert hall and something happening almost every weekend all summer long, from the big flea market Memorial Day Weekend to Old Time Radio Days in late August. The Brownville Methodist Church is the oldest Methodist church in Nebraska still holding services every Sunday. Another local landmark, the Muir House, has a third-floor observatory. Several other fascinating buildings may be seen in the town's historic district, an area roughly bounded by First, Seventh, Nemaha, and Richard streets.

Missouri River at Brownville.

From Brownville, continue west on US 136 to Auburn, another interesting little town known as southeast Nebraska's antiques capital with about thirty dealers at last count. From Auburn, head north on US 75. The southeastern corner of the Cornhusker State is quite pretty, with lush, rolling green hills and prosperous-looking farms. Twenty-five miles north of Auburn, the highway reaches Nebraska City. This area is especially lovely in springtime when the apple trees are decked out in blossoms. Nebraska City's attractions include Arbor Lodge State Historical Park and the Morton Orchard and Tree Farm, both of which commemorate the life of J. Sterling Morton, the founder of Arbor Day. Lewis and Clark camped July 18-19, 1804, near what is now Riverview Marina State Recreation Area, a Missouri River access point just north of Nebraska City.

OMAHA, COUNCIL BLUFFS, AND FORT ATKINSON

Lewis and Clark conducted their first council with an Indian tribe at a Nebraska site called Council Bluffs, not to be confused with the Iowa city of the same name. Early in August 1804, the captains met with a group of Oto and Missouri Indians at the site about fifteen miles north of downtown Omaha. Fort Atkinson State Historical Park marks the site today, but before heading there, visitors may want to stop to see several points of interest in the Omaha-Council Bluffs area.

For starters, there's the new Western Historic Trails Center, located about a half-mile south of Interstate 80's Exit 1-B in Council Bluffs. The center includes exhibits on the Lewis and Clark Expedition as well as on the Mormon, Oregon, and California trails. Hiking trails lead to the nearby Missouri River banks. The center is open from 9 a.m. to 5 p.m. daily except Thanksgiving, Christmas, and New Year's Day. Admission is free. Call (712) 325-4900 for more information.

The city of Council Bluffs also has established a small park at its Lewis and Clark Monument on the bluffs north of town. The stone-plaza monument offers an outstanding view of the Missouri River, Omaha, and Council Bluffs. The site is also a favorite with red-tail hawks, which are often seen riding the thermals above the bluffs. It's a splendid place for a picnic.

To get to the overlook, take North 16th Street and turn right at the sign for Big Lake Park. Drive beneath a railroad trestle into the park and skirt its edges on the road. Past a second railroad trestle, turn left on North 8th Street. After about 0.3 mile, turn left again. The entrance to the park is 0.7 mile up the hill on the left.

Omaha's N.P. Dodge Park also pays tribute to the corps' first encounter with native people. A small plaque in the parking lot near the camping area notes that the expedition camped just across the river. Dodge Park has plenty of big grassy areas for a variety of sports, as well as a bridle trail and horse camping area. An RV dump station is available.

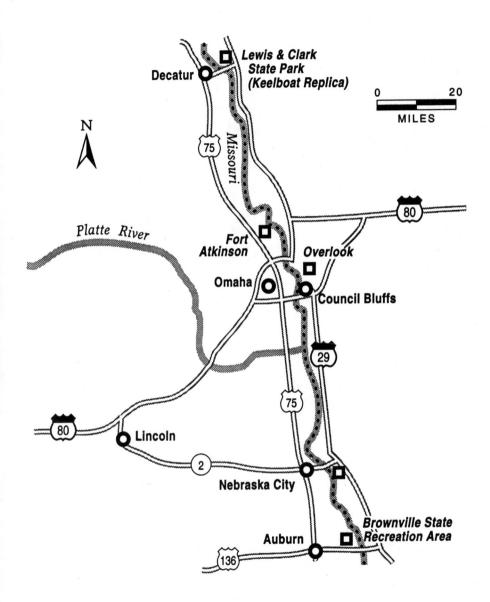

N

Decatur

Lewis & Clark
State Park
(Keelboat Replica)

0   20
MILES

75

Missouri

Platte River

80

Fort
Atkinson

Overlook

Omaha

Council Bluffs

29

75

80

Lincoln

2

Nebraska City

Brownville State
Recreation Area

Auburn

136

Lewis and Clark overlook, Council Bluffs, Iowa.

To get to Dodge Park from Council Bluffs, take Interstate 29 north, then I-680 west over the Mormon Bridge, then follow the signs to the park.

Fort Atkinson is located just east of the town of Fort Calhoun, situated north of Omaha along US 75. Archaeological crews from the Nebraska Historical Society conducted digs at the site during the 1950s, hoping to establish the location of the fort's walls, gates, and outbuildings. All records at the fort indicated it was the site of the Indian council. But sometime after 1827, when the fort was decommissioned, the Missouri River shifted course and is now about three miles east of the original bluff. Moreover, the face of the land is much different now than nearly two hundred years ago, with scrub trees and brush covering the face of the bluffs, and it is impossible to tell exactly where the council was held. Still, one can walk the grounds secure in the knowledge it was near here the first momentous encounter took place.

For a while, it looked like the council was not to be. In late July, camped down in the vicinity of the Platte River, Drouillard and Cruzatte went out in search of the Indians, only to learn the Otos had moved onto the plains for their annual buffalo hunt. Dejected, the explorers moved upriver. But just a few days later, Drouillard located a Missouri Indian who said that while most of the Otos were off on the buffalo hunt, a hundred or so Indians were camped nearby. On July 29, the captains sent one of the French boatmen, Liberte, with the Missouri Indian to locate the Indians and invite them to council.

The Corps of Discovery moved upriver, arriving at the bluff July 30. Captains Lewis and Clark walked up the bluff together and marveled at a landscape far different than any they'd yet seen. "This prairie is covered with grass of ten or twelve inches in height, soil of good quality and at the distance of about a mile still farther back the country rises about eighty or ninety feet higher, and is one continued plain as far as can be seen," Clark wrote. "From the bluff on the second rise immediately above our camp, the most beautiful prospect of the river up and down and the country opposed presented itself which I ever beheld."

Back at camp, the men waited. The Indians finally arrived late on August 2, and the captains suggested they meet the next morning. Lewis, aided by Clark, stayed up late that night writing the first speech he would make to the Indians. It was an important occasion, the first instance in which the party would attempt to fulfill one of the principal orders set forth by President Jefferson. "In all your intercourse with the natives treat them in the most friendly and conciliatory manner which their own conduct will admit," Jefferson wrote. "Allay all jealousies as to the object of your journey, satisfy them of its innocence, make them acquainted with the position, extent, character, peaceable and commercial dispositions of the U.S., of our wish to be neighborly, friendly and useful to them, and of our dispositions to a commercial intercourse with them."

The next day, Lewis told the Otos all that and more. In a long speech, he explained how the Missouri River was now controlled by the United States—the Great Father in Washington—and that, if the Indians honored that sovereignty, there would be good trading for all. The Indians followed with a speech of their own, "promising to pursue the advice and directions given them that they were happy to find that they had fathers which might be depended on," Clark wrote. The speeches were accompanied by gifts to the Otos, and by a demonstration of the corps' airgun, an example of new American technology that never failed to amaze the natives. It is true the captains were disappointed that they were unable to meet with the main chiefs of the Otos and Missouris. On the other hand, this first encounter with the Indians had gone smoothly. All in all, the council had to be considered a success.

Fort Atkinson's visitor center offers a slide show explaining the Louisiana Purchase and Lewis and Clark Expedition, in addition to the fort's military history. Fort Atkinson served as an important outpost for frontier exploration and trapping until it was abandoned in 1827, replaced by Fort Leavenworth, which was better situated to protect traffic on the Santa Fe Trail.

A walking trail leads from the visitor center to the fort's reconstruction. The fort consisted of a rectangular formation of one-story barracks built from horizontal logs. The barracks opened out upon an enclosed parade ground. Other buildings included a large council house for negotiating with the Indians, a grist mill, a schoolhouse, and a brick kiln.

Fort Atkinson's visitor center is normally open daily Memorial Day Weekend through Labor Day Weekend from 9 a.m. to 5 p.m. During late April and May and September and October, the visitor center is open weekends from 10 a.m. to 5 p.m. Several living history days set each spring, summer, and fall concentrate on military activities at Fort Atkinson. For more information, call (402) 468-5611.

Fort Calhoun is a tiny town of small, neat houses, and a few home-style restaurants. In addition to Fort Atkinson, Fort Calhoun is home to the Washington County Historical Museum. From here, the expedition continued north to present-day Blair, Nebraska, a bustling community that serves as gateway to the De Soto National Wildlife Refuge. From Blair, travel north on US 75 (in Nebraska) or I-29 (in Iowa) to Onawa, Iowa, home of the Hawkeye State's version of Lewis and Clark State Park.

SIDETRIP: OMAHA AND COUNCIL BLUFFS ATTRACTIONS

With a population of about 625,000 people, Omaha-Council Bluffs is the last major metropolitan area near the Lewis and Clark Trail until Portland, Oregon. As such, it offers quite a lot in the way of recreation, visitor attractions, culture, and shopping.

The Joslyn Art Museum, 2200 Dodge St., is recognized as one of the Midwest's best. Housed in a marble Art Deco building, the Joslyn's collections include works from ancient Greece and Egypt and from the European masters. It may be best known, however, for its outstanding collection of art depicting the American West, especially the work of Swiss artist Karl Bodmer.

Bodmer's work is of great interest to Lewis and Clark buffs chiefly for its depiction of the Upper Missouri, a region Bodmer traversed with his boss, Alexander Phillip Maximilian, Prince of Wied, on the steamboat *Yellow Stone*, in the 1830s. Bodmer's paintings depict in image much of what Lewis and Clark noted in their journals thirty years earlier. He also is known for his many beautiful Indian portraits.

The Henry Doorly Zoo, another popular Omaha attraction, is located at Deer Park Boulevard and South 10th Street Zoo highlights include a huge open-air aviary and the Lied Jungle, stocked with rain forest plants, animals, birds, and fish from Asia, Africa, and South America. A children's petting zoo, aquarium, educational center, and steam train ride are also among the exhibits and activities.

Other sightseeing possibilities in Omaha include Father Flanagan's Boys Town, two miles west of I-680 on US 6; the Omaha Children's Museum, packed with hands-on activities at 500 S. 20th St.; horse racing at Ak-Sar-Ben May through August; and the Great Plains Black Museum, 2213 Lake Street. Omaha was also the site of the Mormons' winter headquarters as they moved west during the mid-1840s. A center commemorating the trek is located at 3215 State St.

Council Bluffs, Iowa, weighs in with several attractions of its own. Bluffs Run Greyhound Park features year-round parimutuel racing with a dining room and sports bar. Railroad fans will enjoy trips to the RailsWest Railroad Museum at 16th Avenue and South Main Street; the Golden Spike Monument at South 16th St. and 9th Avenue; and the Grenville M. Dodge Home at 605 3rd St., erected in 1869 by the Civil War general and railroad builder. Council Bluffs also is the northern terminus of the Wabash Trace Nature Trail, a sixty-three-mile route through rural southwestern Iowa.

Annual events in the area include the Renaissance Faire of the Midlands, held the second weekend each June at Iowa Western Community College in Council Bluffs; the Phantasmagoric Arts Festival, held each August in Council Bluff's Bayliss Park; and the Omaha Summer Arts Festival, also held each June. For more information about Omaha, call (800) 332-1819, or stop by the visitor center near I-80's 13th St. exit. To learn more about Council Bluffs, stop by the visitor center at the RailsWest Museum, or call (712) 325-1000.

LEWIS AND CLARK STATE PARK (IOWA)

Although it is located along the Corps of Discovery's route, nothing really remarkable happened at Iowa's Lewis and Clark State Park. The expedition camped in the vicinity on August 10, 1804, on the far side near the present-day KOA campground. The site is definitely worth a visit, however, because it is home to a marvelous full-scale replica of the expedition's keelboat, as well as its two pirogues.

The keelboat replica was planned and constructed under the supervision of Butch Bouvier, a local woodwright, history aficionado, and boat buff. To created the replica, Bouvier used both William Clark's drawings of the keelboat and his own research into early 19th century boat building. Its hull was launched in 1987, and its deck, mast, sidewall lockers, and cabins were added later. In fact, visitors who stop by the park early in the season may find volunteers on the scene, making new improvements to the project. Bouvier also built a small model of the boat that now sits in the park superintendent's office.

The boats are usually on view from mid-May through August. The best time to visit, however, may be during the Lewis and Clark Festival the second weekend each June. Events include music and dancing, historical presentations, a buffalo burger feed, a black powder shoot, quilt and art shows, tomahawk throw, a pancake feed, fun run, and Lewis

Butch Bouvier and Les Peary with a keelboat replica at Lewis and Clark State Park near Onawa, Iowa.

and Clark pageant. Visitors may even get a chance to help the crew in the keelboat if they come in costume.

Like its Missouri neighbor, Iowa's Lewis and Clark State Park rests on the shore of an oxbow lake. Blue Lake was part of the river in 1804 and now serves as nucleus of a state park that offers a campground with boat access, a beach, and good fishing opportunities. Picnic areas and hiking trails make the park a nice spot for day use, too. For more information, call (712) 423-2829.

The town of Onawa is just east of the park. It boasts what is supposed to be the widest Main Street in America, a claim to fame celebrated the third Saturday in each June with an old-fashioned dance, car show, and "cruise." Onawa also lures visitors with Casino Omaha, a twenty-four-hour gaming emporium stocked with hundreds of slot machines and a variety of tables. For entertainment of a different sort, the town also serves as the northern gateway to the Loess Hills, a land formation found only two places in the world: western Iowa and China.

BLACKBIRD HILL

From Onawa, cross the toll bridge over the Missouri River into Nebraska and rejoin US 75 at Decatur. Somewhere between here and Macy ten miles to the north is Blackbird Hill, grave of the chief of the Omahas.

After the meeting at Council Bluffs, the Corps of Discovery once again started up the Missouri. It wasn't long before one of the privates, Moses Reed, requested permission to go back and retrieve a knife he said he'd left at the council site. Soon, however, it became apparent Reed had deserted, the second man to do so in one week. Liberte, sent earlier to call the Otos to council, had also disappeared.

The captains sent a four-man search party to bring the deserters back. Meanwhile, the main party moved farther upriver in hopes of meeting the Omahas. On August 11, 1804, they came upon a mound about three hundred feet high, marked at the top with a post. It was Blackbird's grave. Lewis, Clark, and ten of their men decided to climb up, have a look, and pay their respects—even if Blackbird was the sort of man who won respect out of fear, not admiration. For a brief time, the Omahas had enjoyed great power under Blackbird. He frequently used arsenic to poison his rivals, and by this and other means, he and his tribe waged a war of terror over any party trying to pass through their country. But Blackbird's reign was cut short when a smallpox epidemic swept through the Omaha village, reducing its population from seven hundred to no more than three hundred.

In Blackbird's day, and in the time of Lewis and Clark, Blackbird Hill offered a commanding view up and down about seventy miles of the Missouri River. These days, timber growth has obscured what once was a fine view, and the site on the Omaha Indian Reservation is off limits to

View of Missouri River from Blackbird Hill wayside, Nebraska.

the general public. But a road wayside area about 3.5 miles southeast of the actual site provides a similar hilltop view of the Missouri, along with interpretation of Omaha history. The overlook is situated along US 75 about 2.5 miles north of Decatur.

The Omahas' earliest known home was the Ohio River Valley. Like Lewis and Clark after them, the Omaha people knew how tough it was to battle the Missouri upstream, and their name means "against the current." By 1700, the tribe had migrated to the Blood Run site about 100 miles north of the Blackbird Hill area, and moved several more times around the vicinity before building their "Big Village" about twenty miles north of Blackbird Hill in 1775. Creation of this village (called *Tonwontongathon* in the Omaha language) coincided with Blackbird's rise to power.

A shelter at the site recreates the look of an Omaha earth lodge, although, at just thirty feet in diameter, it would have been considered small. Many lodges spanned up to sixty feet in diameter, able to accommodate large families and their horses. The exhibit notes how two men of the Lewis and Clark Expedition—Pierre Cruzatte and Francois Labiche—were sons of Omaha mothers and thus began the tribe's long history of U.S. military service.

Another exhibit at the wayside explains the Missouri River Corridor Project, which seeks to re-establish some of the waterway's natural habitat that was inadvertently degraded or destroyed by river channelization and stabilization. Ultimately, the project aims to renovate oxbow lakes and other floodplain wetland sites to provide breeding, rearing, and feeding areas for fish, migratory waterfowl, and native species. Proponents also hope to restore and interpret sites important to the region's early history and culture, as well as provide increased recreational access.

The Corps of Discovery located the main Omaha village August 14 and hoped for a council, but again, the village was nearly deserted. Finally, on August 17, the search party returned with Reed in tow, accompanied by three Indian chiefs who had been traveling with Reed and who hoped to make peace with the Omahas. Liberte, for his part, had been caught but got away.

Found guilty of desertion the next day, Reed was sentenced to run four times through a gauntlet of his peers, who beat him with willow switches. This shocked the visiting Indian chiefs, who "petitioned for pardon of this man," Clark wrote. But after the captains explained the necessity for such punishment, "they were all satisfied with the propriety of the sentence," Clark added. Afterward, the mood turned merrier as everyone celebrated Captain Lewis's thirtieth birthday with an extra measure of whisky and dancing.

Continue north on US 75 through some very pretty hill country. The Omaha Nation runs a bingo and casino hall located south of Macy, and the town is the site of the annual Omaha powwow the weekend nearest the full moon of August. Daily events begin at 1 p.m., and the public is welcome. Winnebago, ten miles to the north, serves as headquarters for the Winnebago Indian Reservation. Its powwow takes place the last full weekend in July, and a one-time admission is good for all four days of events. From Winnebago, it is less than a half-hour's drive to Sioux City, Iowa.

SERGEANT FLOYD MONUMENT

It seems almost unbelievable that during more than two-and-a-half-years in the wilderness, facing everything from grizzly bears to rattlesnakes to occasionally hostile Indians and frequently extreme weather, only one member of the Lewis and Clark Expedition died. The Sergeant Floyd Monument in Sioux City pays tribute to that man.

The Omahas never returned to their village during the corps' brief respite there, so a council was held with the visiting Oto and Missouri chiefs on August 19. "We showed them many curiosities and the airgun which they were much astonished at," Clark wrote. But by the end of the day, the captains' attention had turned to Sergeant Charles Floyd, who was clearly very ill with what the captains believed was a bilious colic. "We attempt to relieve him without success as yet, he gets worse and we are much alarmed at his situation," Clark wrote. On July 31, Floyd him-

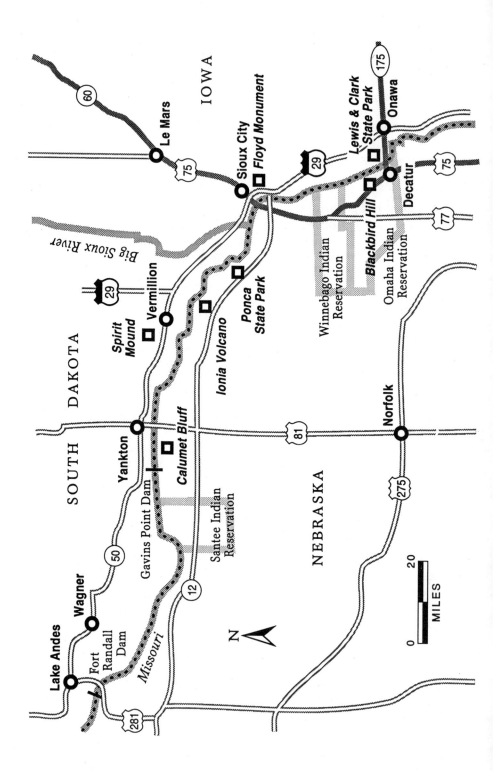

IOWA

SOUTH DAKOTA

NEBRASKA

Le Mars

Sioux City

Floyd Monument

Lewis & Clark State Park

Onawa

Decatur

Winnebago Indian Reservation

Blackbird Hill

Omaha Indian Reservation

Big Sioux River

Vermillion

Spirit Mound

Ionia Volcano

Ponca State Park

Norfolk

Yankton

Calumet Bluff

Gavins Point Dam

Santee Indian Reservation

Wagner

Lake Andes

Fort Randall Dam

Missouri

N

MILES

0 20

self had written in his journal, "I am very sick and has been for sometime but have recovered my health again." That statement has led modern doctors and historians to believe Floyd actually suffered from an infected appendix—an ailment no doctor of the time could have cured.

On the morning of August 20, 1804, the corps proceeded upriver as usual. But by noon, Floyd had taken a turn for the worse. The party halted to prepare a warm bath for their colleague. But before it was ready, Floyd turned to Clark and said, "I'm going away. I want you to write a letter." Those were the sergeant's last words.

The corps saw another riverside bluff a mile or so away and decided it would be a fitting final resting place for their comrade. Floyd was wrapped in a blanket, carried to the hilltop, and buried with full military honors. Patrick Gass was selected to replace the fallen sergeant. The bluff on which Floyd was buried was named after him, as was a small stream in the vicinity.

Over the next few decades, Sergeant Floyd's grave became something of a 19th-century tourist attraction. The corps visited on its way home in 1806; others who stopped by probably included artists George Catlin and John Audubon and Maximilian, Prince of Wied. According to Roy Appleman, author of the National Park Service guide to Lewis and Clark sites, an 1857 flood swept away part of the bluff, reportedly exposing some of poor Floyd's bones. The remains were rescued and reburied

View from the Sergeant Floyd Monument at Sioux City, Iowa.

about two hundred yards back from the face of the bluff in an unmarked grave—but that site was nearly forgotten when dirt from railroad construction was dumped nearby. Finally in 1900, the current one hundred-foot concrete obelisk was erected and Floyd's remains once again interred. The monument was dedicated in 1901, the first site ever to be registered as an official National Historic Landmark.

To visit the site, travel 0.5 mile east and 0.5 mile north of I-29's exit 143. A plaque on the monument reads: "In commemoration of the Louisiana Purchase made during the administration of Thomas Jefferson, third president of the United States, April 3, 1803; of its successful exploration by the heroic members of the Lewis and Clark Expedition; of the valor of the American soldier; and of the enterprise, courage and fortitude of the American pioneer, to whom these great states west of the Mississippi River owe their secure foundation."

Below the monument, a rock wall provides a panoramic overlook. Today's view, dominated by highways and railroad tracks, isn't especially scenic, but an interpretive panel points out several spots of historic note, including the approximate site of Floyd's death and the mouth of the Floyd River, where Lewis and Clark camped after the burial.

The sergeant's memory is preserved elsewhere in and around Sioux City, too. Floyd Boulevard is one of the town's main thoroughfares, and a small town south of Sioux City is named Sergeant Bluff. Most prominent, however, is the Sergeant Floyd Riverboat Museum and Welcome Center. The drydocked *Sergeant Floyd*, once a diesel inspection boat, plied the Missouri River for fifty years as flagship of the U.S. Army Corps of Engineers construction fleet. The boat now serves as a museum focusing on Missouri River history, but it also includes memorabilia from the Lewis and Clark Expedition. Travel information and gifts are also available. The center is located at 1000 Larson Park Road (Exit 149 off of I-29). Hours are 8 a.m. to 6 p.m. Monday through Saturday and 10 a.m. to 6 p.m. Sunday from May through September. Off-season, the center is open 9 a.m. to 5 p.m. Monday through Saturday and noon to 5 p.m. Sunday.

The Sioux City Public Museum, located in a former mansion at 2901 Jackson St., includes displays on anthropology, archaeology, natural history, science, and military memorabilia. The Sioux City Art Center at 513 Nebraska St. offers changing exhibits of contemporary artwork from the Upper Midwest. Sioux City's big annual festival, Rivercade, is held in late July. For more information on area events and attractions, stop by the welcome center or call (800) 593-2228.

From Sioux City, continue north on I-29 to Vermillion, South Dakota, home of Spirit Mound.

SPIRIT MOUND

At their meetings with the Oto Indians, the explorers heard a story they found foolish and fascinating at the same time. "In a northerly direction from the mouth of this creek in an immense plain a high hill is situated, and appears of a conic form, and by the different nations of Indians in this quarter is supposed to be the residence of devils," Clark wrote on August 24, 1804, as the party approached present-day Vermillion, South Dakota. "They are in human form with remarkable large heads, and about eighteen inches high, that they are very watchful and armed with sharp arrows with which they can kill at a great distance; they are said to kill all persons who are so hardy as to attempt to approach the hill.... So much do the Omaha, Sioux, Otos and other neighboring nations believe this fable, that no consideration is sufficient to induce them to approach the hill."

At first, the captains decided to sail on by the trail leading to Spirit Mound. But they reconsidered and, as David Lavender wrote in *The Way to the Western Sea*, "curiosity and conscience got the best of them. Just suppose such creatures did exist and they left the discovery to someone else?"

So Lewis, Clark, and nine other men made the trip on August 25. It was an oppressively hot day, and it took nearly three hours to reach the landmark. Lewis's dog, Seaman, collapsed on the way; he was almost joined by his master, who two days earlier had mildly poisoned himself while tasting the minerals of a bluff the party had encountered near Sioux City. But they finally made it and were rewarded, not by death, but by an astounding view of the surrounding plains. Clark described it thus: "From the top of this mound we beheld a most beautiful landscape; numerous herds of buffalo were seen feeding in various directions; the Plain to the north-northwest and northeast extends without interruption as far as can be seen."

The explorers concluded it must have been the swirl of birds and insects on the mound that produced the Indian legends—that, and the fact the mound did stand out quite remarkably from the surrounding landscape. They soon retreated to the Vermillion River where, hungry and thirsty, they found water and a variety of delicious fruits including grapes, plums, and currants.

Spirit Mound is still visible today, located on private land west of South Dakota 19, about eight miles north of Vermillion. An interpretive sign is placed in view of the mound, but the landmark is well worth a closer look, mainly because it is one of just a few places along the Lewis and Clark Trail that today's traveler can know with certainty he or she is standing in the exact spot the explorers stood. To get permission stop at the farm house at the site.

The view from atop Spirit Mound is indeed beautiful. In recent years, the landmark has become a focus of preservation efforts, particularly since the site now abuts a feedlot that is steadily eroding the bluff. A private group is now seeking to raise about one million dollars to buy the site, restore the area, build a visitor center and walking trail, and maintain the property. Donations or requests for more information may be sent to the Spirit Mound Trust, c/o the South Dakota Preservation Office, 3 E. Main St., Vermillion, SD 57069.

Vermillion is a pleasant college town of about ten thousand people. The South Dakota state legislature named Vermillion the site of the university in 1862, but classes weren't held until twenty years later. Vermillion was originally located closer to the river, but a big flood in 1881 forced the town to move atop the bluffs.

The local Lions club has established a public campground right along the business route on the edge of town; in addition to RV space, the park offers lots of shade trees and a playground for kids. Another park, Prentice Park, has a swimming pool with a water slide and a Frisbee golf course. Vermillion's cultural attractions are centered on the University of South Dakota campus and include the Shrine to Music Museum, home to more than six thousand rare and antique instruments, and the W.H. Over State Museum.

Spirit Mound near Vermillion, South Dakota.

From Vermillion, it's about a half-hour's drive to Yankton on South Dakota 50. Two towns along the way are running a good-natured battle about just which one really produces more hay. Gayville's sign says it is the "hay capital of the world," while Meckling goes Gayville one better, claiming it is "hay capital of the universe."

RIVERS AND LAKES: THE NEBRASKA-SOUTH DAKOTA BORDER

Next to the Missouri Breaks section in Montana, the sixty or so miles of Missouri River northwest of Sioux City to Gavins Point Dam are the least changed from the days of Lewis and Clark. Upstream, the river also flows free from the mouth of the Niobrara River to Fort Randall Dam. Snags, sandbars, islands, eroding banks, and a merrily meandering channel are all still alive and well on the Nebraska-South Dakota border.

In spite of that, it's the lakes—not the river—that are the real star attractions in the area. Perhaps because the river can only be accessed at a few places (including Ponca and Niobrara state parks in Nebraska and Clay County Park and Yankton Community Park in South Dakota), Lewis and Clark Lake upriver from Gavins Point overshadows the wild Missouri, its shores teeming with one campground, beach, and boat ramp after another. Most of the two million or so annual visitors have recreation on their minds, but it's also possible to find a healthy dose of history, notably at the Gavins Point Dam Visitor Center, located on the Nebraska side of the river west of Yankton.

The center sits atop Calumet Bluff. The expedition camped from August 28 to September 1, 1804, on the bottomlands below and held a council with the friendly Yankton Sioux, with Pierre Dorion—who had joined the group some weeks before—serving as translator. The council and the Lewis and Clark Expedition in general are the subject of excellent interpretation at Gavins Point. Other exhibits talk about the Missouri River, one offering this quote from Stanley Vestal: "There are streams that have no story except that of the people on their banks. But the Missouri River is a story in itself, and no idyll or eclogue either, but a heroic poem, an epic. It is a thoroughly masculine river, a burly, husky bulldozer of a stream which has taken upon the biggest job of moving dirt in North America. It has been well named 'the Big Muddy.'" The river exhibit also notes how glacial movement created the differences in terrain seen north and east of present-day Lewis and Clark Lake (where rolling hills, lakes, and marshes predominate) and the high plains to the west, an area never touched by the glaciers.

The center has many exhibits geared to kids (but interesting to adults, too). One asks questions about birds, with the answers hidden beneath flaps. For example: "Can you name the bird that builds a nest twenty feet deep and ten feet wide that weighs two tons?" (Answer: the bald eagle.) Other exhibits examine endangered wildlife. Another interesting display shows how tornados form and includes incredible photos of a funnel cloud sweeping across Lewis and Clark Lake in April 1985. The area is on the northern edge of the Midwest's tornado belt.

Gavins Point Dam itself is interpreted as well. The structure was started in 1952 and completed in 1955, a rolled earth and chalk dam 74 feet high and 8,700 feet long including the spillway. The width at the top is thirty-five feet and maximum width at the base is six hundred feet. More than seven million cubic yards of earth fill were used to complete the dam.

Slide presentations are shown daily, and picnic and playground facilities are located outside. Tours of the dam are also available daily through the summer and by appointment the rest of the year. Gavins Point Dam Visitor Center is open seven days a week from 9 a.m. to 5 p.m. from Memorial Day through Labor Day, and 8 a.m. to 4:30 p.m. weekdays the rest of the year. For more information, call (402) 667-7873.

There are probably a thousand or more campsites surrounding Lewis and Clark Lake, but since they manage to fill up fast on many summer weekends, it's important to stake a place early. The campgrounds all look quite inviting, but in wet years, they can be abuzz with annoying gnats and small black flies. The usual insect repellents seem to have little power over these cursed critters, but South Dakota park personnel say a dab of vanilla extract may ward them off for a while. Try that, or play it safe and find a motel room in Yankton.

Other than the insect swarms, this is a splendid area, flanked by heavily treed, rolling hills. A nature foot trail in the Gavins Unit of South Dakota's Lewis and Clark State Recreation Area leads to a commanding view of the Missouri River bluffs. An interpretive shelter imparts information on the expedition's travels through the area.

Yankton, South Dakota, is a good-sized town with many hotels and restaurants. Many businesses cater to vacationers, but local people clearly enjoy the abundant recreation access, too. A popular bike path stretches from Yankton eight miles out to the Lewis and Clark state recreation areas. Most of the trail is fairly flat, aside from a formidable hill just west of town. The *Far West* riverboat, named for Captain Grant Marsh's famous Missouri River vessel, offers a variety of sailings April through October, including historical cruises at 3 p.m. weekdays and 1 and 3 p.m. weekends. Lewis and Clark Marina just west of Gavins Point Dam (on the Nebraska side) rents and services boats for do-it-yourself sailors.

It's a half-day's drive from Yankton to Pierre, South Dakota's capital and site of Lewis and Clark's fearsome confrontation with the Teton Sioux. Cross-country travelers will probably want to make a beeline for Pierre, although it's also possible to dawdle a while on Nebraska 12. On the Nebraska side, the community nearest the dam is Crofton, which

Lewis and Clark Lake on the Nebraska-South Dakota border.

calls itself "the friendliest town by a dam site." It has a few restaurants and a nine-hole golf course with a view of the lake. Campers are welcome to spend one night free in Crofton's city park. Longer stays cost $2 per night, with a limit of seven days.

Newcastle, thirty-some miles east of Crofton, is best known as home of the Ionia Volcano. Clark reported here that the bluff felt hot to the touch, and later fur traders frequently noticed dense smoke and fire in the vicinity. In 1839, J.N. Nicollet tried to prove the phenomenon was not of volcanic origin, theorizing that the decomposition of beds of iron pyrites in contact with water resulted in a heat capable of igniting other combustible materials. Still, volcano stories persisted, spurred on by an earthquake in 1877. The next year, a flood undermined the bluff and nearly wiped out the town of Ionia. Volcano tales sputtered out soon after, and around 1900, scientists finally learned the heat was generated by the oxidation of shale.

Ponca State Park about fourteen miles east of Newcastle has good camping, cabins, swimming, and picnicking, but not much to specifically attract the Lewis and Clark sleuth. A three-mile trail leads to the Three State Overlook, where visitors can see from Nebraska across the Missouri River into South Dakota and Iowa. Here, the expedition is briefly given its due on a historical marker.

West of Crofton, a drive of about thirty miles puts the traveler at Niobrara State Park. This popular site offers fishing, swimming, boating,

Ponca State Park, Nebraska.

camping, hiking, and an excellent network of horseback riding trails that traverse the river bluffs. An interpretive shelter briefly outlines area history. The expedition camped in the area early in September 1804, and the junction of the Niobrara and Missouri rivers is sometimes called Lewis and Clark Point. From Niobrara, it's another thirty-seven miles west to US 281, which leads north across Fort Randall Dam to I-90 west of Mitchell, South Dakota.

The Fort Randall Dam area also has its share of activities and attractions. Missouri River Adventures based in Wagner specializes in one-day scenic floats and charter boat trips; call (605) 384-5526. Lyons Enterprises' Lewis and Clark Expeditions guides fishing and hunting trips and rents houseboats from its base fourteen miles west of Platte on South Dakota 44. Jim Lyons's number is (605) 337-3581. And the Fort Randall Casino and Hotel deals up gambling, entertainment, and dining twenty-four hours a day ten miles west of Wagner on South Dakota 46.

You can always tell when you're close to a major hydropower dam, which, near the Missouri River in the Dakotas, is just about everywhere. Huge high-tension electrical power poles dot the landscape, ready to carry electricity across the heartland. Dayton Duncan thought they looked like "giant kachina dolls, totems of the triumph and power of science." They also seem to resemble a company of robots transfixed on the high plains, arms outstretched, their huge and powerful legs cemented to the ground.

In the expedition's day, however, it was nature that commanded the men's attention. Paul Cutright, in his book *Lewis and Clark: Pioneering Naturalists*, called the twenty days the expedition spent between the Niobrara and Teton rivers the trip's most exciting period of zoological discovery. They saw pronghorn antelope, bison, wolves, magpies, coyotes, jackrabbits, and the curious "barking squirrels," better known today as prairie dogs. The latter was especially elusive. Private John Shields killed the first one, which was cooked for dinner, but finding another sample to send back to President Jefferson proved quite difficult. "Having no further luck with their guns, they resorted to digging," Cutright wrote. "After going down six feet and finding the runways seemed bottomless, they gave that up and tried flooding. This became a full-scale operation, with all members of the corps participating except a guard left with the boats. They spent a major portion of the day carrying water from the river and pouring it into the subterranean passageways. Though they persisted until nightfall, they succeeded in capturing only one, flushing it out alive. Clark had better luck a few days later. 'I killed four,' he reported, 'with a view to have their skins stuffed.'"

I-90 meets the Missouri River at Chamberlain, known for its walleye fishing and pheasant hunting. The U.S. Army Corps of Engineers runs a nice campground near downtown at American Creek, a waterway named by Lewis and Clark in mid-September 1804. Chamberlain already has many motels, and a major new resort, Cedar Shores, was expected to open in 1994. From Chamberlain, follow South Dakota 50 north to South Dakota 34, which leads west past the Big Bend of the Missouri to Pierre.

PIERRE AND THE TETON COUNCIL SITE

The expedition had a close call on the night of September 20-21, 1804, while camped in the vicinity of what is now West Bend State Recreation Area. "At half past one o'clock this morning the sand bar on which we were camped began to undermine and give way which alarmed the sergeant on guard," Clark wrote. "The motion of the boat awakened me; I got up and by the light of the moon observed that the sand had given away both above and below our camp and was falling in fast. I ordered all hands on as quick as possible and pushed off, we had pushed off but a few minutes before the bank under which the boat and pirogues lay gave way, which would certainly have sunk both pirogues."

This was an unnerving episode, to be sure, but it soon faded with the events of the next few days. The expedition entered what is now the Pierre area on September 23, camping near present-day Antelope Creek. That evening, three Sioux boys swam to the camp and told the explorers that two Teton Sioux villages were not far upriver. "We gave those boys

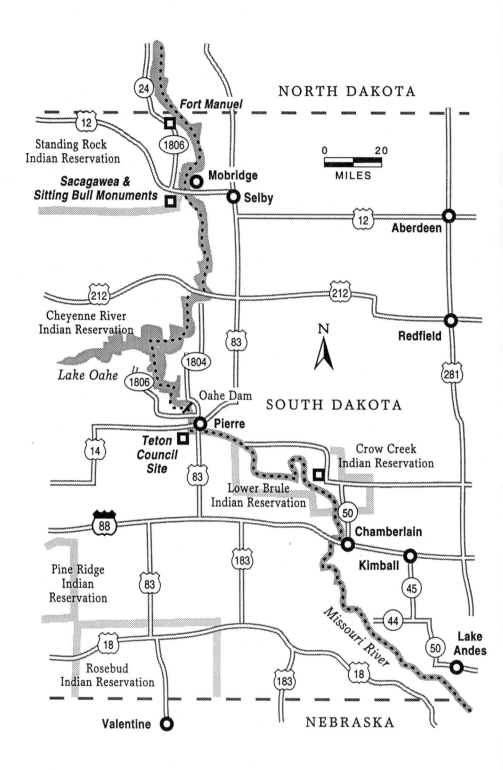

two carrots of tobacco to carry to their chiefs, with directions to tell them that we would speak to them tomorrow," Clark wrote.

On the twenty-fourth, Lewis and Clark somewhat nervously prepared for their meeting with the Teton Sioux—a tribe other Indians had mentioned with much fear and loathing. The boats moved thirteen miles to the mouth of the Bad River, which the explorers renamed the Teton River, perhaps in hopes of placating the Sioux. (It is once again known today as the Bad River.) Several chiefs arrived that evening, and arrangements were made for a council the next day.

The meeting took place at noon on the twenty-fifth on a sandbar in the mouth of the Bad River. Three Teton Sioux chiefs—Black Buffalo, The Partisan, and Buffalo Medicine—were on hand. But both sides soon found they were barely able to communicate: Pierre Dorion had stayed back with the Yankton Sioux, and no one else in the corps knew enough Sioux to translate. It was finally decided to employ Cruzatte, who knew Omaha, to translate through a member of that tribe made prisoner by the Sioux. Almost immediately, the Sioux showed signs of greediness, laughing and sneering at the gifts given them. They said the explorers must either trade with the Sioux alone or give up one of their pirogues and its cargo in tribute.

The captains attempted to lighten the mood by rowing the chiefs out to the keelboat and staging the usual airgun demonstration, accompanied by a measure of whisky for each Indian. The airgun failed to impress the Sioux, and the whisky only made matters worse: The chiefs pretended to be drunk and started falling about the deck. Exasperated, the captains shipped the Indians back to shore on the white pirogue. But as the boat reached the sand, one Indian hugged the mast and others grabbed its mooring rope—a signal they intended to seize the pirogue by force. The Partisan again told Clark the explorers would not be permitted to pass farther upriver.

At that, the captains' moods changed from wariness to anger. Clark brandished his sword, and Lewis swiftly loaded the keelboat's swivel guns and ordered the crew to man their rifles. The Indians, in turn, strung their bows and pulled arrows from their quivers. Black Buffalo, the main chief, grabbed the towrope and ordered his warriors to let go, but repeated that the river was closed to the whites. Clark stood in the water, sure he could not chance a retreat. But he ordered his men to row the pirogue to the keelboat, pick up reinforcements, and return to shore. Together, they finally faced down the Sioux.

Incredibly, the captains agreed to Black Buffalo and Buffalo Medicine's request that they, along with two other Sioux, be permitted to spend the night on the keelboat. No one slept well that night. On the twenty-sixth, the boats traveled upriver to the second and larger Sioux village. Here, the whites were treated with deference: Lewis and Clark were even carried to the village aloft on a buffalo robe. Much entertainment and feasting followed over the next two days, but the explorers remained wary, particularly since the Sioux continued to insist they be allowed to sleep on the keelboat, and because several Omaha prisoners warned Cruzatte the Sioux were simply biding time while plotting the white men's destruction.

Hearing that news, the captains decided to leave on the morning of the twenty-eigth. But before they could cast off, Sioux warriors again grabbed the keelboat's cable. Black Buffalo, on the keelboat and expecting a ride upriver, said his people demanded more tobacco. Disgusted, Clark tossed tobacco to the men holding the cable and grabbed the rope away from them. The Sioux tried to reclaim the rope, but the boats made a clean getaway.

"The four-day ordeal was over," Roy Appleman wrote. "Against weaker men, the Tetons would have triumphed. Only sleepless vigilance, excellent judgment, and bold determination had saved the day. For the time being at least, the two captains had gained much prestige and established U.S. authority over this stretch of the Missouri.... The news spread rapidly up and down the river and promised a peaceful welcome for the explorers among the upriver tribes."

The exact site of the September 25, 1804, encounter with the Sioux has been lost in the mouth of the Bad River, but Fort Pierre's Lilly Park has a sign marking the approximate location. Situated on Fort Pierre's south side where the Bad River meets the Missouri, Lilly Park is fairly scruffy looking, but it does offer free camping with a seven-day limit. The second Sioux encounter site is unmarked, but it probably took place on the west river bank about four miles north of Fort Pierre and two miles south of Oahe Dam. A county road leading along the river offers access at several points. Below Oahe Dam, the Missouri again looks much as it did in the early 1800s.

Another site associated with the expedition is Farm Island State Park, located just east of Pierre on South Dakota 34. Expedition member John Colter is said to have hunted here just before the encounter with the Sioux, who may have stolen his horse. Later, other members of the expedition may have stopped on the island to pick up game Colter had shot.

The state park was actually on the island until the completion of Big Bend Dam downriver at Fort Thompson. That dam created Lake Sharpe, and park officials feared it would inundate the island, so they moved the park's buildings and campground to the mainland. One feature remained unmoved, however. Today, a simple monument marking Lewis and Clark's visit is no longer accessible, situated as it is in a slough, swamped by reeds and cattails. Park staff say canoeists or other boaters may be able to find it, but the plaque on the monument was stolen several years ago. A photo of the monument remains on display at the park visitor center.

Farm Island is still well worth visiting for its good camping, fishing, boating, and swimming. The island itself has returned to a near-wilder-

Missouri River near the Teton Council site, South Dakota.

ness state, most of it accessible only on foot. A park naturalist conducts guided interpretive hikes in summer. Walkers, joggers, and bird watchers favor the trail in the warmer months, while cross-country skiers find its flat terrain ideal for easy winter outings.

The town of Pierre itself is named for Pierre Chouteau, but the name is pronounced PEER—no one seems to know why. Fort Teton, built at the present site of the town of Fort Pierre, was established in 1817 and is credited with being the state's first continuous settlement. But the white man's history at Pierre dates back before those days, and even before the time of Lewis and Clark. In 1743, Chevalier and Louis La Verendrye, two explorers from French Canada, planted a lead plate on a hill in what is now Fort Pierre, claiming the region for the King of France. Like Lewis and Clark sixty years after them, the Verendryes were looking for a route to the Pacific Ocean. They'd come down the Missouri River and traveled as far west as the Black Hills before returning to present-day central South Dakota.

The plate was covered with rocks and remained hidden for 170 years. In 1913, three students from Fort Pierre High School found the plate. A monument was built to the Verendryes, and Gutzon Borglum—sculptor of Mount Rushmore—was the keynote speaker at its dedication in 1933. The Verendrye Plate was a top historical find since it provided a key to early white exploration of region.

The plate is now on display at the South Dakota Cultural Center, located near the Capitol grounds in Pierre. Built for the state centennial in 1989, the 63,000 square foot building is completely underground, reminiscent of Arikara earth lodges that used to dot the Missouri River valley. The center's symbol is the Sioux Horse Effigy, occasionally on loan to other museums nationwide; it's also the symbol seen on South Dakota historical highway markers statewide. Actor Kevin Costner and his wife, Cindy, helped the center compile some of its exhibits on Native American history.

Costner has ties to another Pierre-area attraction, the Houck Buffalo Ranch, where parts of *Dances With Wolves* were filmed. The ranch is located about twenty-five miles north of Oahe Dam on South Dakota 1806, but don't be disappointed if you don't spy any buffalo once you get there. This is the nation's largest private buffalo ranch, and with more than fifty-thousand acres to roam, it's no surprise the shaggy beasts don't hang out by the roadside.

But ranch personnel do offer tours. The best time to visit is generally late spring to early summer, before the prairie gets too dry and fires become a hazard. Tours last anywhere from twenty-five minutes to an hour, depending on how long it takes to find buffalo, and you can also ask to see sites where the filmmaking took place. Minimum tour cost is $20 for up to four people, with each extra person costing an additional $5. Call (605) 567-3624 at least a day or two in advance to make an appointment.

South Dakota State Capitol, Pierre.

Fans of Dayton Duncan's *Out West* will no doubt want to make a pilgrimage to the D&E Cafe at 115 W. Dakota in Pierre, where Duncan chowed down dinner for less than four dollars and two dollars for breakfast, including newspaper and tip. Prices have risen a bit since Duncan's mid-1980s visit, but the D&E is still one heck of a deal. Other places worth a stop in Pierre include the beautiful State Capitol grounds, the South Dakota Discovery Center and Aquarium, and Steamboat Park, with great playground equipment for the kids. For more information on Pierre, call (800) 962-2034.

SIDETRIP: OTHER SOUTH DAKOTA ATTRACTIONS

For a state with well under a million people and an off-the-beaten-path location, South Dakota does a remarkably good job promoting itself. Visitors following the Lewis and Clark Trail will mostly be immune to the relentless public relations campaign that is I-90, but as long as you're in the area, you may want to check out some of South Dakota's myriad claims to fame, some dubious, others divine.

The closest big-name attraction to our route is the Corn Palace in Mitchell, a Moorish-inspired monument to agriculture at Sixth and Main streets. Built in 1892, the palace is decorated inside and out with thousands of bushels of native corn, grain, and grasses. It's also the site or the inspiration for all of Mitchell's big annual events: the Corn Palace Stampede Rodeo in late July, and the Corn Palace Festival and Corn Palace Polka Festival, both in mid- to late September.

Heading west on I-90, Badlands National Park is accessible via exits 131 (Cactus Flat) and 110 (Wall). The Badlands are known for their raw, rugged landscape and some of the world's finest fossil beds, formed about 37 million years ago during the Oligocene epoch. Backcountry adventure abounds, with the Castle Trail particularly acclaimed for its varied prairie topography and wealth of wildlife, including pronghorn antelope, bison, badgers, coyotes, and prairie dogs.

For a quick look at the Badlands, drive the forty-mile loop road (South Dakota 240) between Cactus Flat and Wall. Primitive camping is available, as are cabins at the Sioux-run Cedar Pass Lodge, located south of Cactus Flat. The White River Visitor Center, on the Pine Ridge Reservation in the park's South Unit, features displays and programs on Sioux history. For a very different look at South Dakota, visit the Pine Ridge Indian Reservation south of the Badlands. This was the site of the 1890 Wounded Knee Massacre, where more than 350 Indians were killed by federal troops.

West of the Badlands, the traveler enters the famous Black Hills region. Wind Cave National Park, adjacent to Custer State Park on South Dakota 87, offers daily subterranean tours during the summer. The excursions range from short candlelight walks to more strenuous spelunking missions. Jewel Cave National Monument, fourteen miles west of Custer, South Dakota, on US 16A, is one of the longest caves in the world. It, too, offers tours, as do a number of privately held caves scattered throughout the area. Custer State Park is known for its eighteen-mile wildlife loop drive and abundant recreation.

The Black Hills were named by the Lakota Sioux for the dark appearance of their coniferous forests. The Sioux considered the land sacred, and their rights to it were assured in a treaty signed in 1868. But the United States government broke the pact during the gold rush of the late 1870s. In recent years, the Supreme Court offered the Sioux $200 million as compensation for loss of their lands, but the Sioux are not interested. They want only the land, and their claim remains mired in federal bureaucracy.

Today's Black Hills are heavily commercialized, but their beauty remains mostly intact. Check with the USDA Forest Service office in Custer for maps and information on the area's many scenic byways (and for restrictions on motor homes and trailers, which may have trouble negotiating the region's roads).

Mount Rushmore is probably the best-known Black Hills attraction. Created under the direction of Gutzon Borglum, it features the sixty-foot-high heads of presidents George Washington, Thomas Jefferson,

Abraham Lincoln, and Theodore Roosevelt, all bathed in floodlights each night at dusk.

The Crazy Horse Memorial near Custer was started in 1947 by sculptor Korczak Ziolkowski to honor Chief Crazy Horse and the Native Americans. When completed, it will measure 563 feet high and 641 long, which would make it the largest statue in the world. It, too, is lit nightly at dusk.

Although gambling continues to proliferate throughout the United States, western South Dakota remains famous for its small gaming towns, perhaps because visitors feel a bit wilder when they gamble in the West. After all, it was in Deadwood that Bill Hickok was shot in the back while playing poker in 1876. He's buried alongside Calamity Jane (who claimed she was his secret bride) in Mt. Moriah Cemetery overlooking the city.

Nearby, the town of Lead (rhymes with greed) is famous for its Homestake Gold Mine, largest in the Western Hemisphere. And in early August, Sturgis attracts hordes of Harley enthusiasts for the Black Hills Motorcycle Classic. Spearfish is home to the Black Hills Passion Play, presented Sunday, Tuesday, and Thursday from June through August. For more information on South Dakota, write the state Department of Tourism, Capital Lake Plaza, Pierre, SD 57501, or call (800) 843-1930 or (800) 952-2217 in South Dakota.

THE LAKE OAHE REGION

Travelers who haven't realized it already will probably note north of Pierre that South Dakota has devised an ingenious way of marking state routes closest to the Lewis and Clark Trail. The road on the east side of the Missouri River is South Dakota 1804 (for the year the corps first passed through), and the one on the west side is South Dakota 1806 (named for the year the expedition returned). North Dakota continues this system, but no other states have adopted it. It's important to note that neither of the routes proceeds in a continuous fashion along the river; each frequently sputters out near the shores of Lake Oahe. The quickest way north is US 83 to Selby, then US 12 to Mobridge.

Northcentral South Dakota is dominated by Lake Oahe, the massive manmade body of water created by Oahe Dam and the largest of the four Missouri River reservoirs in South Dakota. The rolled-earth dam north of Pierre was dedicated by President John F. Kennedy in 1963. It is 245 feet high, 9,300 feet long, and backs up a lake capable of storing some 23.5 million acre-feet of water. "Oahe" is a Sioux word meaning "foundation" or "a place to stand on."

Lake Oahe offers 2,250 miles of shoreline, and thirty-nine separate recreation areas dot its length from Pierre to Bismarck, North Dakota. Some of them—including those at Okobojo Point, Little Bend, Sutton Bay, Whitlock Bay, Swan Creek, and Indian Creek—are in the vicinity of campsites used by Lewis and Clark. Primitive camping is available at nearly all the sites, and about half have boat ramps.

Onida is one of a handful of towns right along US 83. It has a park with a pool and playground on the southeast side of town; a free parking area (with no facilities) just south of town is best suited for self-contained RVs.

Gettysburg is home to the Dakota Sunset Museum at 207 W. Commercial Ave., open afternoons daily between Memorial Day and Labor Day. In addition to exhibits of items used by Gettysburg settlers, the museum displays the Medicine Rock, a huge boulder held sacred by the Sioux.

Located five miles east of US 83, Gettysburg has golf, tennis, and swimming facilities, along with free camping in its city park. Gettysburg is also gateway to the popular East and West Whitlock Bay recreation areas on Lake Oahe. West Whitlock State Recreation Area was once a popular Mandan and Arikara campsite, and a replica Arikara earth lodge may be seen.

Selby is at the intersection of US 83 and US 12, and it's here the traveler can turn west for Mobridge. Campers are welcome to stay free at Selby's park near the end of Dakota Street.

It was in this vicinity near the North Dakota border that the expedition was greeted by the Arikara Indians and enjoyed an encounter far different from that with the Teton Sioux. They stayed several days, held a council, and traded gifts with the natives. For the first time in a year, some of the men apparently took their hosts up on what Clark termed a "curious custom...to give handsome squaws to those whom they wish to show some acknowledgements to." The Indians, for their part, were especially fascinated with York, the first black man they had ever seen. "Those Indians were much astonished at my servant," Clark wrote. "All flocked around him and examined him top to toe."

With about 4,000 people, Mobridge serves as the "big town" for northcentral South Dakota. The community reportedly got its name when somebody wired that Missouri river had been bridged, or "Mobridged," for short. Mobridge is known for its walleye and pike fishing, sailboarding, and the annual Sitting Bull Stampede Rodeo July 2-4. The Klein Museum on US 12 displays prairie and Indian artifacts and items from local history.

Aside from the lake recreation, Mobridge's big draw is the Sitting Bull Monument on a ridge west of Lake Oahe. To get there, take US 12 west out of Mobridge, then turn left on South Dakota 1806 and drive south four miles. You really can't miss it: Just look for a billboard nearly as big as the monument itself.

South Dakotans claim this is the burial place of Sitting Bull, the great Sioux leader killed in the area in 1890. He was originally buried at Fort Yates, North Dakota, just over the border, but Mobridgers maintain the body was moved to its "rightful" place in 1953. Many in North Dakota disagree, however; they say the South Dakotans got the wrong bones. In any case, a second Sitting Bull gravesite may be seen south of the town of Fort Yates, North Dakota. The Mobridge monument is a seven-ton granite bust carved by Korczak Ziolkowski, the same sculptor who started the Crazy Horse carving near Custer, South Dakota.

Mobridge's Sitting Bull site is also notable for its monument to Sacagawea, the Shoshoni woman who would join the Lewis and Clark Expedition during its 1804-1805 winter stay in North Dakota. Although some reports had Sacagawea living to be an old woman and dying in Wyoming, most historians agree she actually passed away and was buried at Fort Manuel, a fur trading post. On December 20, 1812, a clerk who compiled the daily journal of events at the fort wrote, "This evening the wife of Charbonneau, a Snake squaw, died of a putrid fever. She was a good and the best woman in the fort, aged about twenty-five years." Fort Manuel was probably located near what is now the west shore of Lake Oahe a few miles south of the North Dakota border. There is no interpretation of the site, but we will learn much more about Sacagawea as we follow Lewis and Clark west.

From the Sitting Bull and Sacagawea monuments, return to US 12 and cross back over to South Dakota 1806 heading north. From here, it is a short drive over the North Dakota border.

View of Lake Oahe at Mobridge, South Dakota.

LODGING

BROWNVILLE, NEBRASKA

Thompson House Bed & Breakfast, (402) 825-6551, Fifth and College St. No children under 12.

AUBURN, NEBRASKA

Anna Belle's Bed and Breakfast, (402) 274-4274, 1302 P St.

Auburn Inn, (402) 274-3143, 517 J St. $40-$55.

NEBRASKA CITY, NEBRASKA

Apple Inn, (800) 659-4446, 502 S. 11th. $35-$49.

Days Inn, (800) 647-1343, 1715 S. 11th. $33.

GREATER OMAHA, NEBRASKA/COUNCIL BLUFFS, IOWA

American Family Inn, (402) 291-0804, 1110 Fort Crook Rd. S. (Bellevue), $36-$40.

Best Western White House Inn, (800) 528-1234, 305 Fort Crook Rd. N. (Bellevue), $39-$43.

Days Inn-Downtown, (800) 325-2525, 3001 Chicago. $68.

Heartland Inn, (800) 334-3277, I-80 Exit 5 (Council Bluffs). $45-$51.

Howard Johnson Lodge and Suites, (800) IGO-HOJO, 35th and Broadway (Council Bluffs). $50-$64.

Interstate Inn, (712) 328-8899, I-80 and South 24th St. (Council Bluffs).

Motel 6, (712) 328-8300, 1846 N. 16th St. (Council Bluffs). $30.

Sleep Inn, (800) 221-2222, 2525 Abbott Dr. $39-$50.

BLAIR, NEBRASKA

Blair House Motel, (402) 426-4801, West US 30. $25-$40.

Starlite Motel, (402) 426-4874, 648 River Rd. $25-$40.

ONAWA, IOWA

Midway Motel, (712) 423-2101, I-29 Exit 112. $35.

SIOUX CITY, IOWA

Best Western Regency Executive, (800) 528-1234, 130 Nebraska St. $65.

Elmdale Motel, (712) 277-1912, US 75 at 22nd St. $28.

Fairfield Inn, (800) 228-2800, 4716 Southern Hills Dr. $46-$52.

Marina Inn, (800) 798-7980, 4th and B St. (South Sioux City, Nebraska). $60-$74.

Park Plaza Motel, (800) 341-8000, 1201 1st Ave. (South Sioux City, Nebraska). $35-$37.

Riverboat Inn, (712) 277-9400, 701 Gordon Dr. $41.

Sioux City Hilton, (800) HILTONS, 707 4th St. $78.

VERMILLION, SOUTH DAKOTA

Comfort Inn, (800) 221-2222, 701 W. Cherry St. $35-$70.

Coyote Motel, (605) 624-2616, 402 N. Dakota. $22-$34.

Goebel House Bed & Breakfast, (605) 624-6691, 102 Franklin St. $35-$45.

Prairie Inn, (605) 624-2824, 912 N. Dakota. $36-$39.

Super 8 Motel, (800) 800-8000, 1208 E. Cherry. $40.

Tomahawk Motel, (800) BUD-HOST, SD 19 and Business Route 50. $26-$46.

YANKTON, SOUTH DAKOTA

Days Inn, (800) 325-2525, 2410 Broadway Ave. $45.

Lewis & Clark Resort, (605) 665-2680, at Lewis & Clark Lake Rec. Area. $48-$70.

Mulberry Inn Bed & Breakfast, (605) 665-7116, 512 Mulberry St.

Starlite Inn Motel, (800) 658-5570, SD 52 and 4th St.

Super 8 Motel, (800) 800-8000,
SD 50 East. $35.

Yankton Inn, (605) 665-2906, East SD 50. $44-$54.

TYNDALL, SOUTH DAKOTA

Tyndall Shady Rest Motel, (605) 589-3980, three blocks off SD 50. $28-$36.

LAKE ANDES, SOUTH DAKOTA

Sands Motel, (605) 487-7621, junction of US 18, US 281, and SD 50.

PLATTE, SOUTH DAKOTA

Kings Inn, (605) 337-3385, SD 44. $28-$31.

CHAMBERLAIN, SOUTH DAKOTA

Hillside Motel, (605) 734-5591, 502 E. King. $24-$35.

Lake Shore Motel, (605) 734-5566, 115 N. River St. $36.

Oasis Inn, (800) 341-8000, I-90 Exit 260. $37-$60.

River View Ridge Bed & Breakfast, (605) 734-6084, north on SD 50.

Super 8 Motel, (800) 800-8000, I-90 Exit 263. $49-$59.

PIERRE, SOUTH DAKOTA

Best Western Ramkota Inn Rivercentre, (800) 528-1234, 920 W. Sioux. $51-$64.

Governor's Inn, (800) 341-8000, 700 W. Sioux. $38-$50.

Oahe Lodge, (605) 224-9340, SD 1804 north of Pierre. $35 and up.

Pierre Motel, (605) 224-9266, 914 N. Euclid. $26-$28.

Spring Creek Resort, (605) 224-8336, 10 miles north of Oahe Dam on SD 1804. $55.

State Motel, (800) 658-3940, 640 N. Euclid. $36-$40.

ONIDA, SOUTH DAKOTA

Wheatland Inn, (605) 258-2341, 200 S. Main St.

GETTYSBURG, SOUTH DAKOTA

Harer Lodge Bed & Breakfast, (605) 765-2167, west of town within walking distance
of Lake Oahe.

Trail Motel, (800) 341-8000, 211 E. Garfield. $30-$45.

MOBRIDGE, SOUTH DAKOTA

East Side Motel and Cabins, (605) 845-7867, 510 E. 7th Ave. $30-$40.

The Mark VI Motel, (605) 845-3681, 317 E. US 12.

Mo-Rest Motel, (605) 845-3668, 706 W. Grand Crossing.

Super 8 Motel, (800) 800-8000, US 12. $38.

Wrangler Motor Inn, (800) 341-8000, US 12. $47-$57.

CAMPING

BROWNVILLE, NEBRASKA

Brownville State Recreation Area, 0.5 mile southeast of town. Primitive sites.

Indian Cave State Park, (402) 883-2575, nine miles south on NE 67, then five miles east NE 64E.

NEBRASKA CITY, NEBRASKA

John Brown's Cave Camper Site, (402) 873-3925, from junction of NE 2 and US 75, 1.5 miles north, 0.5 west, then one block south on 19th St.

Riverview Marina State Recreation Area, northeast of town on US 73/75 and NE 2. Primitive sites.

GREATER OMAHA, NEBRASKA/COUNCIL BLUFFS, IOWA

N.P. Dodge Park, (402) 444-4673, I-680 30th Street exit, follow signs.

Friendship Park, (712) 328-4963, I-29 Exit 53A, then west on 9th Ave. (Council Bluffs).

Lake Manawa State Park, (712) 336-0220, south of Council Bluffs on IA 192.

ONAWA, IOWA

Interchange RV Campground, (712) 423-1387, from junction of I-29 and IA 175, go one block east on IA 175, then one block south to campground.

KOA-Onawa, (712) 423-1633, one mile west from I-29 on IA 175, then 1.5 miles north on county road.

Lewis and Clark State Park, (712) 423-2829, one mile west from I-29 on IA 175, then one mile north on IA 324.

SIOUX CITY, IOWA

KOA-North Sioux City, (605) 232-4519, on west side of I-29 between Exits 2 and 4 (North Sioux City, South Dakota).

Scenic Park, (402) 494-2452, from junction of US 20, 77, and 73, [US 75?] six blocks east on 4th St. (South Sioux City, Nebraska).

Stone State Park, (712) 255-4698, five miles north of I-29 on IA 12.

YANKTON, SOUTH DAKOTA

Lewis and Clark Lake/Corps of Engineers, (605) 667-7873, west of town on SD 52.

Lewis and Clark State Recreation Area (Nebraska), northwest of Crofton on Lewis and Clark Lake.

Lewis and Clark State Recreation Area (South Dakota), (605) 668-3435, west of town on SD 52.

CHAMBERLAIN, SOUTH DAKOTA

American Creek Campground, (605) 734-6772, two miles north of I-90 Exit 263 on Lake Francis Case.

Familyland Campground, (605) 734-6959, I-90 Exit 260 (Oacoma).

KOA-Chamberlain, (605) 734-5729, I-90 Exit 265.

PIERRE, SOUTH DAKOTA

Downstream Area/Missouri River, (605) 224-5862, north of Pierre below Oahe Dam on Lake Oahe.

Farm Island State Recreation Area, (605) 224-5605, four miles east on SD 34.

West Bend State Recreation Area, (605) 875-3220, twenty-six miles east on SD 34 and 9S.

GETTYSBURG, SOUTH DAKOTA

River Edge Campsite, ten miles west of US 83 on US 212.

South Whitlock Resort, (605) 765-9762, eight miles west of US 83 on US 212.

West Whitlock State Recreation Area, (605) 765-9410, thirteen miles west of US 83 on US 212, then nine miles north.

SELBY, SOUTH DAKOTA

Hilltop Motel and Campground, (605) 649-7622, north on US 12.

Lake Hiddenwood State Park, (605) 649-7876, two miles east, then three miles north on US 12/83.

MOBRIDGE, SOUTH DAKOTA

Indian Creek, (605) 224-5862, two miles east on US 12, then one mile south, on Lake Oahe.

Indian Memorial, three miles west on US 12, on Lake Oahe.

RESTAURANTS

BROWNVILLE, NEBRASKA

Riverview Restaurant, (402) 825-3011, US 136. Full menu and keno lounge.

AUBURN, NEBRASKA

Darling's Cafe, (402) 274-4125, 520 J St. Fish, prime rib, Sunday buffet.

Korner Kitchen, (402) 274-3015, "one block east of the stoplight." Weekend breakfast buffet.

The Wheeler Inn, (402) 274-3681, 1905 J St. Steaks, seafood, salad bar.

NEBRASKA CITY, NEBRASKA

Embers Steak House, (402) 873-6416, Junction of US 75 and NE 2. American cuisine with children's menu.

GREATER OMAHA, NEBRASKA/COUNCIL BLUFFS, IOWA

The Aquarium, 1850 S. 72nd, (402) 392-0777. Unusual dining room features walls of live fish from around the world.

Burke's Family Restaurant, (712) 366-2217, I-80 at I-29 (Lake Manawa exit, Council Bluffs). Open 24 hours.

Club 64 Restaurant & Lounge, (712) 323-6464, 701 McKenzie (Council Bluffs). Prime rib, steaks, seafood, and pizza.

O.J.'s Cafe, 9201 N. 30th., (402) 451-3266. Homemade Mexican food. Closed Mondays.

Romeo's Mexican Food and Pizza, (712) 323-0042, 19th and Broadway (Council Bluffs). Casual dining; take-out available.

Ross' Steak House, 909 S. 72nd, (402) 393-2030. Popular place for lunch and dinner.

Szechwan Chinese Restaurant, (712) 325-1782, 2612 W. Broadway (Council Bluffs). Chinese food.

Spaghetti Works, (402) 422-0770, 502 S. 11th St. Spaghetti and more in downtown Omaha.

Summer Kitchen Cafe, 7855 S. 83rd, (402) 592-8017. "A taste of summer all year long."

SIOUX CITY, IOWA

Cucos Mexican Restaurante, (712) 252-1169, 1122 Pierce St. Mexican and American food.

Green Gables, (712) 258-4246, 1800 Pierce St. Longtime family owned restaurant.

Horizon Family Restaurant, (712) 255-1658, 1220 Tri-View Ave. (I-29 Hamilton Exit). Open 24 hours, breakfast anytime.

Plum's Restaurant, (712) 276-5000, 4280 Sergeant Rd. Full menu including heart-healthy meals.

VERMILLION, SOUTH DAKOTA

Chae's, (605) 624-2294, 8 W. Main St., Korean, Chinese and American food.

Emma's Kitchen, (605) 624-9337, 13 W. Main St., Downtown eatery with outdoor courtyard.

Prairie Inn, (605) 624-2657, 912 N. Dakota., Homestyle food, Sunday brunch.

Recuerdo de Mexico, 112 E. Main St., (605) 624-6445. Mexican food.

MECKLING, SOUTH DAKOTA

Toby's Lounge, SD 50, (605) 624-9905. Broasted chicken, shrimp, and fish.

YANKTON, SOUTH DAKOTA

The Galley Restaurant, (605) 665-3255, at Lewis & Clark State Recreation Area. Waterfront dining.

Jodean's Steak House, (605) 665-9884, US 81. Weekend smorgasbord, Sunday brunch.

The Library Restaurant, (605) 665-0186, 401 Capitol St. Wide menu including Cajun and Oriental dishes.

Mom's Picnic Place, (605) 665-4405, SD 52. Daily specials, located near Lewis & Clark Lake.

Quarry Steak House, (605) 665-4337, SD 52 near the lake. Prime rib and nightly specials.

River City Cafe, (605) 665-4662, 202 W. 3rd. Breakfast and lunch specializing in hamburgers, pies, muffins.

CHAMBERLAIN, SOUTH DAKOTA

Al's Oasis, (605) 734-6054, I-90 Exit 260. Truck stop cafe.

Caldwell's American Creek Restaurant, (605) 734-5692, north end of Main St. Full menu with daily specials.

Casey's, (605) 734-6530, Welcome West Plaza at I-90 Exit 263. Homemade soups, pies, specials.

Rainbow Cafe, (605) 734-5481, Main St. in downtown Chamberlain. Home cooking.

PIERRE, SOUTH DAKOTA

D&E Cafe, (605) 224-7200, 115 W. Dakota. Home cooking at rock-bottom prices.

Kozy Korner Family Restaurant, (605) 224-9547, 217 E. Dakota. Specialties include soups and cream pies.

Rivercentre Cafe, (605) 224-6877, in the Best Western Ramkota Inn. American cuisine.

Pizza Ranch, (605) 223-9114, next to the bridge in Fort Pierre.

Town & Country Restaurant, (605) 224-7183, 808 W. Sioux (next to the bridge). Open 24 hours.

ONIDA, SOUTH DAKOTA

Fireside Restaurant & Lounge, (605) 258-2377, US 83.

GETTYSBURG, SOUTH DAKOTA

Bob's Resort, (605) 765-2500, at the Lake Oahe bridge. Char-broiled steaks.

MOBRIDGE, SOUTH DAKOTA

Dakota Country Restaurant, (605) 845-7495, 122 W. Grand Crossing.

Dean's Fast Food, (605) 845-2843, US 12 and Seventh Ave. W.

Harvest Family Dining, (605) 845-3717, 209 Main.

The Wheel Family Restaurant, (605) 845-7474, West US 12. Large menu and salad bar with view of Lake Oahe.

Sacagawea Statue on the North Dakota State Capitol grounds, Bismarck.

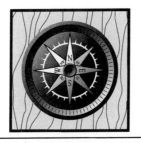

CHAPTER FIVE

NORTH DAKOTA AND EASTERN MONTANA

About five o'clock this evening one of the wives of
Charbonneau (Sacagawea) was delivered of a fine boy.
- Meriwether Lewis, February 11, 1805,
Fort Mandan, North Dakota

FORT ABRAHAM LINCOLN STATE PARK

The Lewis and Clark Expedition entered North Dakota on October 14, 1804, and returned to the present North Dakota-South Dakota border twenty-two months later, en route home from the Pacific. All told, the corps spent a total of 212 days in North Dakota. And since the party made its first winter camp there, Lewis and Clark and their men ended up staying longer in North Dakota than in any other state through which they passed.

Across the South Dakota-North Dakota border, the first town the traveler comes to is Fort Yates, headquarters of the Standing Rock Indian Reservation. There really is a "standing rock" on a pedestal near the Missouri River/Lake Oahe shore, and a plaque explains how the reservation got its name: "A famous sacred stone which many years ago came into possession of the Sioux. According to Dakota legend, it is a body of a young Indian woman with her child on her back who were left in camp when she refused to accompany the tribe as they moved south. When others were sent back to find her, she was found to have turned to stone. This stone is held in reverence by the Sioux and is placed here overlooking the waters in the empire once held by the mighty Sioux Nation."

The corps' camp of October 15, 1804, is in the middle of Lake Oahe, just northeast of Fort Yates. During the day, the corps saw many Indians on both sides of the river and stopped to eat and trade with about thirty Arikaras. Once camped, Lewis and Clark visited a nearby Arikara village. They scouted the area for a possible wintering location, but finding wood and game scarce, decided to press farther north. We shall do the same; it is about an hour's drive from Fort Yates to Fort Abraham Lincoln State Park, located just south of the town of Mandan. Note that North Dakota Highway 24 swings off to the west about twenty miles north of Fort Yates, but North Dakota 1806 hugs the Missouri River and proceeds north to the park.

The corps camped in the vicinity of what was later Fort Abraham Lincoln on October 20, 1804, and August 18, 1806. These were short stays, but at present, the state park at the site is the best-interpreted spot along the Lewis and Clark trail in North Dakota. Although this particular village was abandoned by the time the expedition arrived, the reconstruction here shows better than anywhere else what the captains probably encountered during their time with the Mandans. For travelers who can stop only one place in North Dakota, this is the best bet.

The park's highlight is On A Slant Village, with its earth lodge replicas. The village, sacred to the Mandan people, received its name from the sloping ground on which it was situated. During the 1804 visit, Clark wrote: "Camped on the leeward side above a bluff containing coal of an inferior quality. This bank is immediately above the old (deserted) village of the Mandans." The village included about seven or eight acres of land, and a 1937 survey of the site found the ruins of seventy-five earth lodges.

Studies of tree rings in the area indicate the village was occupied from about 1650 to 1750. After that, the Mandan population was reduced by a smallpox epidemic and pressure from other marauding tribes. In 1804, as Clark noted, the village was in ruins and the tribe had moved about sixty miles upriver to the Knife River Villages. The Mandan moved into North Dakota from the south, and other ruins are present from the South Dakota line north to the Fort Berthold Indian Reservation, where the Mandan's descendants live today.

The village's earth lodge replicas are typical of those used by the Mandans before they were forced onto the reservation. Twenty to forty feet in diameter, the earthlodges were owned and primarily built by the tribe's women, with some help from the men. The lodges' main supports were ten to fifteen feet high and made of logs from nearby trees. Over the framework, the Indians placed a thick mat of willows followed by a layer of grass and thick layer of earth. A well-constructed earth lodge would last about ten years.

Visitors can actually walk inside several of the structures. Interpretive panels describe lifestyle, legends, and ceremonies. One lodge shows how such a dwelling may have been furnished, complete with an adult's bed, a small replica of a sweat lodge, and a horse stall.

The Ark of the Lone Man, centrally located in the village, is a special point of interest. According to Mandan legend, the Lone Man saved the Indian nation from a great flood by building a palisade around the village. The ark, a symbolic shrine, became a site for religious ceremonies. A red cedar post represents the lone man, and a circular willow band marks the high water of the flood.

The park's visitor center has good interpretation of Lewis and Clark's travels through the area, with a replica elk hide journal, peace medal, and espontoon such as that Lewis carried. Mandan culture is well represented, too, by artifacts ranging from pieces of decorated pottery to projectile points. Other exhibits explain the area's heritage of fur trade, railroading, homesteading, and the military. There's also a boxful of dried

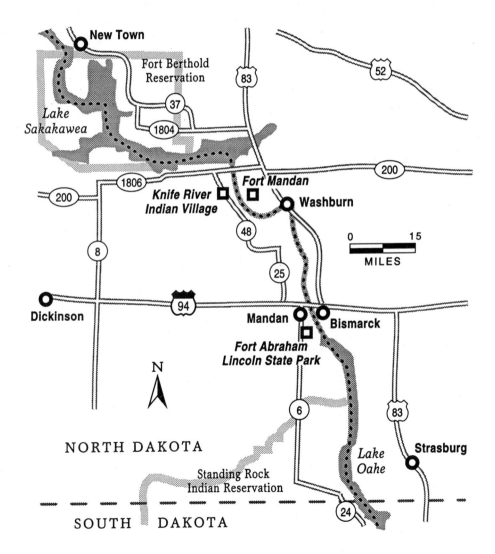

The Lewis and Clark *riverboat at Bismarck, North Dakota.*

medicinal plants. Each specimen includes a drawing of the plant in its native state and possible uses. The patio between the museum and the trading post has a native Mandan Indian garden.

Fort Abraham Lincoln itself was in operation from 1872 through 1891, providing protection for railroad workers and survey parties, as well as settlements that sprung up in the area. The infantry soldiers stationed at the post found they were no match for the Sioux, who were excellent horsemen. In response, Congress authorized the addition of a calvary post, and Lieutenant Colonel George Armstrong Custer arrived with the Seventh Calvary in the autumn of 1873. From here, Custer led expeditions into the Black Hills. When he discovered gold amid the sacred Sioux lands, it marked the beginning of the end for the Sioux way of life.

Tensions rose between the whites and the Indians. Ultimately, it was from Fort Abraham Lincoln that Custer led his troops to the Battle of the Little Big Horn, where he and 265 others were killed by Sioux and Cheyenne warriors led by Sitting Bull and Crazy Horse. Military-oriented exhibits explain the events leading up to the battle, and the trading post offers an excellent selection of the many books written about Custer.

Fort Abraham Lincoln was abandoned in 1891. Most of its original structures were torn down by 1900, with wood from the site reportedly used to construct many buildings in the Bismarck-Mandan area. But several buildings have been reconstructed, including Custer's home.

Activities abound at Fort Abraham Lincoln. Living history demonstrations are offered, and junior ranger programs for kids ages eight through twelve are held on several Saturdays during the summer. Special events held each year usually include astronomy programs, concerts, a fiddle fest, hot-air balloon rally, and walking tours.

During the summer months, the Fort Lincoln trolley runs along the Heart and Missouri rivers between the Third Street Station in Mandan and the state park. The *Lewis and Clark* riverboat, headquartered at Bismarck, also makes regular trips to Fort Abraham Lincoln. To top it off, the park has a modern campground with nearly one hundred sites and river access.

Fort Abraham Lincoln State Park is open daily from 8 a.m. to dusk all year. The museum is open daily from 9 a.m. to 9 p.m. Memorial Day through Labor Day; 9 a.m. to 5 p.m. from the day after Labor Day through November 30; and by appointment the rest of the year. Admission is $3 per vehicle, with a separate charge for admission to the Custer House. For more information, call (701) 663-1464 or (701) 663-9571.

Bismarck/Mandan is one of North Dakota's more populous areas, with about 65,000 people calling the two cities home. Bismarck is also the state capital, and several points of interest are found at the capitol

Mandan earthlodge replica at Fort Abraham Lincoln State Park, North Dakota.

complex. The capitol itself is unusual among statehouses: It looks more like an office building than a seat of government. The nineteen-story Art Deco-inspired building is nicknamed the "skyscraper of the prairies." A statue of Sacagawea—or "Sakakawea," as she is known in North Dakota—stands nearby.

The North Dakota Heritage Center also makes its home on the capitol grounds. A large main gallery traces the evolution of human and natural history in North Dakota. Exhibits include a mounted grizzly bear, along with this journal entry from Sergeant Gass: "These bears are very numerous in this part of the country and very dangerous as they will attack a man at every opportunity." Amateur ornithologists will love the extensive displays on North Dakota's birds of wetlands, woodlands, and prairie. There's something for everyone here, from a special section called Fort Kidd for the youngsters to an abundance of nostalgia for the older folks. The center is open from 8 a.m. to 5 p.m. Monday through Thursday, 8 a.m. to 8 p.m. Friday, 9 a.m. to 5 p.m. Saturday, and 11 a.m. to 5 p.m. Sunday. It is closed Easter, Thanksgiving, Christmas, and New Year's Day.

The stretch of the Missouri River from south of Bismarck north to Garrison Dam remains free-flowing. At nearly one hundred miles long, this segment provides good boating opportunities for visitors eager to experience a bit of what the river was like two hundred years ago. Access points are available up and down the river, or leave the work to someone else and go aboard the *Lewis and Clark* riverboat, an all-weather cruise vessel with sailings Memorial Day through Labor Day (including a 1 p.m. daily departure for Fort Abraham Lincoln, where passengers may lay over for about two hours). Call (701) 255-4233 for more information.

The Bismarck area has a fair number of art galleries for a community of its size. Among the most notable are the Mandan Depot, specializing in Native American arts and crafts at 401 W. Main St. in Mandan; the Heritage Center museum store; and Bismarck Art and Galleries Association at 422 E. Front Ave. in Bismarck. Other attractions include the Dakota Zoo, five major golf courses, and several annual powwows. For more information on Bismarck/Mandan, call (701) 222-4308.

FORT MANDAN

As the expedition moved north through the Dakotas, the need to find a place to spend the winter became increasingly acute. Beginning in late October 1804, the journal entries mention bitter winds and snow. On October 26, roughly 1,600 miles from Camp Wood, the Corps of Discovery reached the new villages established by the Mandans, Minitaris (later known as Hidatsa), and Amahamis.

About 4,400 people lived in five separate villages. They greeted the white men warmly, and the captains quickly decided this would be a

Fort Mandan replica near Washburn, North Dakota.

good place to spend the winter months. After several days of searching, a suitable spot was found for a fort. It was there, on the Missouri's east bank about six miles below the mouth of Knife River, that Fort Mandan was built.

Construction started November 2, using cottonwood logs cut nearby. Two sides of the V-shaped fort held four rooms each to house the men and their belongings. Each room was fourteen feet square, seven feet high, and equipped with a fireplace. The third side was blockaded by "amazing long pickets." The men occupied the still-unfinished buildings November 16, and the two captains moved into their quarters four days later. The party at that point numbered about forty-five.

The expedition spent a long winter in a variety of pursuits, chief among them finding enough food. Trade with the Indians brought corn, squash, and berries. Meat was obtained by daily hunting parties. Game was abundant, but many of the animals were in such poor shape during the colder months that only the choicest parts—such as buffalo tongue, heart, and liver—could be used. There were many wolves in the area, and harvested animals left overnight without protection were often found completely devoured by the time the men returned to retrieve the game.

They also found themselves expending much energy to stay warm: In his journal entry of December 8, Clark reported several cases of frostbitten feet and, in the case of York, a frostbitten male organ. On December 12, he wrote, "We do not think it prudent to turn out to hunt in such cold weather," and on December 13, more of the same: "The thermometer stands this morning at twenty below zero, a fine day." In all, the temperature dipped below zero, once as low as forty-eight below, a total of forty days.

Despite the bitter cold, a steady stream of visitors came to the fort all winter long. The captains spent many hours talking with the Mandans, mostly seeking to learn as much as they could about the tribes and the country still to come, but also eager to cement relations for future trading. Lewis, Clark, and company were far from the first white men to arrive in this area. Traders, mostly French, had been operating in the area for perhaps a half-century or more, and the captains conferred with some of them during their stay. It was also here the men met Charbonneau and Sacagawea, who were to become among the most famous members of the party.

Lewis and Clark had just hired an interpreter, René Jessaume, who had moved into Fort Mandan with his wife and child. When Charbonneau offered his services, the captains said they had no need for him. But Charbonneau wouldn't take no for an answer. He finally sold the captains on the idea by promising that Sacagawea could help the expedition communicate with—and perhaps obtain horses from—her people, the Shoshonis, once the party reached the Rocky Mountains.

No one knows whether Sacagawea had much say in the matter. Just a few years before, at age twelve, she had been kidnapped near present-day Three Forks, Montana. She later was either sold to or won by Charbonneau and now, just sixteen or seventeen years old, was about to give birth to her first child. But despite her youth, Sacagawea more than earned her place in history over the next two years as an indispensable member of the expedition, and one of its most controversial.

Much of the controversy surrounds just how to spell and say her name: there are three predominant versions. Scholars generally agree on the spelling—Sacagawea—used throughout this book, pronouncing it "Sah-CAH-ga-we-a." But the spelling Sacajawea, pronounced "Sah-cah-ja-WE-a," is probably more popular and widespread, especially in the Pacific Northwest. The third version is the one used most often in the Dakotas: Sakakawea, pronounced "Sa-KAH-ka-we-a."

In addition, Sacagawea is frequently—but erroneously—viewed as the expedition's guide, a myth perpetuated by several books written in the early twentyth century. Although she didn't exactly guide the expedition, Sacagawea's assistance proved invaluable when the party reached the Great Divide of western Montana and Idaho. Here, Sacagawea was able to identify landmarks and serve as an intermediary when—in an unbelievable coincidence—the corps came upon the Shoshoni village led by Chief Cameahwait, Sacagawea's long-lost brother. Sacagawea helped the expedition in other ways, too: Since a war party would not travel with a woman and a baby, she and her baby, Jean Baptiste—or Pomp, as Captain Clark nicknamed him—served as signals of the Corps' peaceful intentions. She also gathered plants and herbs for food and medicine.

For a long time, Fort Mandan was the least-interpreted major site along the Lewis and Clark Trail. This was finally remedied with the 1997 opening of the North Dakota Lewis and Clark Interpretive Center at Washburn. Exhibits at the center give an overview of the expedition, paying special attention to the Fort Mandan Winter of 1804-1805, and Native American artifacts representing nearly every tribe the explorers encountered on the way west. Visitors can try on a buffalo robe or a weighted cradle board much like that Sacagawea used to carry her baby. This also is home to one of four complete sets of prints from the 1833-1834 travels of Swiss artist Karl Bodmer, who made extensive sketches of the Missouri River landscape and peoples.

On Saturday mornings in the summer, school-age children are welcome to take part in the center's Lewis and Clark Explorer's Club. Free with admission, the club allows young visitors to pursue an activity that their 19th century counterparts may have enjoyed. Past sessions have included doll making, basket weaving, and making "dream catchers." Adults are welcome to participate too.

The center is located at the junction of U.S. Highway 83 and North Dakota Highway 200A. From Memorial Day through Labor Day, it is open daily from 9 a.m. to 7 p.m. Central Time; the rest of the year, the hours are 9 a.m. to 5 p.m. Admission is $2 for adults and $1 for students (kindergarten through college); members of the North Dakota Lewis and Clark Bicentennial Foundation, which operates the center, are admitted free.

After you've seen the center, plan a trip to the nearby reconstructed Fort Mandan site less than two miles away. The replica, approximately ten miles downstream from the original fort site, was built in the 1970s by local volunteers. It's now run under the auspices of the state bicentennial foundation, which is adding onsite interpretation and living history. For information on either the interpretive center or the Fort Mandan reconstruction, call (701) 462-8535.

Washburn is thirty-eight miles north of Bismark via U.S. Highway 83. The town celebrates its trail heritage each June with the Lewis and Clark Days, which include a parade, buffallo barbecue, re-enactments, lectures, and demonstrations.

On Christmas Day 1804, the captains found their crew "merrily disposed." "We fired the swivels at daybreak and each man fired one round," wrote Sergeant Ordway. "Our officers gave the party a drink of (rum). We had the best to eat that could be had, and continued firing, dancing, and frolicking during the whole day. The savages did not trouble us as we had requested them not to come as it was a great medicine day with us. We enjoyed a merry Christmas during the day and evening until nine o'clock—all in peace and quietness."

On February 11, as Lewis noted, Sacagawea gave birth to her son, Jean Baptiste, the newest member of the Lewis and Clark Expedition. "It is worthy of remark that this was the first child which this woman had borne, and as is common in such cases her labor was tedious and the pain violent," Lewis wrote. Jessaume, the interpreter, suggested to Lewis that a small portion of rattlesnake's rattle "never failed to produce the desired effect, that of hastening the birth of the child." Lewis just happened to have a rattle in his possession and gave it to Jessaume. "Whether this medicine was truly the cause or not I shall not undertake to determine, but I was informed that she had not taken it more than ten minutes before she brought forth."

On April 7, 1805, the keelboat and eleven men were sent back downriver under the command of Corporal Richard Warfington and accompanied by a vast array of specimens for President Jefferson. Items shipped back included Indian artifacts, sixty plant specimens, many animal skins and skeletons, and four living magpies. Later that same day, the captains and the remainder of the party resumed the upriver trip in six newly built canoes and the two old pirogues.

KNIFE RIVER INDIAN VILLAGES

From Washburn, it's a short drive on North Dakota 200A to the Knife River Indian Villages Historic Site, near the small town of Stanton. This site, administered by the National Park Service, offers another haunting hint at what life was like in the area when Lewis and Clark arrived.

Start with a stop at the visitor center, where a short film—shown on request—sets the scene by featuring the words of Buffalo-Bird Woman, one of the last Hidatsa to know the old ways. "Sometimes at evening I sit looking out on the big Missouri. The sun sets and dusk steals over the water," she says. "In the shadows, I seem again to see our Indian village with smoke curling upward from the earth lodges. And in the river's roar, I hear the yells of the warrior, the laughter of little children as of old. It is but an old woman's dream. Again I see but shadows and hear only the roar of the river and tears come into my eyes. Our Indian life, I know, is gone forever."

Gone, perhaps, but not forgotten. A trail from the headquarters building winds past what once was the Awatixa Xi'e, or Lower Hidatsa Site. When the earth lodges collapsed, they left circular mounds of earth around hardened, saucer-like floors, surprisingly close together. The Hidatsa had plenty of room to spread out, so the depressions' proximity suggests the village was quite close-knit, perhaps to offer protection from raiding tribes. Fifty-one earth lodge depressions are plainly visible from the air.

The Awatixa abandoned this village sometime around 1780 after a smallpox epidemic, but later returned to build a similar village closer to the Knife River. This later village is where Lewis and Clark found the Indians when the expedition arrived late in 1804, and it was probably where Charbonneau and Sacagawea were camped.

Here, the trail dips down to the Knife River. If a civilization can be known by its trash, this is where visitors get an even more intimate glimpse at the village. Molehill-like mounds two to four feet high near the village edge are middens, or garbage heaps. Here, archaeologists

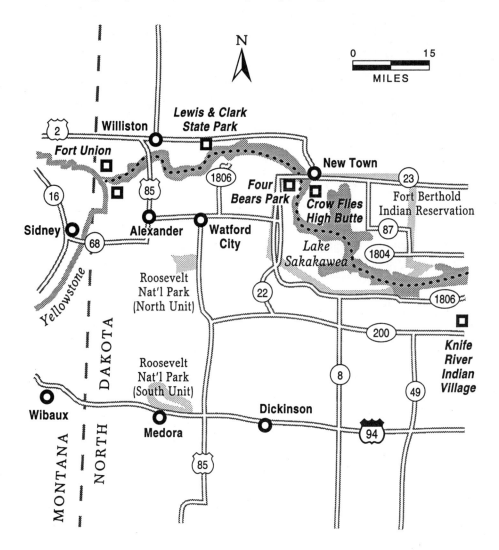

Knife River.

have found broken pottery and bone tools, and sharp observers can see other remnants emerging from the eroding bluff.

A forty-foot diameter full-size earth lodge is being constructed east of the existing visitor center at Knife River. When completed, it will offer a center for demonstrations of life in an earth lodge village. Several other trails are accessible at the site, including the Two Rivers Trail, offering a seven-mile roundtrip over mostly level terrain. A few picnic tables and grills are available on the grounds of the visitor center.

Knife River Indian Villages Historic Site is open from 8 a.m. to 8 p.m. daily from Memorial Day through Labor Day, and from 8 a.m. to 4:30 p.m. daily the rest of the year. During the summer, demonstrations are usually given on Saturdays and Sundays at 2 p.m. Mountain Time; topics range from "Tattooing and Body Ornamentation" to our heroine, Sacagawea. For more information, call (701) 745-3309.

Stanton is a tiny town with very basic visitor services and an Indian display at the courthouse. Many local people work in nearby Beulah, home of the huge Great Plains Synfuels, where lignite coal is turned into natural gas, or at other plants in this energy-rich region.

SIDETRIP: MEDORA AND THEODORE ROOSEVELT NATIONAL PARK

When he first ventured out to North Dakota's Badlands in 1883, Theodore Roosevelt was a sickly young New York State legislator who hoped some time hunting in the Wild West might cure his body and spirit. Like so many before him—and since—Roosevelt fell madly in love with the region and proceeded to spend several years living and ranching in the Dakotas in the mid-1880s before returning to public service as a Spanish-American War hero and, ultimately, as president.

The wealthy French Marquis deMores liked North Dakota, too, so much so he founded a town on the frontier and named it for his bride, Medora von Hoffman. Within a few years, he had established a brick-yard, packing plant, stage line, Catholic church, and several stores and saloons.

Today, the town of Medora serves as the southern gateway to Theodore Roosevelt National Park, and, together, they are North Dakota's most popular summer vacation destinations. Location hasn't hurt: The town and park sit right along Interstate 94 in the state's south-west corner. Although this is a bit off the Lewis and Clark Trail, it would be easy enough to detour west on I-94 from Bismarck, visit the Medora area and both the south and north units of Roosevelt National Park, then pick up the Corps of Discovery's route at Williston. North Dakota's "Rough Rider" country may also be a viable stop for travelers who return east on interstates 90/94. This route also traverses Captain Clark's home-ward journey along the Yellowstone River, a trip examined later in this chapter.

Medora is a very small town totally oriented to tourism. Attractions are numerous, ranging from the Medora Musical, performed nightly dur-ing the summer at the new Burning Hills Amphitheatre, to the Chateau de Mores State Historic Site, where the marquis's twenty-eight room mansion includes many original furnishings and family possessions. The Medora Doll House claims to have a thousand dolls and antique toys from the eighteenth through twentieth centuries, and the Museum of the Badlands displays exhibits on Native Americans, wildlife, early fur trad-ing, and the pioneer days.

Roosevelt was the best advertisement for one of the area's favorite pursuits: horseback riding. "There are few sensations I prefer to that of galloping over these rolling limitless prairies or winding my way among the barren fantastic and grimly picturesque deserts of the so-called Bad-lands," he wrote. Medora Stables offers trail rides ranging from one to three hours long from its headquarters on the east side of town (near the Bad Lands Motel), as does Peaceful Valley Ranch, seven miles north of town in the national park.

Theodore Roosevelt National Park encompasses more than seventy thousand acres in its two major units and at Roosevelt's Elkhorn Ranch, about thirty-five miles north of Medora. Huge herds of roaming American bison are a major attraction in both the south and north units, and pronghorn antelope, mule deer, elk, bobcats, and coyotes are among the other resident animals. Each unit has a designated scenic drive, a thirty-six mile loop in the south and a fourteen-mile route in the north, as well as hiking and nature trails. Early mornings or late afternoons are the best time to see the park's legendary colored plateaus, bluffs, and buttes. If you're near the south unit and have time for just a brief stop, try the Painted Canyon Visitor Center seven miles east of Medora on I-94.

The park is open all year, although weather conditions generally close some roads during the winter. Campgrounds are situated in both units, and backcountry camping is also available, by permit.

For more information on Theodore Roosevelt National Park, call (701) 623-4466 (South Unit) or (701) 842-2333 (North Unit). For more information on Medora, call the Medora Chamber of Commerce at (701) 623-4910.

LAKE SAKAKAWEA COUNTRY

Lake Sakakawea, like Lake Oahe, is one of the nation's largest manmade lakes, 178 miles long with a storage capacity of 24.6 million acre-feet and 1,600 miles of shoreline. The lake is the product of Garrison Dam, another of the six Pick-Sloan projects on the Missouri River. Built by the U.S. Army Corps of Engineers at a cost of $294 million from 1947 through 1954, Garrison is the third-largest earth-filled dam in the United States, after Fort Peck and Oahe. It is 210 feet high and 11,300 feet long. Engineers used 1.5 million cubic yards of concrete in its construction, enough to build a two-lane road 400 miles long.

Despite the superlatives, Lake Sakakawea is relatively easy to break down to a more manageable size, especially along its more accessible northern shores. Secluded bays lure anglers with champion-size walleye, northern pike, smallmouth bass, sauger, chinook salmon, and striped bass. Several state parks, though popular, leave the visitor plenty of room to breathe. North Dakota is one of the smallest Western states in total land area—69,299 square miles—but that's still nearly twice the size of Indiana and more than fourteen times the size of Connecticut.

From Stanton, North Dakota 200A (soon ND 200) winds north before turning east at Pick City. Riverdale, four miles east, is the headquarters for Garrison Dam. Here in the power plant lobby, visitors can see displays on the dam, along with a 100-square-foot mural of Sacagawea and Pomp, painted by Clarence Cuts the Rope, a Hidatsa Indian. Lake Sakakawea State Park is also nearby, with three hundred campsites and some of the lake's best salmon fishing.

From Riverdale, drive another nine miles east to US 83, which heads north, cutting between Lake Sakakawea and the much smaller Audubon

Lake Sakakawea from Crow Flies High Butte near New Town, North Dakota.

Lake. North of the lakes, turn west on North Dakota 37 which, combined with North Dakota 1804, leads all the way to Williston, a distance of about 150 miles. Fort Stevenson State Park is near Garrison, with attractions including a prairie dog town, 105-site campground, and abundant walleye fishing.

The expedition had its share of exciting and dangerous events in this area. On April 13, 1805, the white pirogue—the boat carrying most of the party's valuables, not to mention the two captains, Sacagawea, Charbonneau, and their son—was suddenly struck by a squall of wind and nearly capsized near the mouth of what is now called Van Hook Arm. On the next day, Lewis wrote they had attained "the highest point to which any white man had ever ascended" on the Missouri, "except for two Frenchmen (one of whom Lapage was now with us) who having lost their way had straggled a few miles farther though to what place precisely I could not learn."

This same day, April 14, the expedition reached the area of Crow Flies High Butte and camped in the vicinity of Bear Den Bay. The winter had hit this area hard: Clark killed a "meager" buffalo bull, and Lewis shot an elk near Indian Creek, so poor it was unfit for use. But they also saw signs of spring: geese nesting in the trees, magpies, black-tailed prairie dogs, and at least two bears.

Parshall, located just off North Dakota 37 before it turns west to New Town, is home to the noted Paul Broste Rock Museum, which displays rocks, fossils, and a large collection of hand-cut rock spheres. New Town is a good place to stop for fuel and food, since few services are available on North Dakota 1804 for the next seventy-five miles or so. From New Town, drive about 2.25 miles west to a small interpretive area that tells the story of *Pe-Ri-Tska-Wa-Ku-Re* ("Crow Flies High"), a Hidatsa chief who was a leader on the Fort Berthold Indian Reservation. He lived at Like A Fishhook village until a disagreement with another chief led Crow Flies High and his followers to leave.

About 1870, Crow Flies High and his band of some 140 Hidatsa settled around Fort Buford near Williston, using that area as a winter base camp and ranging back into what is now the Lake Sakakawea area during the summers. For almost twenty-five years, Crow Flies High and his band were self-sustaining, living without government rations. They were forced back on the reservation in 1894, and the chief died of pneumonia in 1900.

The view from Crow Flies High Butte is beautiful. But the butte itself is also worth a look. Cross the Four Bears Bridge, 0.8 mile long, and look back. Nearby, the Three Affiliated Tribes of the Mandan, Hidatsa, and Arikara operate a museum, casino, and lodge. Several powwows are held each summer on the Fort Berthold Indian Reservation, including Twin Buttes, third weekend in June; White Shield, second weekend in July; Mandaree, third weekend in July; and New Town, second weekend in August.

It was near here on their return trip that Lewis and Clark reunited on August 12, 1806, after separate explorations along the Missouri (Lewis) and Yellowstone (Clark) rivers. One day earlier, Lewis had been seriously injured when nearsighted Private Cruzatte mistook the captain's buckskin-clad legs for an elk and shot him through both thighs. "The wounds bled considerably but I was happy to find that it touched neither bone nor artery," Lewis wrote. And the next day, "At 1 p.m. I overtook Captain Clark and party and had the pleasure of finding them all well. As writing in my present situation is extremely painful to me I shall desist until I recover and leave to my friend Captain C. the continuation of our journal."

Although just nineteen miles from the town of Williston, Lewis and Clark State Park is rarely crowded. The park features rugged Badlands scenery and a nature trail that winds through one of the largest intact native prairies in the North Dakota state parks system. Camping, fishing, and boating are other popular activities.

Williston has only about 13,500 people, but in this country, that's a good-sized town. The traveler will find plenty in the way of budget motels, restaurants, and shopping, along with several pleasant parks. The Upper Missouri Valley Fair is held just north of town in late June, and the local Frontier Museum's displays include a schoolhouse, medical offices, and a pioneer store. Williston is also the gateway to the North Unit of Theodore Roosevelt State Park (take US 85 south through Watford City), and to the Fort Union and Fort Buford historic sites, which we shall look at in the next section of this chapter. The Lewis and Clark Trail Museum in the small town of Alexander (also located south on US 85) is housed in a 1914 school building, with one room dedicated to a scale model of the explorers' winter camp at Fort Mandan.

THE MISSOURI-YELLOWSTONE CONFLUENCE

The Corps of Discovery's excitement grew as they neared the confluence of the Missouri and the Yellowstone, the Missouri's major tributary. The Yellowstone was finally glimpsed on April 25, 1805, by Lewis and four other men walking overland from the Missouri. "When we had proceeded on about four miles, I ascended the hills from whence I had a most pleasing view of the country, particularly of the wide and fertile valleys formed by the Yellowstone and Missouri rivers, which occasionally unmasked by the wood on their borders disclose their meanderings for many miles in their passage through these delightful tracts of country," he wrote. "I determined to camp on the bank of the Yellowstone River which made its appearance about two miles south of

Fort Union on the North Dakota- Montana border.

Visitors watch a blacksmith working at Fort Union.

me. The whole face of the country was covered with herds of buffalo, elk, and antelopes; deer are also abundant, but keep themselves more concealed in the woodland. The buffalo, elk, and antelope are so gentle that we pass near them while feeding without appearing to excite any alarm among them; and when we attract their attention, they frequently approach us more nearly to discover what we are, and in some cases pursue us a considerable distance apparently with that view." True to his word, Lewis and his party did camp on the Yellowstone that night, about two miles south of its confluence with the Missouri.

The next day, Lewis walked to the confluence. En route, he heard several shots, "which announced to me the arrival of the party with Captain Clark...after I completed my observations in the evening I walked down and joined the party at their encampment on the point of land formed by the junction of the rivers; found them all in good health, and much pleased at having arrived at this long-wished-for spot, and in order to add in some measure to the general pleasure which seemed to pervade our little community, we ordered a dram to be issued to each person; this soon produced the fiddle, and they spent the evening with much hilarity, singing & dancing, and seemed as perfectly as to forget their past toils, as they appeared regardless of those to come."

As they had at the spots that would become Fort Osage and Fort Atkinson, Lewis and Clark thought this confluence would be an excellent spot for a military or trading post. The explorers noted the river banks here had a gravel base and were situated well above flood level. Cottonwood and ash trees were available for construction. The site provided a broad vista which would prevent approaching Indians from being concealed—and which would let the Indians see any trading post from quite a distance. On his return trip in 1806, Lewis surveyed and charted the land near the confluence.

Several years went by before anyone took advantage of the idea, but in 1829, John Jacob Astor's American Fur Company built Fort Union here. Under the supervision of Kenneth McKenzie, the fort's first bourgeois (or superintendent), the new fort became a beacon on the Plains. Indians came to trade: first beaver skins; then tanned buffalo robes, elk, antelope, wolf, otter, hedgehog, and even mice. With these, the natives could obtain iron goods, tools, blankets, food, and more. The Assiniboine, Crow, Cree, Blackfoot, and Hunkpapa Sioux were among the tribes that visited Fort Union to trade.

Famous white visitors also came to see Fort Union: George Catlin, Prince Maximilian and Karl Bodmer, John Audubon, Jim Bridger, and Father Pierre De Smet were among those who visited the post in its heyday. During those peak years, the fort employed up to 100 people, including clerks, hunters, craftsmen, herders, and traders. It was always a busy place.

Busy, that is, until about the time of the Civil War. By then, smallpox, white westward expansion, and tensions with the Sioux had altered life on the Plains. In 1864, General Alfred Sully described Fort Union as "an old dilapidated affair, almost falling to pieces." Fort Union's era was almost over, but another era—that of Fort Buford—was about to begin.

Fort Union was located two miles from the confluence, but Fort Buford, the new infantry post established in 1866, was built overlooking the river junction. The post eventually housed six companies of infantry and calvary and served as a vital link in American military strategy of the mid- to late-twentyth century. It was here that Sitting Bull surrendered in 1881; here, too, where Chief Joseph of the Nez Perce was imprisoned after his Montana capture just forty-two miles from freedom at the Canadian border. Fort Buford remained in use until 1895, when widespread white settlement of the area made it no longer necessary.

For many decades, Fort Union and Fort Buford were mostly forgotten, but the sites have seen a dramatic upturn in interest and visitation in recent years. Fort Union National Historic Site was a grassy plain when the National Park Service acquired the land in 1966; today, much of the fort has been reconstructed, including the fabulous bourgeois house. Daily tours, living history demonstrations, and special interpretive programs are planned throughout the summer, including the annual Fort Union Trading Post Rendezvous typically held the third weekend of June. The fort is open daily from 8 a.m. to 8 p.m. Central Time Memorial

Day through Labor Day and 9 a.m. to 5:30 p.m. the rest of the year except Thanksgiving, Christmas, and New Year's Day. Admission is by donation. For more information, call (701) 572-9083.

Fort Buford State Historic Site is located just a few miles east of Fort Union. The old field officers' quarters now house a museum that tells the fort's history, and a stone powder magazine and military cemetery are among the other fort remnants still standing. The site is open annually from mid-May through mid-September, from 8 a.m. to 5 p.m. daily with off-season tours offered by appointment. Admission is $1.50, or .75 cents for kids ages seven through twelve. A picnic area is nearby. Call (701) 572-9034 for more information.

The Missouri and Yellowstone rivers meet almost smack-dab on the North Dakota-Montana border. From here, most travelers following the Lewis and Clark Trail proceed west, most likely on US 2—Montana's "Hi-Line"—although several other routes offer reasonable, even tempting, alternatives. We will look at the first of these in the section below, and conclude this chapter with a trip across the Hi-Line.

HOMEWARD BOUND: CLARK ON THE YELLOWSTONE RIVER

When Lewis and Clark reached the Pacific, their trip was only half over, geographically speaking. And as much country as they'd covered heading west, the captains knew there was much they'd been unable to explore. So even before they left Fort Clatsop, their second winter camp, Lewis and Clark had decided they'd split up near what is now Missoula, Montana, and take separate routes back to the Missouri-Yellowstone confluence.

Clark chose the southerly route, traveling through the Big Hole, over Bozeman Pass, and onto the Yellowstone River—the section we will follow here. This route actually has little in the way of Lewis and Clark interpretation except for one very notable exception: It was along the Yellowstone, east of present-day Billings, that Clark carved his name at Pompey's Pillar. To this day, it is the only remaining documented physical evidence of the expedition. For that reason, this particular side trip—though long—is well worth the traveler's time if it can be included in the itinerary.

Anyone who lives in the East or Upper Midwest may want to make this trip, as Clark did, on their own way home. (In that event, it will be necessary to read this particular section backward.) But the side trip may also be done while heading west by detouring from Fort Union to I-94 (via Montana 200 and 16), then on to Pompeys Pillar near Billings. From there, the traveler could continue on into Billings and take US 87 north, resuming the corps' westward trek at Great Falls or Fort Benton. Most of the country along the Missouri River to the north is inaccessible by mo-

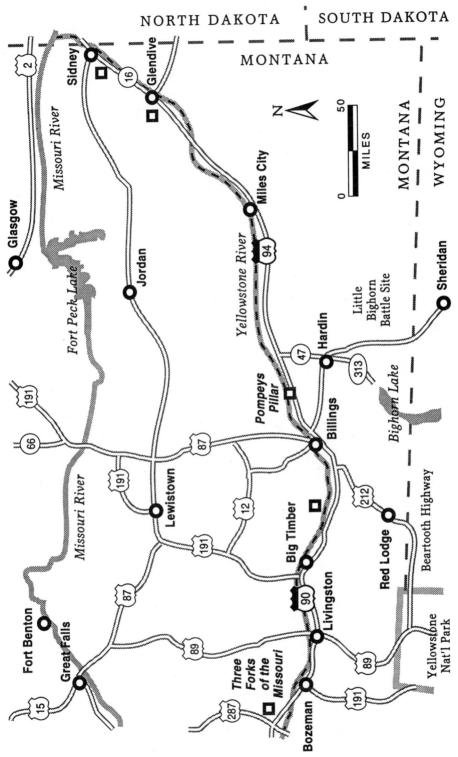

tor vehicle, anyway, so this detour, although about one hundred miles longer than the alternatives, remains an option. What's a hundred miles in Montana, anyway?

Eastern Montana has a reputation as a desolate, barren country. The region's topography certainly differs from the mountainous west, and sheer size and the vast distance between highway exits may be the reason some folks consider it monotonous. But eastern Montana has its own raw beauty and plenty of recreational and historical diversions, too.

Sidney, Montana, is the major town along the lower Yellowstone Valley. Long an agricultural center, Sidney enjoyed an oil boom in the late 1970s and early 1980s. Things have calmed down since then, but much of the energy-driven development may still be seen in the new stores and restaurants of this friendly town.

Sidney's pride is the Mon-Dak Heritage Center, a bright, airy museum with changing art exhibits and a fascinating walk-through streetscape on its lower level. One painting, "Lewis and Clark Arriving at the Confluence," by Barbara Schaffner, remains on permanent display near the museum entrance. Other exhibits include fossils, dinosaur bones, a gun collection, and numerous photographs.

From Sidney, follow the Yellowstone Valley down Montana 16 to Glendive. (If you're in the mood to fish, try your luck at catching the boneless, bottom-dwelling paddlefish, a species unique to this part of the country. You'll need a state license and a copy of the fishing regulations.)

A Lewis and Clark buff's license plate.

Glendive is the gateway to Makoshika State Park, three miles south of town in the badlands. Sightseeing, rock hunting, and hiking are popular activities at Makoshika, and the area has also yielded some major dinosaur fossil finds. Glendive also marks the entrance to I-94.

The next major town, Miles City, is seventy-five miles west. Nestled at the mouth of the Tongue River, Miles City relishes its image as a cowboy's town. But this is also a commercial center for southeast Montana, and there are plenty of modern-day visitor amenities. The Miles City Jaycee Bucking Horse Sale, held the third weekend of May, is one of the biggest of its kind: Rodeo folks from many states visit to see and buy some of the wildest broncs this side of Dodge. The Range Riders Museum and historic Montana Bar at 612 Main St. are among Miles City's other attractions.

Although home to only about 2,500 people, Forsyth is notable for some interesting architecture, especially the Rosebud County Courthouse, a Classical Revival building with a copper dome, murals, and stained glass. It dates from 1911.

The Little Big Horn Battlefield is accessible via Exit 49 from I-94. Follow Montana 47 thirty miles south to I-90, then another fifteen miles to the battlefield. It was here General George Armstrong Custer and the Seventh Calvary made their last stand against the Sioux and Northern Cheyenne.

And finally, at long last, Pompeys Pillar National Landmark is found at Exit 23 on I-94. A historical marker and large version of the familiar Lewis and Clark trail sign help point the way.

Clark and his party arrived here July 25, 1806. Looking up at the monolith two hundred feet high and four hundred paces in circumference, he pronounced it "a remarkable rock" and named it Pompys Tower for Sacagawea's son, who by then was seventeen months old and much attached to Clark (the affection was mutual).

Approaching the pillar, the visitor can't help but feel a real sense of excitement. Here is one of the few sites where little imagination is required: Captain Clark's signature is right there, plainly visible behind the protective glass casing. Looking at the signature, many visitors wonder: Was Clark that tall? Did someone boost him up to make his mark? Actually, the bluff around the signature has eroded since 1806.

After viewing the signature, continue on to the viewpoint on the pillar's west edge. It's a bit of a climb, but hikers are richly rewarded with a sublime view. Clark likely stood on this exact spot, and it is fun to imagine what the surrounding land may have looked like in his day. No interstate, no neatly plowed rectangles of farmland, no houses, no cars. But some things haven't changed much, chief among them the sprawling horizons and the wild, free-flowing Yellowstone, one of the only great Western rivers still unfettered by dams. Clark found two piles of stones placed by Indians at the summit, along with many animals and designs carved on the steep rock faces.

Pompeys Pillar's development as a visitor attraction is something of a recent phenomenon. Montana's first historic marker was a protective grid over the signature, placed by the Northern Pacific Railroad in 1882. The grid did the job, but it also made viewing quite difficult. Some seventy years later, Don C. Foote, the landowner, replaced the grid with bulletproof glass. Ultimately, the Footes sold the site to the Bureau of Land Management, and the site was finally dedicated as a National Historic Landmark in 1992. The name Pompeys Pillar was first seen upon the publication of the Lewis and Clark journals in 1814.

Several plaques sit at the base of the pillar, among them one dedicating the site to "the vision and spirit of the individuals who passed this way and left an indelible mark on the history of this great nation." The site also includes a riverside picnic area, rest rooms, and small visitor center. Several dugout canoe replicas are also on display, the product of a Lewis and Clark float re-enactment a few years back.

The visitor center offers several interpretive programs for all ages. There's also a replica of the signature for people unable to view the original up the grade, along with a closed-circuit camera monitor beaming the real thing into view. Hours are 8 a.m. to 8 p.m. every day. For more information, call (406) 657-6262.

William Clark's signature at Pompeys Pillar east of Billings, Montana.

Several outfitters lead river trips down the Yellowstone and stop at Pompeys Pillar. A one-day canoe excursion, named the "Voyage of the Bird Woman" in honor of Sacagawea, is led by Thomas R. White, owner of Voyagers of the Roche Jaune (the French term for Yellowstone). Call (406) 652-0054 or write to P.O. Box 80804, Billings, MT 59108 for details. Yellowstone River Expeditions, (406) 652-7561, specializes in jetboat trips through the area.

From Pompeys Pillar, it's just about a half-hour's drive to Billings, the biggest city in Montana with about 82,000 people. Attractions include the Pictograph Caves seven miles southeast of town near I-90's Lockwood exit, where Indian rock paintings have been uncovered by archaeologists; the gracious 1903 Moss Mansion, 914 Division St.; and a horse-drawn trolley tour that leaves every thirty minutes daily (except Sunday) June through mid-September from Broadway and 1st Avenue North.

Billings has its share of interesting museums. The Peter Yegen Jr. Yellowstone Country Museum displays a variety of Indian, pioneer, and cowboy artifacts at Billings Logan International Airport, while the Western Heritage Center (2822 Montana Ave.) features changing exhibits on the region's history and culture. Oscar's Dreamland, five miles southwest of town on Wise Lane, has one of the world's largest collections of historic farm machinery, and the Yellowstone Art Center (located in the original county jail at 401 N. 27th St.) focuses on contemporary Western works.

For some spur-of-the-moment recreation, Billings has a good selection of parks, including Riverfront Park right along the Yellowstone and Lake Elmo, north of town in Billings Heights. The Mustangs, a Cincinnati Reds farm team, play June through August at Cobb Field on North 27th St. The Billings Night Rodeo is held at 8 p.m. nightly all summer long at the 4 Cross Arena (I-90 Exit 446). Major shopping areas include downtown Billings, with specialty shops and a factory outlet mall, and the West End, home of the Rimrock Mall, Billings' largest, with about ninety stores. Stop by the Billings Chamber of Commerce's headquarters at I-90's Exit 450 for more local information or call (800) 735-2635.

From Billings, the traveler can either head north on US 87 toward Great Falls and Fort Benton to pick up the westward trek or follow Captain Clark's route in reverse along I-90 all the way to Three Forks—another major junction for the expedition. Highlights of this latter option might include the following:

*Park City (Exit 426). It was near here where Clark and his party actually started their Yellowstone river trip, after following the waterway for some distance overland. Near what is now called the Buffalo Mirage Access, Clark finally found some trees suitable for canoe building. The state-run access area offers camping, fishing, boat ramps, and picnic tables.

Montana Centennial Trail Drive Statue at the Billings visitor center.

*Big Timber (Exit 377). Another Yellowstone River access point, although the major attraction here is probably Big Timber Waterslide, a water-park complex with a half-dozen large waterslides, Olympic-size swimming pool, bumper boats, and more.

*Livingston (Exit 322) and Bozeman (Exit 309). It was between these two towns, guided in part by Sacagawea, that the Clark party crossed Bozeman Pass and descended to the Yellowstone Valley. Both cities are major recreation areas and gateways to Yellowstone National Park (see the sidetrip near the end of Chapter Six).

*Three Forks (Exit 278). On their 1804 westward trip, Lewis and Clark finally discovered the Missouri River headwaters here. Eastbound in 1806, the Clark party split up at the Three Forks, with Sergeant Ordway and nine others pushing down the Missouri to rendezvous with Captain Lewis, and Clark and twelve others continuing overland to the Yellowstone.

THE HI-LINE

Now we return to Fort Buford for travelers who want to follow the corps' westward journey up the Missouri.

Past the Missouri-Yellowstone confluence, it becomes difficult to follow Lewis and Clark's route by land. Two motor routes parallel the Missouri, but neither very closely. Backroads provide access to the river, but these offer little more than a few miles of riverbank driving. The traveler's best bet is to hightail it for Fort Benton, where—if your schedule permits—outfitters can help you backtrack a ways on the stretch of water that most closely resembles the waterway Lewis and Clark experienced—the Upper Missouri Wild and Scenic River.

But first, we must get across a huge chunk of northeast Montana, a land so vast that high school sports teams frequently must travel all day to reach their opponents. The two major routes across this part of the state are US 2 and Montana 200/US 87. US 2—often called the Hi-Line, after the Great Northern Railway route it paralleled—is the more popular and practical of the two.

Urged on by Great Falls founder Paris Gibson and copper baron Marcus Daly, rail magnate James Hill decided northern Montana was ripe for settling. Towns like Glasgow, Zurich, Havre, and Malta were named in hopes of appealing to would-be European immigrants; in some instances, Great Northern employees reportedly spun the globe, closed their eyes, and jabbed their finger at the whirring sphere. Whatever town they hit, that was the new settlement's name.

Many emigrants arrived between 1910 and 1918, eager to claim their land and start farming. For a while, the homesteaders flourished; wet weather and World War I led to inflated grain prices. But a long drought set in about 1918, and many settlers left just as soon as they'd come. However, today days, northeastern Montanans generally do well with wheat, often planted in strips to help control wind erosion.

It's some 350 miles from the North Dakota border to Fort Benton, way too much ground to cover thoroughly when Lewis and Clark lore is the primary objective. So let's take a brief look at highlights of the Hi-Line:

*When folks think of Montana, many think about cowboys, and several outfitters around the state offer honest-to-goodness cattle-drive vacations for anyone willing to pay the price. Gene and Marsha Foss of Culbertson, Montana, offer several drives each summer. The six-day rides are geared to people with all levels of riding experience, and the Fosses have guided people from as far away as Hong Kong and Switzerland. For more information, write Gene Foss, HC 69 Box 97, Culbertson, MT 59218, or call (406) 787-5559.

*It was somewhere here along the Missouri that the Corps of Discovery had its first encounter with a grizzly bear. The date was April 29, 1805. "I walked on shore with one man. About 8 a.m. we fell in with two

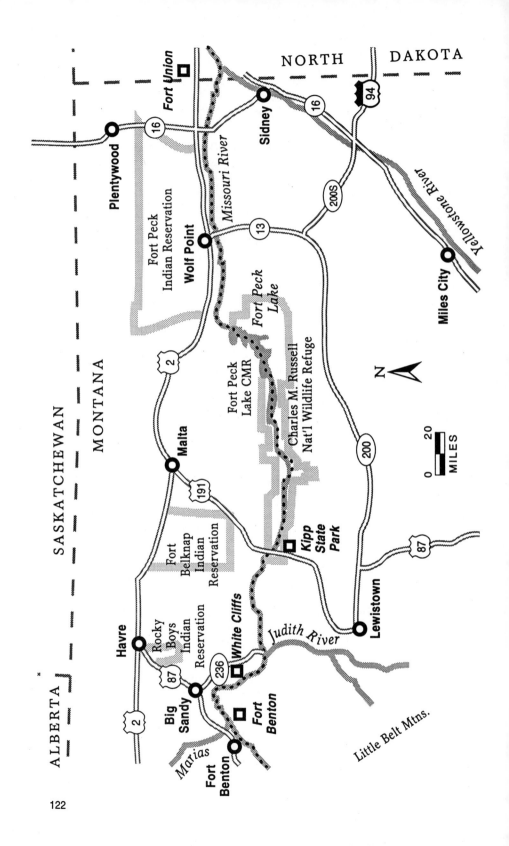

brown or yellow bear, both of which we wounded. One of them made his escape, the other after my firing on him pursued me seventy or eighty yards, but fortunately had been so badly wounded that he was unable to pursue me so closely as to prevent my charging my gun; we again repeated our fire and killed him," Lewis wrote.

*Coming from the North Dakota border, Wolf Point is the first major town along the Hi-Line. Wolf Point pays tribute to our heroes at Lewis and Clark Memorial Park, situated several miles east of town on the Missouri River. The town's major event is the Wolf Point Stampede, Montana's oldest rodeo and one of its best. A shared celebration of cowboy and Indian culture, the event takes place the second weekend of July.

*Nashua and Glasgow, less than an hour west of Wolf Point, are the jumping-off spots for Fort Peck Dam, largest and westernmost of the Pick-Sloan Plan impoundments. The earth-filled dam is more than 21,000 feet long, 3,500 feet wide at its base, and 250 feet high. The dam created Fort Peck Lake, with a storage capacity of 19 million acre-feet of water and a surface area of 249,000 acres. The lake stretches about 150 miles west, more than the distance spanned between Pittsburgh and Cleveland, while its total shoreline—nearly 1,600 miles—is longer than that of California.

In addition to Fort Peck, the dam and Fort Peck the lake, there's Fort Peck, the town. Built by the U.S. Army Corps of Engineers to house some of the many thousands who worked on the dam, Fort Peck still boasts some interesting architecture, including the COE office, the Fort Peck Hotel, and the popular Fort Peck Theatre, which presents summer stock shows.

*Fort Peck is also the northern gateway to the Charles M. Russell National Wildlife Refuge, largest in the continental United States at 1.2 million acres. The CMR, as it's known to Montanans, is full of bighorn sheep, pronghorn, deer, elk, and coyotes—everything Lewis and Clark saw except grizzly bears, which now live only in sections of western Montana. Big as it is, the CMR is difficult to access. Get a good local map, exercise caution, and don't even think of exploring the area's back roads if rain is threatening—the terrain quickly becomes an impassible gumbo when wet.

*Glasgow's Valley County Pioneer Museum, just west of town, is one of Montana's better small-town museums. It has several Lewis and Clark exhibits; one tells how Lewis and Clark came to name the Milk River, which the Indians had earlier called "The River Which Scolds at All Others." The expedition reached this largest and most important northern tributary of the Missouri on May 8, 1805. "The water of this river possesses a peculiar whiteness, being about the color of a cup of tea with the admixture of a tablespoonful of milk," Lewis wrote. "From the color of its water we called it Milk River."

Missouri River south of Culbertson, Montana.

  *Western Montana is full of hot springs, but they're something of a rarity in the state's eastern reaches. Sleeping Buffalo Hot Springs Resort near Saco was named for a group of glacial boulders near the Milk River which, from a distance, resemble a herd of sleeping buffalo. These were held sacred by the Indians, with one rock in particular thought to be the leader. Indians sacrificed possessions at this rock, now part of a roadside monument at the hot springs turnoff. Facilities at the resort include several pools, a water slide, golf course, restaurant, and lodging.

  *Malta sits at the terminus of US 191, the best land route to James Kipp Recreation Area, one of the most popular and accessible spots in the CMR. Located just east of the designated Upper Missouri National Wild and Scenic River, Kipp Recreation Area is a frequent destination for longer guided river trips through the corridor. This is also the eastern access point for the Missouri Breaks National Back Country Byway, a route leading to several rugged river overlooks.

  *It was near Chinook that Chief Joseph of the Nez Perce surrendered on October 5, 1877, with his eloquent "I will fight no more forever ..." speech. The site is marked at the Chief Joseph Battlefield sixteen miles south of US 2.

  *Havre is the most populous town on the Hi-Line, home of Northern Montana College, and jumping off spot for Fort Benton, Great Falls, and the rest of the Lewis and Clark route. If you have time, stop by the H. Earl Clack Museum in Havre's Lions Park, where exhibits include some excellent photos of Native American sites and a piece of the Berlin Wall. The park also offers reasonably-priced RV and tent sites, as well as tours of nearby Fort Assiniboine and an area buffalo jump. The museum is open 9 a.m. to 9 p.m. May 15 through September 15. Beaver Creek Park, one of the largest county-run parks in the nation, is south of Havre.

Another alternate route runs about four hundred miles from the Dakota border to Fort Benton, following Montana 200 (from Sidney to Grass Range), US 87 (from Grass Range to Stanford via Lewistown), and Montana 80 (from Stanford to Fort Benton). This is big, wild country, where a dot on the map doesn't necessarily indicate much. As W.C. McRae and Judy Jewell point out in their *Montana Handbook*, "Between Sidney and Lewistown—a distance of almost three hundred miles—Highway 200 passes through only three towns with gas pumps; their *combined* population approaches fifteen hundred people. As it connects up these remote enclaves of humanity, Highway 200 intersects a part of Montana often called the Big Lonely. Unpopulated, marginally productive, and often starkly beautiful, this is one of the last vast frontiers left in Montana."

*Denotes towns along Clark's 1806 homeward route.

LODGING

BISMARCK/MANDAN, NORTH DAKOTA

Best Western Seven Seas Inn, (800) 528-1234, 2611 Old Red Trail (Mandan). $56.
Bismarck Motor Hotel, (701) 223-2474, 2301 E. Main Ave. $27-$29.
Expressway Inn, (800) 456-6388, 200 E. Bismarck Expressway. $35-$40.
Holiday Inn, (800) HOLIDAY, 6th and Broadway. $54-$64.
Kelly Inn, (800) 635-3559, 1800 N. 12th St. $44-$48.
Select Inn, (800) 641-1000, 1505 Interchange Ave. $30-$33.

WASHBURN, NORTH DAKOTA

ScotWood Motel, (701) 462-8191, 1323 Frontage Rd. $33.

STANTON, NORTH DAKOTA

Hiawatha Motel, (701) 745-3204, 418 Van Slyck.

GARRISON, NORTH DAKOTA

Garrison Motel, (701) 463-2858, 0.25 mile east on ND 37. $27.
Indian Hills Resort, (701) 743-4122, ND 1804 west of Garrison on Good Bear Bay. Cabins and condos for rent.

PARSHALL, NORTH DAKOTA

Parshall Motor Inn, (701) 862-3127, North Main St.

NEW TOWN, NORTH DAKOTA

Cottage Motel, (701) 627-4217, Main St.

Sunset Motel, (701) 627-3316, ND 23 E.

West Dakota Inn Motel, (701) 627-3721, ND 23 E.

WILLISTON, NORTH DAKOTA

Airport International Inn, (701) 774-0241, US 2 and US 85 N.

El Rancho Motor Hotel, (701) 572-6321, 1623 2nd Ave. W. $37.

Select Inn, (800) 641-1000, 213 35th St. $36.

Super 8 Lodge, (800) 800-8000, 2324 2nd Ave. W. $27-$34.

Travel Host, (701) 774-0041, 3801 2nd Ave. W.

*SIDNEY, MONTANA

Lone Tree Inn, (406) 482-4520, 900 S. Central. $38.

Park Plaza Motel, (406) 482-1520, 601 S. Central.

Richland Motor Inn, (406) 482-6400, 1200 S. Central. $43.

*GLENDIVE, MONTANA

Best Western Holiday Lodge, (800) 528-1234, 222 N. Kendrick. $54.

El Centro Motel, (406) 365-5211, 112 S. Kendrick Ave. $28.

Jordon Motor Inn, (406) 365-3371, 223 N. Merrill Ave. $44.

*MILES CITY, MONTANA

Buckboard Motel, (406) 232-3550, 1006 S. Haynes Ave. $31.

Budget Host Custer's Inn, (800) 456-5026, 1209 S. Haynes Ave. $34.

Super 8 Motel, (800) 800-8000, MT 59 S. $36.

*FORSYTH, MONTANA

Best Western Sundowner Inn, (800) 528-1234, 1018 Front St. $52.

Restwel Motel, (406) 356-2771, 810 Front St. $29.

*BILLINGS, MONTANA

Airport Metra Inn, (406) 245-6611, 403 Main. $34.

The Billings Inn, (800) 231-7782, 880 N. 29th St. $37-$41.

Elliott Inn, ((800) 333-6311, I-90 Exit 446. $45-$49.

Juniper Motel, (406) 245-4128, 1315 N. 27th St. $41.

Overpass Motel, (406) 252-5157, 615 Central Ave. $27.

Ramada Inn, (800) 228-2828, 1223 Mullowney Ln. $57.

Sheraton Billings Hotel, (800) 325-3535. $55-$82.

*COLUMBUS, MONTANA

TownHouse Inn, (800) 442-4667, 602 8th Ave. N. $43-$46.

*BIG TIMBER, MONTANA

C.M. Russell Lodge, (406) 932-5244, I-90 Exit 367. $39.

*LIVINGSTON, MONTANA

Budget Host Parkway Motel, (406) 222-3840, 1124 W. Park. $44-$46.

Del Mar Motel, (406) 222-3120, I-90 business loop. $42.

Paradise Inn, (800) 437-6291, I-90 Exit 333. $45.

Talcott House Bed & Breakfast, (406) 222-7699, 405 W. Lewis. $55-$65.

*BOZEMAN, MONTANA

The Bozeman Inn, (406) 587-3176, 1235 N. 7th Ave. $49.

Gallatin Gateway Inn, (406) 763-4672, twelve miles southwest on US 191.

Holiday Inn, (800) HOLIDAY, 5 Baxter Ln. $71.

Lewis and Clark Motel, (406) 586-3341, 824 W. Main St. $49.

Royal 7 Motel, (406) 587-3103, 310 N. 7th Ave. $37.

Torch & Toes Bed & Breakfast, (800) 446-2138, 309 S. Third Ave.

CULBERTSON, MONTANA

Diamond Willow Inn, (406) 787-6218, US 2. Under $40.

Kings Inn, (406) 787-6277, 408 6th St. E. $30.

WOLF POINT, MONTANA

Big Sky Motel, (406) 653-2300, US 2 E. Under $40.

Homestead Inn, (800) 231-0986, 101 US 2 E. Under $40.

Sherman Motor Inn, (800) 952-1100, 200 E. Main. $30.

GLASGOW, MONTANA

Campbell Lodge, (406) 228-9328, 534 3rd Ave. S. $30-$34.

Cottonwood Inn, (800) 321-8213, US 2 E. $46-$51.

La Casa Motel, (406) 228-9311, 238 1st Ave. N. Under $40.

MALTA, MONTANA

Edgewater Inn, (800) 821-7475 (in state) or (406) 654-1302, 101 US 2 W. $40-$60.

Maltana Motel, (406) 654-2610, 138 S. 1st Ave. $32.

CHINOOK, MONTANA

Chinook Motor Inn, (406) 357-2248, 100 Indiana Ave. under $40.

HAVRE, MONTANA

El Toro Inn, (800) 422-5414 (in state) or (800) 735-2794, 521 1st St. $42.

Super 8, (800) 800-8000, 1902 US 2 W. $39.

TownHouse Inn, (800) 442-4667, 629 W. 1st St. $49-$53.

CAMPING

BISMARCK/MANDAN, NORTH DAKOTA

Bismarck KOA, (701) 222-2662, 3720 Centennial Rd.

Colonial Motel and Campground, (701) 663-9824, 4631 Memorial Hwy. (Mandan).

Fort Abraham Lincoln State Park, (701) 663-9571, south of Mandan on ND 1806.

Hillcrest Acres Campground, (701) 255-4334, from East Bismarck Expressway, 1.25 miles east on Old Hwy. 10.

Mandan Camping Area, (701) 667-3280, four blocks west of ND 1806 on Third St. (Mandan).

WASHBURN, NORTH DAKOTA

Fort Mandan Historical Site, (701) 462-8129, west of town.

City Park, free overnight camping.

PICK CITY, NORTH DAKOTA

Lake Sakakawea State Park, (701) 487-3315.

GARRISON, NORTH DAKOTA

Fort Stevenson State Park, (701) 337-5576, three miles south.

Indian Hills Resort, (701) 463-2102, thirty-one miles west.

WILLISTON, NORTH DAKOTA

Buffalo Trails Campground, (701) 572-3206, four miles north via US 2 and US 85.

Lewis and Clark State Park, (701) 859-3071, sixteen miles east on ND 1804.

Lund's Landing, (701) 568-3474, twenty-four miles east on ND 1804.

*GLENDIVE, MONTANA

Green Valley Campground, (406) 365-4156, I-94 Exit 212.

Glendive Campground, (406) 365- 6721, I-94 Exit 215.

Makoshika State Park, (406) 365-8596, two miles south east on Snyder Ave.

*MILES CITY, MONTANA

KOA-Miles City, (406) 232-3991, I-94 Exit 135.

*BILLINGS, MONTANA

Big Sky Campground, (406) 259-4110, 5516 Laurel Rd.

Billings Metro KOA, (406) 252-3104, 3087 Garden Ave.

Garden Avenue RV Park, (406) 259-0878, I-90 Exit 450.

*LAUREL, MONTANA

Pelican RV Park, (406) 259-8211, 3444 S. Frontage Rd.

*COLUMBUS, MONTANA

Itch-Ke-Pe Park, (406) 322-5313, on south edge of town.

*BIG TIMBER, MONTANA

KOA-Big Timber, (406) 932-6569, I-90 Exit 377.

*LIVINGSTON, MONTANA

Big Spur Campground, (406) 222-7600, 10.5 miles south on US 89.

KOA-Paradise Valley, (406) 222-0992, ten miles south on US 89.

Livingston Inn & Campground, (406) 222-1122, I-90 Exit 333.

*BOZEMAN, MONTANA

Bear Canyon Campground, (406) 587-1575, I-90 at Bear Canyon Rd.

Bozeman Hot Springs KOA, (406) 587-3030, 81123 Gallatin Road (US 191).

Lexley Acres, (406) 388-6095, I-90 Exit 298 (Belgrade).

Manhattan Camper Court, (406) 284-6930, I-90 Exit 288 (Manhattan).

Sunrise Campground, (406) 587-4797, I-90 Exit 309.

CULBERTSON, MONTANA

Bicentennial Park, south side of town. Free camping with RV hookups.

WOLF POINT, MONTANA

R.B.W. Campground, (406) 525-3740, seven miles east on US 2.

Rancho Motel & Campground, (406) 653-1940, 1.25 miles west on US 2.

GLASGOW, MONTANA

Shady Rest RV Park, (800) 422-8954, US 2 and Lasar Dr.

Trails West Trailer Park & Campground, (406) 228-2778, 1.5 miles west on US 2 at Skylark Rd.

MALTA, MONTANA

Edgewater Campground, (800) 821-7475, US 2 W.

HAVRE, MONTANA

Beaver Creek Park, (406) 395-4565, south of Havre via 5th Ave.

Earl Clack Museum & Campground, (406) 265-9913, in Lions Park on US 2.

Evergreen Campground, (406) 265-8228, south of town on US 87.

Fresno Reservoir, west of Havre on US 2.

Havre RV Park, (406) 265-8861, 1300 1st St.

KOA of Havre, (406) 265-9722, nine miles east on US 2.

RESTAURANTS

BISMARCK/MANDAN, NORTH DAKOTA

Captain Meriwether's Landing & Pasta Co., (701) 224-0455, at the *Lewis and Clark* Riverboat Landing. Family dining on the Missouri River.

The Drumstick, (701) 223-8449, 307 N. Third. Open 24 hours except Sundays and holidays.

Little Cottage Cafe, (701) 223-4949, 2513 E. Main. Homemade soups, pies, and pastries.

Paradiso, (701) 224-1111, 2620 State St. Mexican dining.

Seasons Cafe, (701) 258-7700 ext. 1850, 800 S. Third St. (in the Radisson Inn Bismarck). Featuring regional American specialties.

WASHBURN, NORTH DAKOTA

Dakota Farms, (701) 462-8175, US 83 bypass. Wide menu with daily specials.

COLEHARBOR, NORTH DAKOTA

83 Cafe, (701) 442-3294, US 83.

GARRISON, NORTH DAKOTA

Lake Road Restaurant, (701) 463-2569, ND 37. Breakfast all day, sack lunches to go.

Stone Inn Supper Club & Lounge, (701) 337-5590, ND 37 E. Nightly specials, prime rib Fridays and Saturdays.

NEW TOWN, NORTH DAKOTA

Scenic 23 Supper Club & Lounge, (701) 627-9494, east of town on ND 23. Steakhouse.

WILLISTON, NORTH DAKOTA

Analene's Country Restaurant, at Lund's Landing, twenty-four miles east on ND 1804. Pan-fried walleye, view of Lake Sakakawea.

Gramma Sharon's, US 2 and US 85. Open 24 hours at the Conoco Truck Stop.

Pierce's Steakhouse, (701) 572-4751, 18 2nd St. E. Steak and seafood. Closed Sundays.

Trapper's Kettle, (701) 774-2831, north on US 2 and US 85. Informal American dining.

*SIDNEY, MONTANA

Lalonde Restaurant, (406) 482-1043, 217 S. Central Ave. Lunch specials, Sunday buffet.

New Hunan Restaurant, (406) 482-1118, 821 Central Ave. Chinese and American food.

South 40 Restaurant, (406) 482-4999, 207 2nd Ave. N.W. Wide menu including entrees, burgers, soup and salad bar.

*GLENDIVE, MONTANA

The Montana Inn, (406) 365-2024, I-94 and MT 200 S. All-you-can-eat smorgasbord.

Twilite Dining & Lounge, (406) 365-8705, 209 N. Merrill. Prime rib, steak, chicken, and seafood.

*MILES CITY, MONTANA

Flying J Restaurant, (406) 232-4121, I-90 Baker Exit. Truck stop eatery open 24 hours a day.

Louie's Olive Dining Room, (406) 232-7621, 501 Main. Steaks and seafood.

*FORSYTH, MONTANA

Blue Spruce Cafe, (406) 356-7955, 109 S. 10th Ave. Specializing in homegrown beef.

Speedway Diner, (406) 356-7987, 811 Main. Daily specials, homemade pies, salad bar.

*BILLINGS, MONTANA

The Cattle Company, (406) 656-9090, in the Rimrock Mall. Steaks, prime rib, seafood, salads.

Dos Machos, (406) 652-2020, 24th St. W. Mexican-American food.

George Henry's Restaurant, (406) 245-4570, 404 N. 30th St. Food made from scratch in early American atmosphere.

Jake's, (406) 259-9375, 2701 1st Ave. N. Steaks, ribs, seafood.

Miyajima Gardens, (406) 245-8240, 5364 Midland Rd. Japanese dining.

Vinnie's Italian Kitchen, (406) 256-8484, 119 N. Broadway. Authentic Italian cuisine.

*LAUREL, MONTANA

Little Big Men Pizza, (406) 628-8241, 220 First Ave S. Pizza and more.

*COLUMBUS, MONTANA

Apple Village Cafe, (406) 322-5939, I-90 Exit 408. Sunday brunch, salad bar.

*BIG TIMBER, MONTANA

Country Pride, (406) 932-4419, I-90 Exit 367. Family dining.

Prospector Pizza Plus, (406) 932-4846, 121 McLeod St. Pizza, sandwiches, salad, ribs.

*LIVINGSTON, MONTANA

Livingston Bar & Grill, (406) 222-7909, 130 N. Main. Montana trout, beef, and buffalo burgers.

Trail Ride Inn, (406) 222-1071, 1306 E. Park. Casual American dining.

*BOZEMAN, MONTANA

John Bozeman's Bistro, (406) 587-4100, 242 E. Main. American food, generous portions.

Spanish Peaks Brewery and Italian Cafe, (406) 585-2996, 120 N. 19th. Microbrewery/restaurant featuring brick-oven pizza, pasta, and seafood.

Western Cafe, (406) 587-0436, 443 E. Main. Down-home diner with famous cinnamon rolls.

CULBERTSON, MONTANA

M & M's Place, (406) 787-5362, 14 E. Sixth. Family restaurant.

Wild West Diner, (406) 787-5374, 20 E. Sixth.

WOLF POINT, MONTANA

Pat's Pizza and Family Restaurant, US 2, (406) 653-2577. Pizza, subs, and more.

Sherman Motor Inn (406) 653-1100, 200 E. Main. Wide menu.

GLASGOW, MONTANA

Johnnie Cafe, (406) 228-4222, 433 First Ave. Open 24 hours.

Sam's Supper Club, (406) 228-4614, 307 First Ave. N. Here's the beef.

MALTA, MONTANA

Hitchin' Post, (406) 654-1882, US 2. Western home cooking.

Westside Restaurant, (406) 654-1555, US 2 W. Wide menu.

HAVRE, MONTANA

Andy's Supper Club and Lounge, (406) 265-9963, 658 1st St. W.

4B's Restaurant & Black Angus Supper Club, (406) 265-9721, 604 W. 1st St. Open 24 hours with wide menu.

Iron Horse Pancake House, (406) 265-7891, 335 1st St.

Navlika's, (406) 265-5426, 415 1st St. W. Italian fare and homemade pies.

Wild and scenic Missouri River.

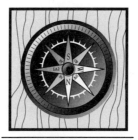

CHAPTER SIX

CENTRAL MONTANA

*The hills and river cliffs which we passed today exhibit a
most romantic appearance...it seemed as if those scenes of vi-
sionary enchantment would never have an end.*
 - Meriwether Lewis, May 31, 1805,
on the Upper Missouri River

THE MISSOURI RIVER BREAKS

The country around Montana's Upper Missouri Wild and Scenic
River looks like a blank spot on many maps, but it is far from barren.
And with its slow pace and near total lack of modern intrusions, the Up-
per Missouri is perhaps the single best place to get a feel for what the
Lewis and Clark Expedition really saw and experienced on its journey.

For many travelers, this is easier said than done. If you are trying to
trace the entire Lewis and Clark Trail over a two-week vacation, you
probably won't have time for even a short Missouri River sojourn. But if
you do have extra days, either now or in the future, this is a good place
to consider spending them.

In a way, this river's "wild and scenic" designation may give people
the wrong idea. The Upper Missouri is certainly scenic, but there are
very few rapids. "Gentle and Scenic" would be a more apt description.
This is a place where it's easy to kick back, daydream, read, ruminate, or
do absolutely nothing at all. Best of all, a boat offers a view of the river
that is all but impossible to experience otherwise. A river trip is just
about the only way to see the White Cliffs section, for example. Someone

Looking at tepee rings on the Missouri River Breaks, Montana.

with a four-wheel drive vehicle could drive down to a few isolated spots on the river but would be unable to get a broad picture of the terrain.

Several outfitters lead guided tours of the Wild and Scenic Missouri, with most trips leaving from Fort Benton and heading downriver—not upstream as the Corps of Discovery did in the spring of 1805. The best known is probably Missouri River Outfitters, once run by Bob Singer, and now operated by Larry and Bonnie Cook. The Cooks offer two- to seven-day outfitted canoe trips, canoe rentals for do-it-yourselfers, and two- to five-day excursions on motorized, weatherized pontoon boats.

Both Cooks are Fort Benton area natives and former teachers with a genuine love for the river, eager to share their wealth of stories of the Missouri's natural and human history. They wear traditional river clothing, and their boat flies a fifteen-star flag, the same style in use during the Lewis and Clark expedition.

The motorized trips travel downriver about eight miles an hour. On board, passengers can browse books depicting sketches and paintings by Swiss artist Karl Bodmer, who traveled through the area with Prince Maximilian of Germany in 1833. It's remarkable to see how little the country has changed.

Most sights are on the river, but the Cooks also allow time for exploration along the banks. A hillside behind one favorite campsite still bears

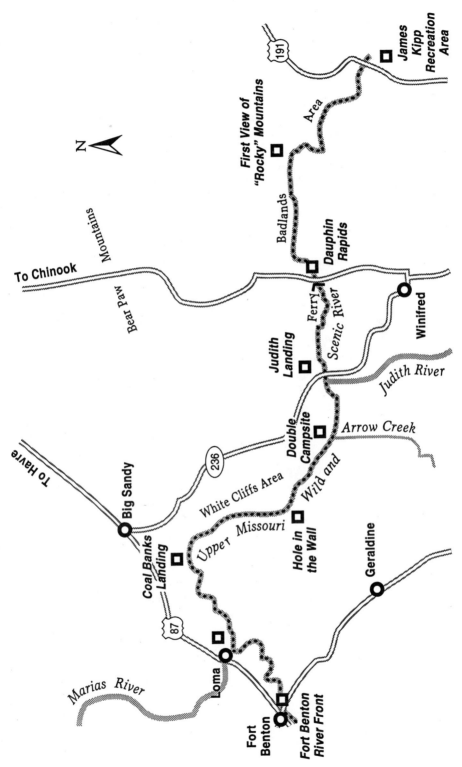

N

To Chinook

Bear Paw Mountains

First View of "Rocky" Mountains

James Kipp Recreation Area

191

Badlands Area

Dauphin Rapids

Ferry

Scenic River

Judith Landing

Winifred

Judith River

To Havre

Big Sandy

236

Double Campsite

Arrow Creek

Coal Banks Landing

White Cliffs Area

Upper Missouri

Wild and

Hole in the Wall

Geraldine

87

Loma

Marias River

Fort Benton

Fort Benton River Front

signs of Indian tepee rings and burial grounds. More strenuous hikes are possible to such landmarks as Hole-in-the-Wall. Some longer trips also venture into the Badlands section, an area even less visited than the White Cliffs. Here, the Cooks can lead participants on hikes with incredibly rugged vistas and abundant wildlife.

The trips are fully outfitted; participants are asked to bring only a sleeping bag, clothing, and personal effects. The motorized trips easily accommodate people of all ages, and the Cooks try to vary each cruise's activities to suit the participants' interests and physical abilities. The food isn't necessarily gourmet, but it is good and plentiful. Breakfasts typically include such fare as pancakes and sausage one morning, French toast and scrambled eggs the next. Dinner might be steak, corn, and oat bran muffins or pork chops and salad.

People interested in a river cruise should contact the Cooks no later than November of the year before they'd like to float. At least 10 people are needed for the motorized trips, although the Cooks can sometimes accommodate smaller groups on previously arranged cruises. Cost in 1998 was $175 per person per day with a two-day minimum. Adventurous sorts seeking more independent travel may prefer the solitude of a canoe journey, which usually lasts from two to seven days. Canoes can be lashed together so even inexperienced canoeists can maneuver the craft downriver. For more information, write Missouri River Outfitters, P.O. Box 762, Fort Benton, MT 59442, or call (406) 622-3295.

A few other established outfitters on the Upper Missouri include Montana River Outfitters (Craig Madsen), 1401 5th Ave. S., Great Falls, MT 59405; Rose River Inn (Gar Wood), Loma, MT 59461; and Voyageurs of the Roche Jaune (Thomas R. White), P.O. Box 80804, Billings, MT 59108. The Bureau of Land Management maintains a list of river permittees, and the roster may change from year to year. For a copy of the latest list (or for more information on floating the river on your own), contact the BLM Lewistown District Office, Airport Road, Lewistown, MT 59457.

Camping conditions along the river are primitive and serene. There are several marked sites along the route; others have just evolved from word-of-mouth use. One designated site, Hole-in-the-Wall, offers a few soft-sided shelters for canoeists caught on the river in bad weather. The Steamboat Rock/Dark Butte area is another favorite with river travelers. Steamboat Rock is the largest columnar sandstone bluff along the river, and the surrounding landscape is filled with other fascinating rock formations, many easily accessible by scrambling.

The Lewis and Clark Expedition had its share of excitement during its ascent of the Upper Missouri. May 14 was a particularly eventful day, starting with another bear encounter. Six men in the two rear dugout canoes spied a sleeping grizzly—an easy catch, they figured. But this bear

The Corps of Discovery "At Lemhi," oil on canvas by Robert F. Morgan. Photo courtesy of the Montana Historical Society.

Rolling hills of South Dakota near Pierre (left). Photo courtesy of the South Dakota Department of Tourism.

Buffalo display in the W.H. Over State Museum Vermillion, South Dakota (below). Photo courtesy of the South Dakota Department of Tourism.

Wild and Scenic Missouri River, Montana. Photo by Michael S. Sample.

Square Butte near Ulm, Montana. Photo by John Reddy.

Rainbow over the Montana plains near the Rocky Mountain Front (left). Photo by Doug O'Looney.

Arrowleaf-balsamroot blooming near the Rocky Mountain Front northwest of Great Falls, Montana (below). Photo by John Reddy.

Gates of the Mountains tour boat (left). Photo by Darrin Schreder.

Lochsa River in Clearwater National Forest, Idaho (right). Photo by George Wuerthner.

Fall colors along the Missouri River (below). Photo by Michael S. Sample.

*View of Trapper Peak in the
Bitterroot Mountains near Darby,
Montana (left).* Photo by Michael S.
Sample.

*Fall colors along the Bitterroot River
(below).* Photo by Michael S.
Sample.

*Placid waters of the lower
Snake River near Lewiston-
Clarkston on the Idaho-
Washington border (left).*
Photo by Julie Fanselow.

Looking west toward Hood River, Oregon, with autumn colored cherry orchards in the Columbia River Gorge National Scenic Area (above). Photo by Steve Terrill.

Mural of Corps of Discovery on the Oregon Historical Building, Portland (left). Photo by Larry Geddis.

Fort replica at Fort Clatsop National Memorial near Astoria, Oregon (right). Photo by Steve Terrill.

Sunrise over Cannon Beach and Haystack Rock near Ecola State Park, Oregon.
Photo by Larry Geddis.

Floating a section of the Wild and Scenic Missouri River in Montana.

proved a beast to kill. Shot first by four of the men, then by the two others, the wounds only enraged the animal, and he gave chase to the hunters. "In this manner he pursued two of them separately so close that they were obliged to throw aside their guns and pouches and throw themselves into the river," Lewis wrote. When the bear finally succumbed, "they then took him on shore and butchered him when they found eight balls had passed through him in different directions."

Later that day, the party experienced another near mishap with the boats. As with the incident in North Dakota, Charbonneau—surely one of the world's worst boatmen—was at the helm of the usually stable and steadfast white pirogue. "In this pirogue were embarked our papers, instruments, books, medicine, a great part of our merchandise and in short almost every article indispensably necessary to further the views, or insure the success of the enterprise in which we are now launched to the distance of 2,200 miles," Lewis wrote. "Suffice it to say, the pirogue was under sail when a sudden squall of wind struck her obliquely and turned her considerably. The steersman alarmed, instead of putting her before the wind lifted her up into it." Confused, Charbonneau wailed at his misfortune until Cruzatte threatened to "shoot him instantly if he did not take hold of the rudder and do his duty," Lewis recalled. "The waves by this time were running very high but the fortitude, resolution and good conduct of Cruzatte saved her. He ordered two of the men to throw out the water with some kettles that fortunately were convenient, while himself and two others rowed her ashore, where she arrived scarcely above the water." In the next day's journal installment, Lewis also gave credit to Sacagawea, who calmly sat in the back of the pirogue and caught most of the boat's light articles just before they washed overboard. Because of her actions, little of real value was lost.

On May 26, Lewis climbed the river bluffs, "which I found sufficiently fatiguing. On arriving to the summit (of) one of the highest points in the neighborhood I thought myself well repaid for my labor; as from this point I beheld the Rocky Mountains for the first time...These mountains were covered with snow, and the sun shone on it in such manner as to give me the most plain and satisfactory view. While I viewed these mountains, I felt a secret pleasure in finding myself so near the head of the heretofore conceived boundless Missouri, but when I reflected on the difficulties which this snowy barrier would most probably throw in my way to the Pacific and the sufferings and hardships of myself and party in them, it in some measure counterbalanced the joy I had felt in the first moments in which I gazed on them; but as I have always held it a crime to anticipate evils I will believe it a good comfortable road until I am compelled to believe differently."

Lewis's philosophizing makes for compelling reading two hundred years later. Alas, the mountains he saw probably weren't the

Exploring the rugged landscape of unusual rock formations above the Missouri River, Montana.

Rockies...he was still too far away. He had likely either spied the Bear Paw Mountains near Havre or the Big or Little Belt mountains south of Great Falls.

On May 28 Lewis and Clark camped near what is now known as the Judith Landing, today a major access point to the Missouri River. Many boat trips take out here, and primitive camping is available. The Power Norris bridge also spans the river at Judith Landing, with Montana Highway 236 leading north to Big Sandy and south to Lewistown.

The Judith Landing takes its name from the river that runs into the Missouri at the site. At first, Lewis and Clark named it the Big Horn. The next day, however, Clark renamed it the Judith River for his girlfriend in Virginia. Actually, Clark didn't know the young woman all that well: Her real name was Julia Hancock, and her friends called her Judy. Nevertheless, she must have been touched by his tribute, for they later were married.

Lewis and Clark had seen tens of thousands of buffalo by the time they reached this area, but the shaggy beasts were to play prominent roles in their journals over the next few days. On May 29, Lewis wrote, "Last night we were all alarmed by a large buffalo bull which swam over from the opposite shore.... (He)...ran up the bank in full speed directly toward the fires, and was within eighteen inches of the heads of some of the men who lay sleeping." Lewis credited his dog, Seaman, with causing the buffalo to change course, and disaster was averted. Lewis noted the only serious damage done was to a rifle trampled by the buffalo. The gun had been left in the ill-fated white pirogue, and Lewis wrote "it appears that the white pirogue, which contains our most valuable stores, is attended by some evil genie."

Later that day, the explorers found huge mounds of rotting, stinking buffalo. They thought this was evidence of a buffalo jump, a ritual Lewis then described in detail in his journal, but no pishkun has ever been found in the immediate vicinity. Historians now believe the buffalo actually drowned and were dumped at the site on the river's backwater. Nevertheless, this river earned a most unromantic name: the Slaughter River.

Slaughter River is now known as Arrow Creek, an Indian name that actually predated the explorers' trip through the area. It got this moniker from a Blackfeet legend. A poor young man fell in love with a young woman, and they wanted to marry but were discouraged by the man's lack of property. Meanwhile, an evil warrior with many horses, lodges, and wives sought to add the young woman to his harem. Luckily, her father would not sell her to the rich warrior.

As the story goes, the young lovers took a walk up the creek. The evil warrior was waiting to ambush the unsuspecting pair when suddenly they heard a groan. When they investigated, the warrior had been shot with an arrow bearing feathers from a bird no one had ever seen and a projectile point unlike any other. The tribal elders figured the evil warrior must have been shot by the gods, thus paving the way for the young couple's marriage.

The Slaughter River/Arrow Creek campsite is the lone "double camp-site" in Montana, that is, the only place the expedition camped on both its inbound and homeward journeys. The corps stayed here May 29, 1805, and the site was again visited by Lewis and his men on July 29, 1806.

On May 30-31, 1805, the explorers floated through an area now known as the White Cliffs of the Missouri. In one of the journals' most famous passages, Lewis wrote a lengthy description of these fantastic bluffs, noting how water had shaped the rich loam into "a thousand gro-tesque figures," pyramids, and "lofty freestone buildings...their parapets well stocked with statuary...so perfect indeed are those walls that I should have thought that nature had attempted here to rival the human art of masonry had I not recollected that she had first begun her work."

THE MARIAS RIVER AND FORT BENTON

When they reached what is now Loma, Montana, on June 2, 1805, the expedition saw a formidable river, one they'd had no warning of. "An interesting question was now to be determined," Lewis wrote the next day, "which of these rivers was the Missouri...what astonished us a little is that the Indians who appeared to be so well acquainted with the geog-raphy of this country should not have mentioned this river on right hand if it be not the Missouri."

The north fork was whitish-brown, very thick and turbid, looking much like the Missouri, while the south fork was transparent. But after exploring the north branch, Lewis was convinced it flowed in too much of a northern direction to be the right path to the Pacific. Further, he rea-soned, if the river penetrated the mountains, it would be clearer.

Lewis had an experience here not unlike his adventure at the Tavern Cave way back in Missouri. On June 7, while exploring bluffs in the area, "I slipped at a narrow pass of about thirty yards in length and but for a quick and fortunate recovery by my espontoon I should have been precipitated into the river down a craggy precipice of about ninety feet." No sooner had Lewis regained his balance than he heard a voice crying for help. It was Private Richard Windsor, who—having slipped and fallen on the same narrow pass that tripped up Lewis—was hanging on for dear life. Lewis slowly talked Windsor down from the cliff, instructing him "to take the knife out of his belt behind him with his right hand and dig a hole with it in the face of the bank to receive his right foot, which he did, and then raise himself to his knees." That night, the captain was ex-hausted but happy to be alive. After a hearty meal of venison, "I now laid myself down on some willow boughs to a comfortable night's rest, and felt indeed as if I was fully repaid for the toil and pain of the day...."

Statue of Lewis, Clark, Sacagawea, and Pomp at Fort Benton, Montana.

The party spent nine days at this confluence, trying to figure out which way to go. Both leaders were convinced the south fork was the Missouri, but the rest of the men wanted to follow the northern fork. On June 11, 1805, Lewis and four others left to seek the Great Falls of the Missouri down the south fork. If they found the falls, they would know they were on the right path. The expedition's continued survival and success rested on making the correct choice. In the meantime, on June 8, Lewis took his turn at flattering womanhood, naming the mystery stream Marias River, in honor of his cousin, Maria Wood. "It is true that the hue of the waters of this turbulent and troubled stream but illy comport with the pure celestial virtues and amiable qualifications of that lovely fair one," he wrote. "But on the other hand it is a noble river; one destined to become in my opinion an object of contention between the two great powers of American and Great Britain with respect to the adjustment of the Northwesterly boundary of the former."

There were once plans for a town named Ophir at the mouth of the Marias. It was twenty-two miles downriver from Fort Benton, and planners felt that—in low water—if steamboats couldn't reach Fort Benton, they could possibly reach Ophir. There was also plentiful timber for building. Moreover, the town was the idea of men with high connections in Montana's territorial government. Ophir seemed destined for success.

Stock in the company was issued on March 24, 1864, and a charter was obtained eleven months later. All went well for a while: A field manager was hired to build the town, a sawmill was established, and four hundred lots were laid out. But in May 1865, something went awry. One story goes that nine Blood Indians were killed on the streets of Fort Benton, and their bodies thrown into the river. The second story held that during the winter, Charlie Carson, cousin of Kit Carson, was trapping along the Missouri with two buddies when three Bloods stole their horses. Carson and his party pursued the Indians, caught and shot them, and regained their horses. Whatever really happened, a war party of 180 Indians was traveling to Fort Benton for vengeance when they encountered wood cutters building the town of Ophir. Ten whites were killed, and dreams of the town died with them. Nothing remains of the townsite; a few log cabins left over after the massacre eventually were used to feed the fires in steamboat boilers.

Fort Benton has many claims to historical fame, but perhaps none so mighty as its reign during the steamboat era, when as many as ten steamboats a day might tie up at its waterfront. In its heyday, Fort Benton also boasted what was known as "the wildest block in the West," jam-packed with bars, dance halls, and brothels.

The upriver trip from St. Louis usually took sixty to sixty-five days. Passenger fare averaged $150. During the busy year of 1867, about fifteen hundred people traveled to Montana on the steamboats. The river route was also faster and safer than overland routes, which frequently

A drift boat on a section of the Wild and Scenic Missouri River, Montana.

were closed down by Indians. The riverboats were also important to trade and shipping. The all-time peak of river traffic was in 1879, when forty-seven boats carried 9,444 tons of cargo up the river, but railroads started cutting into the riverboat shipping during the 1880s.

Fort Bentonites are proud their town is home to"Explorers at the Marias," the official Montana Lewis and Clark Monument. The riverfront statue was created by Bob Scriver, a prolific Western sculptor from Browning, Montana, to mark the United States Bicentennial in 1976. It depicts Sacagawea and her baby Jean Baptiste in addition to the captains. Scriver spent a year researching the expedition before starting his work on the statue, trying to ensure the accuracy of the equipment, clothing, body features, and faces. For example, the square compass in Clark's hand was modeled from the actual one he used, and Sacagawea is carrying her baby in a blanket because the packboard he rode in earlier was lost overboard a few days before the party's arrival at the mouth of the Marias River.

The finished product is of heroic proportions: one-sixth larger than life-size. The statue weighs 2.5 tons, is 21 feet high, and sits on an 85-ton granite base given as a gift from Tanner Brothers Quarry near Square Butte, Montana. After its casting at the Modern Art Foundry in New York City, the statue was transported cross-country to Montana upright on the bed of a semitrailer, causing many a head to turn.

A four-block walking tour along Fort Benton's levee offers a good look at the town's history. Start in Old Fort Park at the Museum of the Upper Missouri. Pass by the ruins of Fort Benton, a fur-trading post founded in 1846 by Alexander Culbertson; a monument to the Whoop-Up Trail, a route to western Canada popular before the railroads; a replica of the "Mandan" keelboat, built for the film *The Big Sky*; the remains of the *Baby Rose* steamboat, mired in the Missouri mud below the Lewis and Clark statue; and a monument to the Mullan Road, another famous western route that traveled from Fort Benton to Walla Walla, Washington. The walking tour ends at the Grand Union Hotel, once considered the finest between Minneapolis and Seattle.

The Bureau of Land Management also maintains a small museum at 1718 Front St., near the Lewis and Clark statue. Called the Upper Missouri Visitor Center, it features a slide show on the expedition, complete with readings from the journals. This is also a good place to check out detailed, waterproof guides to the Missouri River. The books include information on all aspects of river history and can be returned downstream. At some point, the BLM hopes to build a major interpretive center in Fort Benton to further explain the area's role in America's early days of steamboating, fur trading, and river exploration. In the meantime, the current visitor center is open from 8 a.m. to 6 p.m. daily, Memorial Day through Labor Day weekends.

Fort Benton has several motels, a bed-and-breakfast, and about half a dozen restaurants. Another big local attraction is a memorial to "Shep." This sheepherder's dog, made famous in "Ripley's Believe It Or Not," met every train into Fort Benton for five years after his master's body was taken away by rail. Eventually, Shep was run over by a train, and he was buried on a hillside overlooking the rail depot.

For more information on Fort Benton, call (406) 622-5634. From here, it's a short thirty-five mile drive to Great Falls.

HOMEWARD BOUND: CAMP DISAPPOINTMENT, THE TWO MEDICINE FIGHT SITE, AND GLACIER NATIONAL PARK

As noted earlier, the Marias River had captivated and perplexed the explorers during the 1805 trip through Montana. On his way home in 1806, Lewis was eager to explore the river's upper reaches. His side trip into the area produced perhaps some of the most disappointing and dramatic passages of the entire expedition.

Lewis's main purpose in tracing the Marias River was to see if the river reached far enough north to satisfy the northern boundary agreement of the 1783 Paris Treaty between the United States and Great Britain, which ended the American Revolution. This treaty said the north-

Participants of Lewis and Clark Festival field trip at the Two Medicine Fight Site.

western boundary of the Northwestern Territory would be determined by a line drawn from the northwesternmost point of the Lake of the Woods to the Mississippi River. It was later learned the Mississippi did not reach far enough north to satisfy that article of the treaty, so after the Louisiana Purchase, one of the purposes of the Lewis and Clark expedition was to find a tributary that would fulfill the treaty's requirements. Lewis found the Marias River didn't reach far enough north, either, and that's how he came to name Camp Disappointment.

The Camp Disappointment-Two Medicine region is still quite wild, and the major historic sites here, though marked, are not easy to find. Moreover, the sites are on private land; permission should be obtained, and a four-wheel drive vehicle is necessary to make the final approaches. Alternatively, Great Falls's annual Lewis and Clark Festival (held late each June; see the Great Falls section for more information) offers excellent field trips to the sites on the average of every other year. But even travelers who cannot arrange a tour or don't wish to strike out on their own may find this sidetrip worthwhile since it comes within twenty miles of Glacier National Park and the vacation possibilities there. See more information later in this section.

Camp Disappointment was the farthest campsite north used by the expedition, although not the northernmost point reached by Lewis's party: They actually traveled about two miles farther north on their way to this site. The turnoff is located on U.S. Highway 2 just under twenty

View of Camp Disappointment area near Cut Bank, Montana.

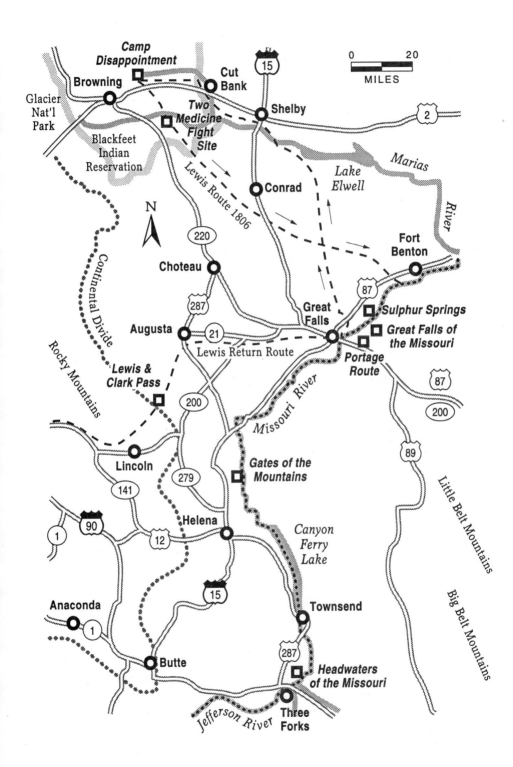

miles west of Cut Bank, Montana, (and fifteen miles east of Browning). Turn north just before reaching the Meriwether grain elevators and drive 3.2 miles north on Montana 444, also known as Meriwether Road. Then turn left, or west, at a fenceline just south of Willow Creek (which is in turn just south of the Cut Bank River). Camp Disappointment is located along a bend in the river a little more than three miles (by farm roads) northwest of the turnoff. A plaque marks the site.

Here, Lewis could see that the Cut Bank River was flowing directly from the mountains to the west, meaning—once again—the river did not meander far enough north to help America's claim. The site further earned its name because of the poor weather Lewis and his men experienced here. Beset by rain and clouds, Lewis was unable to complete the celestial observations he hoped would help pinpoint the camp's location.

Return to US 2 and continue west past a turnout on the north side of the road noting the nearby presence of Camp Disappointment. US 2 soon intersects with US 89 at Browning, headquarters of the Blackfeet Indian Reservation and gateway to Glacier National Park. From Browning, US 2 skims the park's south edge, while US 89 leads north to the Going-to-the-Sun-Road and the heart of Glacier. If you have time for only a day in Glacier National Park, it is perhaps best spent driving at least part of this scenic and amazing fifty-mile road, deservedly one of the world's most famous. Note, however, it is only open from mid-June to mid-October, and certain vehicle length and width restrictions apply.

With its sculpted peaks and numerous lakes, Glacier offers some of the continent's best scenery, along with seven hundred miles of hiking and bridle trails from which to access it. Some of the most beloved include the Alpine Meadow Walk, which jumps off from Logan Pass on Going-to-the-Sun Road, and Avalanche Lake Trail, an easy path featuring scenic waterfalls. Other activities include backpacking, white-water rafting, open-air bus tours, fishing (get a free park permit), and birdwatching.

Glacier visitors can choose from a wide range of accommodations, ranging from designated and backcountry campgrounds to European-inspired lodging at Many Glacier Hotel. For more information on Glacier National Park, call (406) 888-5441.

From Browning, head back toward Great Falls. About ten miles to the southeast, the road crosses the Two Medicine River. Here the Lewis and Clark Expedition had its only armed—and fatal—encounter with Indians.

The Two Medicine Fight Site is even more difficult to find than Camp Disappointment, and a four-wheel drive vehicle is necessary for the last approach. Near the Two Medicine River on US 89, look for a brown metal shed marked "Three Rivers Telephone Co-op" on the north side of the road. Turn north here. The road soon parallels a mile long pishkun (a buffalo jump) and the remnants of the Holy Family Mission, started in 1888 by the Jesuits. The mission was run by the Jesuits and

Ursuline nuns until 1939. In the mid-1960s, thirty-five people were killed and the mission grounds inundated when spring floods swept through this area. Most of the bodies were never recovered. The facility no longer operates as a mission, but Catholic services are still held weekly.

This area also is known as the final resting place of James Willard Schultz. Born in Boonville, New York, in 1859, Schultz moved to Montana at age seventeen. He worked at Joe Kipp's trading post near what is now Conrad and married a Piegan woman. By living with the Blackfeet, Schultz had a ringside seat to the vanishing West—experiences and impressions he recorded in some three dozen books, including *My Life as a Indian*. Schultz died in 1947 and was buried near the irrigation canal beneath the buffalo jump.

The road eventually turns to gravel, then dead-ends at the paved Valier Road (Montana 358). Turn right here and drive south. The road crosses the Two Medicine River again. Another 1.8 miles south, turn right again onto another gravel road at the Stoltz Ranch. This road leads west past three irrigation ditches to a fork about 2.4 miles from the ranch turnoff. After proceeding through (and closing) the gate, bear left to the faint path leading up the ridge. Four-wheel drive is necessary to make this ascent.

Once up on the ridge, look for a small rock cairn on the north side of the road. The rocks form an arrow which points directly to the Two Medicine Fight Site. (Look for the telltale clump of trees and a fence erected by area Boy Scouts.) Even if you cannot locate the cairn, the ridge affords an amazing 360-degree view of this wild, forlorn area and the badlands where dinosaurs once roamed.

The high ridge trail proceeds on past a group of tepee rings and another junction. The right fork is extremely rugged and descends into the badlands and a buffalo jump area; the left loops back to the gate. It's possible to hike to the fight site from the right fork; the site may also be approached by returning to the gate, then driving in a north-northwest direction toward the badlands, parking before the land drops off to the river, and walking the rest of the way.

Historians believe the fight occurred here based on descriptions in Lewis's journals, and the hardy narrowleaf cottonwood tree within the fenced area may well be the very one on the site in 1806. (Two other cottonwoods mentioned fell to fire about 1980.) Plans call for cuttings from the trees' surviving branches to be replanted to take the place of their burned ancestors. Other cuttings from the trees have found their way to other sites around the country, including the Montana State Capitol grounds in Helena.

The site bears a historical plaque mentioning that Lewis and his party camped here July 26, 1806, with eight Blackfeet Indians with whom they'd nervously counciled that evening. They went to bed late and Lewis took the first guard, relieved later by Reuben Field, and then by Joseph Field. Carelessly, Joseph Field laid down his gun next to his brother's and fell asleep.

At daybreak, the Indians awoke first and, seeing the white men's guns unguarded, quickly made a plan of attack. Joseph Field woke up just in time to see an Indian seize the unattended guns. He hollered for his brother, and together they chased after the Blackfeet, "whom they overtook at the distance of fifty or sixty paces from the camp, seized their guns and wrested them from him, and Reuben Field as he seized his gun stabbed the Indian to the heart with his knife," Lewis wrote. "The fellow ran about fifteen steps and fell dead." This was hearsay to Lewis, who was still asleep as the incident began.

In the meantime, Drouillard, too, was locked in a struggle for his gun. This finally awakened Lewis, who realized his own rifle was missing. Lewis reached for his pistol and chased after the Indian who had taken his gun, shouting for the brave to drop the weapon. Sensing failure, the Indian complied.

By this point, the expedition's horses and those of the Blackfeet were galloping away from the scene in two bunches. Drouillard and the Fields brothers chased one group, while Lewis followed the two Blackfeet pursuing the second—straight into a box canyon. Here, one of the Blackfeet jumped behind a pile of rocks; the other turned and took aim at Lewis, who was just thirty steps away. Lewis managed to fire first, striking the Blackfoot in the belly, but the Indian got off a shot, too. "Being bareheaded I felt the wind of his bullet very distinctly," Lewis later wrote. Knowing another Indian was hiding among the rocks, and that the others were still in the area, perhaps with reinforcements on the way, Lewis decided to give up his pursuit of the horses.

The party reclaimed enough of its own mounts—plus four owned by the Blackfeet—and beat a hasty retreat from the Two Medicine River. From there, they rode 120 miles in little more than twenty-four hours, stopping only to eat, catch catnaps, and let the horses graze. Amazingly, they arrived at the Missouri River just in time to find the parties led by Sergeant Gass, who had supervised the rest of the Lewis group around the Great Falls portage, and Sergeant Ordway, leading the group Clark sent down the Missouri from Three Forks.

The entire Lewis contingent, thus reunited, traveled down the Missouri, reaching the Yellowstone confluence within nine days of the Clark attachment—good progress, considering the adventure they'd had.

The Two Medicine Fight could have been a woeful turning point for the expedition. Had Lewis and his men been killed, the journals and his accumulated knowledge of the exploration would have been lost forever. The deaths on the Two Medicine were the only casualties the Lewis and Clark expedition inflicted on the West's native peoples during the corps' 2.5-year journey. While it is sad anyone had to die, it is surely to the captains' credit that nearly all the Indian encounters resulted in friendship and cooperation, not animosity and violence.

Return to the Valier Road and drive south. From Valier, it is fifteen miles east to Interstate 15 and about seventy miles to Great Falls.

GREAT FALLS

Lewis and Clark spent thirty-two days in the Great Falls area, more than any other place other than the sites they made their winter camps. At Great Falls, the explorers expected to encounter one cascade and a portage of no more than a half-mile, easily accomplished in a day. Instead, the corps found five formidable falls and wound up taking two weeks to cover the distance they'd normally travel by water in a single day. The falls, in the order they were reached going up river, were the Great Falls, highest of the series at eighty-nine feet; Horseshoe or Crooked Falls; Rainbow or Handsome Falls; Colter Falls, no longer visible, about a half-mile upriver from Rainbow Falls; and Black Eagle Falls, second-highest with a drop of some fifty feet.

Because of the amount of time the Corps of Discovery spent here, Great Falls has evolved into a major center for modern Lewis and Clark buffs. Here you'll find the new Lewis and Clark National Historic Trail Interpretive Center on the bluffs of the Missouri River. Great Falls also is home to the Lewis and Clark Trail Heritage Foundation, and the foundation's local Portage Route chapter is among the nation's most active. For these reasons, the city is a treasure trove of expedition lore, well worth a stop. If possible, time your visit with the town's annual Lewis and Clark Festival, held late each June about the same time the explorers arrived.

The Great Falls of the Missouri are an apt place to begin any visit to the area. To get there, drive north on US 87 and follow the signs to Ryan Dam. The turnoff is about two miles north of the town of Black Eagle, just across the river from Great Falls. Remember that Lewis and several others had left the Marias River confluence, intent on making sure this south fork was indeed still the Missouri. Toward noon on June 13, 1805, Lewis and Private Silas Goodrich had walked about two miles toward the river when, Lewis wrote, "My ears were saluted with the agreeable sound of a fall of water and advancing a little farther I saw a spray arise above the plain like a column of smoke which would frequently disappear again and an instant caused I presume from the wind which was blowing pretty hard from the southwest. I did not however lose my direction to this point which soon began to make a roaring too tremendous to be mistaken for any cause short of the Great Falls of the Missouri."

Lewis scrambled down a two hundred-foot bluff to witness what he called "the grandest sight" he had ever seen. He and his advance party had a good dinner of buffalo and trout and camped overnight at the site. The next day, Lewis sent Joseph Field down the river with word that the

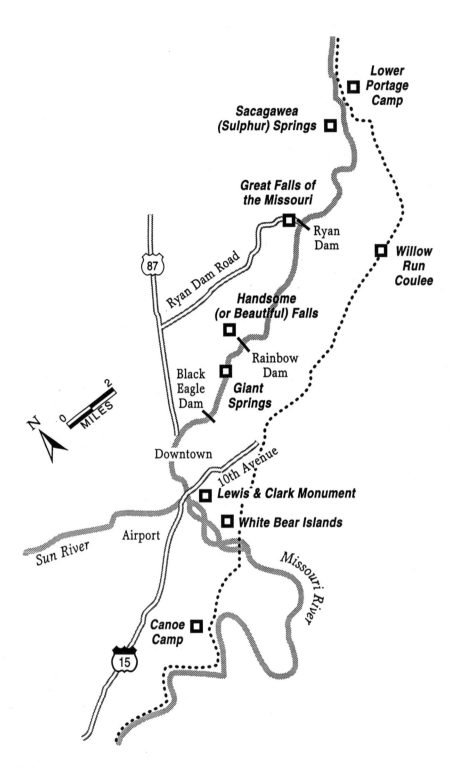

Lower
Portage
Camp

Sacagawea
(Sulphur) Springs

Great Falls of
the Missouri

Ryan
Dam

Willow
Run
Coulee

87

Ryan Dam Road

Handsome
(or Beautiful) Falls

Rainbow
Dam

Black
Eagle
Dam

Giant
Springs

N

2

0

MILES

Downtown

10th Avenue

Lewis & Clark Monument

White Bear Islands

Airport

Sun River

Missouri River

Canoe
Camp

15

The Great Falls of the Missouri River.

Rainbow Falls at Great Falls, Montana.

south fork was the true Missouri. Later, he walked upriver alone five miles and found a nineteen-foot high waterfall with an irregular rock shelf. He named this cascade Crooked Falls. In another half mile he discovered what he called in his journal Beautiful or Handsome Falls, now known as Rainbow Falls. A quarter mile farther, he spotted a small falls, Colter; and finally, two and one half miles more upriver, another large cascade. Nearby, he spied an eagle's nest—the very landmark Indians had mentioned the corps would see past the falls.

Meanwhile, as Lewis was exploring the Great Falls, Clark was attending to Sacagawea, who had been ill for about a week. He bled her and tried purges, poultices, and just about every other remedy in the corps' primitive medical repertoire, but nothing seemed to work. Finally, someone brought water from a sulphur spring located near what had become the party's lower portage camp, and the young woman finally started to improve. Today, the spring is still known as Sacagawea Springs. It is accessible on the north side of the Missouri via a one-mile hike atop the bluffs north of the Morony Dam parking area. The area below Morony Dam is also a popular launching spot for river trips.

Great Falls had long been a key spot in Indian travels through the region. Because the confluence of the Missouri and Medicine (now Sun) rivers boasted the best fording spot for forty miles in any direction, Indians frequently followed the Medicine River to its mouth here before crossing the Missouri and heading for elk and buffalo hunting grounds on the Plains. Today, this junction is overseen from Broadwater Park, off Tenth Avenue South. The park's centerpiece is a heroic-sized bronze statue of Lewis and Clark sculpted by Bob Scriver to commemorate the Montana state Centennial in 1989. In addition to the captains, it shows York and Lewis's dog, Seaman.

Lewis is pointing—but at what? After finding the remaining falls on June 14, Lewis discovered the Medicine River, which Indians at Fort Mandan had told him to expect. Elated, Lewis decided to kill a buffalo and make camp at the site. He picked his target, shot the beast, and stood watching it die, all the while neglecting to reload his rifle. Suddenly, he saw a grizzly bear walking toward him. Lewis headed off toward a tree where he intended to make camp, but the bear followed him. So Lewis switched directions, heading instead for the river, running in until he was waist-deep in water. He planted his feet, grasped his trusty espontoon, and held it menacingly toward the bear—an action that apparently startled the griz. Luckily for Lewis, the bear spun around and ran out of the river, out of sight.

If you have only a short time in Great Falls, spend it at the new Lewis and Clark National Historic Trail Interpretive Center on the Missouri River near Black Eagle Falls. Set to open in the spring of 1998, this 25,000-square-foot facility offers visitors one of the nation's most compelling and comprehensive looks at the expedition and its legacy.

The center's entrance resembles a coulee cutting into the hillside, similar to those the Corps of Discovery encountered on the Great Falls portage. Once inside, get oriented by viewing a short film created especially for the center by noted documentary filmmakers Ken Burns and Dayton Duncan. The film briefly outlines the explorers' outgoing and return journeys; the array of native peoples the expedition met along the way; and the changing landscapes they saw from Camp Wood to the Pacific Ocean.

The center's upstairs exhibits further set the stage for the trip by detailing President Jefferson's instructions to the corps and Lewis' preparation for the journey. Downstairs, the journey unfolds from two perspectives: the expedition's on your left and the Native Americans' on the right. Visitors learn how relations between the explorers and the natives ranged from warm to wary. There are also hands-on stations where, for example, you can try lashing willow onto a boat; test your strength by "pulling" a canoe against a current; decide which way to go at the Marias-Missouri confluence; or try to figure out the modern names of some prairie creatures described by Lewis and Clark.

Other center features include living history exhibits, an outdoor interpretive trail on the area's flora and fauna, a traveling exhibit gallery, a research library, and office for the Lewis and Clark Trail Heritage Foundation. To get to the center, follow River Drive, which runs north and east of Central Great Falls. The turnoff to the center is just across River

Drive from R.O. Speck Municipal Golf Course. For more information including hours of operation and admission cost, still to be set at presstime, call (406) 727-8733.

Near the interpretive center, Giant Springs/Heritage State Park is also worth a stop. Clark discovered the spring on June 18, 1805, and Lewis later said it was the largest he'd ever seen, perhaps the largest in America. Indeed, Giant Springs lives up to its name with a flow of nearly eight million gallons per hour. The water comes from the Madison limestone formations lying beneath most of eastern and central Montana. Rainfall and melted snow soak into the limestone to the Great Falls area, where it flows upward about 700 feet through fractures before being pushed out at Giant Springs. This thirty-eight mile trip takes hundreds of years, but the water gains momentum as it travels until it is pumped out at Giant Springs with a force of about 134,000 gallons per minute. The spring also forms the Roe River, the shortest in the world at just over 200 feet.

The springs are rich in calcium, magnesium, bicarbonate, and sulfate. These minerals are all excellent for producing trout, and a hatchery is located at the site. Visitors may buy fish food to feed the hatchlings—a great source of cheap entertainment! A playground, picnic tables, and big shade trees make this a very pleasant place to visit. Giant Springs/Heritage State Park is open from dawn to dusk, with the fish hatchery open daily from 8 a.m. to 4:30 p.m. For more information, call (406) 454-5840.

Those are the major Great Falls sites, but visitors with the time and inclination may want to try following the entire Lewis and Clark portage route across the southeast edge of town. The trek may still be traced with an excellent map available from the local Lewis and Clark Heritage Foundation chapter. Ask for the "Explorers at the Portage" brochure at the interpretive center, or write the Portage Route Chapter, P.O. Box 2424, Great Falls, MT 59403 for a copy.

To outline it briefly, the portage began at what is now known as Belt Creek, located directly across the river from Sacagawea Springs. There, the corps built two truck frames with wooden wheels to haul their goods overland. From the creek, the trail wound up the coulee and on to the prairie bench. (A farm road now parallels the way.)

Hazards and inconveniences were many. Rattlesnakes were a constant threat all along the portage route, as were prickly pear cactus—the men's soft-soled moccasins were no match for these sharp-spined plants. The expedition's pace was also slowed by ruts gouged by the immense hoofprints of thousands of buffalo. The corps encountered several violent storms, with hail so fierce on one occasion it bloodied several men. Yet despite all the difficulties, Clark noted that "no man complains. All go cheerfully on."

The portage ended at the White Bear Islands, so named because they were teeming with grizzlies. There were three islands when Lewis and Clark camped here, and there are still three today—though not necessarily the same ones the expedition saw. The journals mention that the party drank the last of its spirits here on July 4, 1805. Paris Gibson, the founder of Great Falls, felt the event took place on a knoll north of what is now the Ayrshire Dairy, which overlooks the islands. Gibson commemorated the site with a brass plaque and city park. Both park and plaque are gone now, but the plaque's cement base may still be seen.

Back east, Lewis had concocted the idea of a collapsible iron boat. He had the ninety-pound frame fabricated at Harpers Ferry, and felt that when the explorers needed to leave their dugout canoes behind when trekking overland, they could easily carry the portable boat. Constructed, the boat would be thirty-six feet long and carry at least eight thousand pounds—enough cargo space to replace the two pirogues.

At the upper portage camp at White Bear Islands, Lewis finally had the chance to test his invention. The boat was fitted with twenty-eight elk skins and four buffalo hides, then launched into the river. It floated! But after about five hours, the boat started coming apart at the seams. Without pine trees to make pitch, the men had made do with beeswax, tallow, and charcoal, none of which worked as well. "I need not add this circumstance mortified me not a little," Lewis wrote. "I therefore relinquished all further hope of my favorite boat and ordered her to be sunk in the water...." Meanwhile, Clark took some men and proceeded upstream to find trees suitable for making new canoes of the time-tested dugout variety. The iron boat, whether submerged in the river or cached nearby, has never been found.

Lewis was dejected, but other words he wrote during the portage conveyed a good deal more hope. The captains had earlier toyed with the idea of sending a boatload of men back east from the Great Falls; they now decided not to do so. The party was still small enough, they reasoned, and all available hands might be needed to deal with the unknown ahead. "We have never hinted to anyone of the party that we had such a scheme in contemplation, and all appear perfectly to have made up their minds to succeed in the expedition or perish in the attempt," Lewis wrote. "We all believe that we are now about to enter the most perilous and difficult part of our voyage, yet I see no one repining. All appear ready to meet those difficulties which await us with resolution and becoming fortitude."

Aside from Lewis and Clark, Charlie Russell is Great Falls's major local hero. The famous Western artist lived much of his life nearby and is buried in Highland Cemetery. Russell's influence seems to loom everywhere—his initials are even carved into a hillside by the Missouri riverbank—but the must-see attraction for Russell buffs is the C.M. Russell Museum Complex, located at 400 13th St. N. Here, visitors can see Russell's home, his original log cabin studio, and one of the largest collections of Russell art and personal effects in any one place. The

C.M. Russell Auction of Original Western Art, held mid-March of every year, is one of Great Falls' biggest annual events.

Paris Gibson Square is another favorite with visitors. The square, at the corner of 14th Street and 1st Avenue N., includes the Center for Contemporary Arts and the Cascade County Museum, where changing exhibits and a permanent collection of more than 50,000 objects ensure there's always something new to see. The Museum Cafe here is also one of Great Falls's more interesting places to grab lunch.

Great Falls's biggest recreational asset is the River's Edge Trail, which starts at the Missouri/Sun River confluence and will eventually go all the way out to the Great Falls and Sacagawea Springs. Walkers, strollers, joggers, cyclists, and skaters all will enjoy the route, which is being built on a former railroad bed. The trail also passes the site of Lewis's grizzly bear encounter, which likely took place across the river from the tennis courts and horseshoe pits at a site now known as West Bank Park. Every July 4, Great Falls's annual Meriwether Lewis fun run is held to commemorate what must have been the West's fastest fifty-yard dash. Sacagawea Island, a kind of nature preserve, is also visible in the river nearby.

If you travel to Great Falls by air, be sure to check out the mural by Robert Orduno above the main escalators at the city airport. Measuring ten feet by thirty-five feet, the painting shows the explorers making their portage. For more information on Great Falls, call (406) 761-4434.

From Great Falls, it is possible to take scenic Montana 200 directly to Missoula, a distance of 167 miles. Doing so will mean missing several key chapters in the Lewis and Clark story, but it will also save about 200 miles and a day of rugged travel. Montana 200 also takes the traveler close to the route Captain Lewis used on his return journey in 1806 (see the "Homeward Bound: Lewis Finds a Shortcut" section later in this chapter for details). Travelers who want to continue following the corps' westbound route should leave Great Falls south on I-15. It's seventy-six miles from Great Falls to the Gates of the Mountains, our next major stop.

GATES OF THE MOUNTAINS

Driving south of Great Falls, it soon becomes apparent the Montana plains are ending and giving way to the lofty peaks that gave this state its name. ("Montana" is indeed the Spanish word for "mountain.") The ranges surrounding Great Falls—hardly visible in town but prominent once one leaves—are the Highwoods to the east, Little Belts to the southeast and the Big Belts to the southwest.

A few miles out of town, Square Butte also comes into view. This massive rock table is probably most famous for its appearance in a number of Charlie Russell paintings. But before that, it served as a landmark to the eastbound Meriwether Lewis in 1806, who recognized Square

Gates of the Mountains boat tour.

Butte as he made his way back to the Great Falls. The explorers first saw the butte on the westward trek in 1805 and named it "Fort Mountain."

The area between Great Falls and Helena is sparsely settled, with the few towns along the way catering to tourism and outdoor activities. Near Ulm (Exit 270), the corps camped during July 10-14, 1805, and built the dugout canoes needed to replace Lewis's iron boat. The Ulm Pishkun State Monument preserves a buffalo jump, pictographs, and prairie dog town. Cascade (Exit 256) has a free overnight camping park.

Although I-15 is one of the most scenic interstates found anywhere, the traveler can escape it by taking an even more pleasant recreation road that runs closer to the Missouri River. Access this scenic route at Hardy Creek (Exit 247). From there, the route can be followed as far south as Spring Creek.

Wolf Creek (Exits 226-228) is the access point to Holter Lake, the first of several popular lakes located just minutes from the interstate. Wolf Creek is also headquarters for several river and fly-fishing guide services, including Montana River Outfitters and Missouri River Angler.

But the canyon corridor's primary lure for Lewis and Clark buffs is the Gates of the Mountains boat trip. Even the name sounds wonderfully inviting, a tribute to Meriwether Lewis's poetic imagination. To get there, take Exit 209 to Upper Holter Lake and follow the signs.

By the time Lewis and Clark arrived in this area in mid-July 1805, it had been months since they had seen any Indians (other than Sacagawea, of course). They were starting to get anxious, knowing the party would need horses to travel over the Continental Divide. Moreover, the captains figured they had to be getting close to Sacagawea's home country, the land of the Shoshonis, or Snake Indians, as the white men called them. It was decided they would take turns traveling overland to increase the chances of meeting Indians. Clark and three other men left the canyon on the first expedition, with no clue of the river spectacle they were about to miss.

"This evening we entered the most remarkable cliffs that we have yet seen," Lewis wrote on July 19. "These cliffs rise from the water's edge on either side perpendicularly to the height of 1,200 feet...the towering and projecting rocks in many places seem ready to tumble in on us." Lewis also noted that, although it was getting dark, the men had to keep moving, for there was scarcely a spot on shore where "a man could rest the sole of his foot.... It was late in the evening before I entered this place and was obliged to continue my route until sometime after dark before I found a place sufficiently large to encamp my small party. At length such a one occurred on the larboard side where we found plenty of light wood and pitch pine. This rock is a black granite below and appears to be of a much lighter color above...from the singular appearance of this place I called it the gates of the rocky mountains."

The boat tours here last about 1.75 hours and cover a distance of 6.5 miles on what is now Holter Lake. Guides offer a wealth of information on the canyon's natural and human history, while helping passengers scan the cliffs for bighorn sheep and mountain goats (most likely seen on the right-hand side going into the canyon and the left-hand side going out). Young bald eagles, osprey, cliff swallows, and barn swallows live here, too.

Also in evidence are pictographs, probably two hundred to three hundred years old and of Blackfeet origin. And the tours pass by Mann Gulch, where twelve men lost their lives in a wildfire, August 1949. The fire spread from thirty acres to two thousand acres in less than ten minutes when the winds kicked up, and ended up burning fifteen thousand acres before it was through. The incident made national news at the time and is detailed in *Young Men and Fire*, a book by Montana author Norman Maclean (best known for *A River Runs Through It*).

All trips stop at the Meriwether Picnic Area, believed to be where Lewis and his party found their small campsite. Although these stops are usually brief—just enough time to stretch one's legs and use the restroom—passengers have the option of catching a later boat back to the docks. Those who do so may want to pack a picnic or take the one-mile trail to Coulter Campground, named after the expedition member but spelled differently for some reason. More ambitious backpackers could stay overnight—or longer—and trek into the Gates of the Mountains Wilderness. One popular destination, Refrigerator Canyon, is an eighteen-mile roundtrip from Coulter Campground.

Gates of the Mountains boat tours run Memorial Day Weekend through mid-September. Cruises are offered at 11 a.m., 1 p.m., and 3 p.m. weekdays; 10 a.m., noon, 2 p.m., and 4 p.m. on Saturdays; and every hour from 10 a.m. to 5 p.m. Sundays and holidays during July and August. In June, weekday sailings are set for 11 a.m. and 2 p.m.; with weekend and holiday cruises scheduled at 10 a.m., noon, 2 p.m., and 4 p.m. In September, sailings are at 11 a.m. and 2 p.m. weekdays; and 11 a.m., 1 p.m., and 3 p.m. weekends.

Tickets cost $7.50 for adults, $6.50 for senior citizens (ages sixty and over), and $4.50 for kids four to seventeen. Children under four ride free. Plan to arrive about a half-hour early to buy tickets. Bring a jacket—even hot days can be breezy on the boat—and binoculars. For more information, call (406) 458-5241.

It's a short, twenty-minute drive from Gates of the Mountains to Helena, Montana's charming capital city. A good way to get oriented here is with a hour-long ride on the Last Chance Tour Train, which departs from the Montana Historical Society on the corner of Roberts and 6th Avenue just east of the Capitol. The train—and Montana's downtown pedestrian mall, Last Chance Gulch—take their name from "the Georgians," four weary and despondent Southern gold prospectors who, arriving at what is now Helena in 1864, decided to make one more attempt at locating gold. They struck it rich, as did many others: By the late 1880s, there were more millionaires per capita in Helena than anywhere else in the United States.

Tour train guides point out important state buildings (including Montana's decidedly modest governor's residence), the elegant architectural gems on Last Chance Gulch, and the impressive west-side mansion district. Riders also learn that the Helena Masonic Temple has Meriwether Lewis's Masonic apron, and that a feisty local pilot once flew between the spires of the lovely Cathedral of St. Helena. In all, it's a very entertaining and informative trip. Trains depart every half-hour between 9:30 a.m. and 4:30 p.m. (except 12:30 p.m.) and again at 6:30 p.m. from June 1 through Labor Day.

Before or after the train ride, stop in the Montana Historical Society. Highlights include the Mackay Gallery of Charlie Russell Art, including several paintings and drawings on the Lewis and Clark theme. The Montana Homeland exhibit also has a section on the expedition. The Montana State Capitol, just across Sixth Avenue, also honors Lewis and Clark with grand artworks, including Russell's "Lewis and Clark Meeting the Flathead Indians at Ross' Hole," at twelve feet by twenty-five feet his largest work. Other paintings by E.S. Paxson depict the explorers at the Three Forks and Lewis at Black Eagle Falls. Capitol tours are offered on the hour from 10 a.m. to 5 p.m. Monday through Saturday and from 11 a.m. to 4 p.m. Sunday.

Helena boasts an active cultural scene, much of it revolving around the Myrna Loy Center for the Performing Arts at 15 N. Ewing and the Holter Museum of the Arts at 12 E. Lawrence. The city also has a full calendar of annual events including the Montana Traditional Jazz Festival in late June and the Last Chance Stampede in late July. Like Billings, Great Falls, and Butte, Helena fields a Pioneer League baseball team, the Brewers. Those yearning for more active sports need only look to Mount Helena, where an excellent network of trails offers hiking and mountain biking right out the city's back door. For more information on Helena, call (800) 7-HELENA (out of state) or (406) 442-4120.

A bit out of town, but still close by, Frontier Town is an Old West theme village on the Continental Divide built almost entirely by one man, John Quigley. Aside from an outstanding view, Frontier Town offers a museum, numerous shops, restaurants—even a wedding chapel. A new owner plans to add a blacksmith shop, saddlery, gold-mining exhibit, and other old-time attractions. Frontier Town is located fifteen miles west of Helena on US 12.

From Helena, the Lewis and Clark Trail bends to the southeast, following US 12 to Townsend, then US 287 to Three Forks. En route, travelers may want to stop at Canyon Ferry Lake, one of Montana's most popular recreation areas. The original Canyon Ferry Dam was completed in 1898 to provide power to the booming town of Helena. The present dam, completed in 1954, is 225 feet high and impounds the twenty-five-mile-long Canyon Ferry Lake.

Canyon Ferry Village has a visitor center that is open from noon to 4 p.m. Sunday, Monday, Wednesday, and Friday and noon to 8 p.m. on Saturday during the summer. If the center isn't open, you can still get information at a nearby shelter. Interpretive panels tell about the dam and describe an eighty-five-mile auto tour through the nearby Helena National Forest.

There is scant Lewis and Clark interpretation, and a picnic area on the lake's west shore is named for our heroes, but no camping is allowed. To get there, take Montana 284 southeast from the village, across the dam, and bear left at the Yacht Basin Marina area. There once was a mining town called York near Canyon Ferry, but it was named for New York City, not the York of Lewis and Clark fame.

Canyon Ferry's congested campgrounds seem better suited to RV'ers than tent campers, although a few decent tent sites may be found in the Court Sheriff area's back loop and at Hellgate. Showers are available at some of the nearby commercial establishments including Kim's Marina.

Townsend, twenty-nine miles south of Helena, is a agricultural hub and tourist-oriented community dedicated to serving visitors bound for Canyon Ferry Lake. The Broadwater County Museum at 133 N. Walnut

St., has displays of pioneer artifacts and information on the area's mining history. From Townsend, it is thirty-one miles to I-90 and the Missouri Headwaters.

HOMEWARD BOUND: LEWIS FINDS A SHORTCUT

When the expedition was on its way home in 1806, the captains split up at their Traveler's Rest camp at present-day Lolo, Montana (Chapter Seven). From there, Clark explored the Big Hole Country and Lewis took the Indian road to the buffalo hunting grounds east of the divide. He crossed the Continental Divide at a point now called Lewis and Clark Pass, something of a misnomer since Clark never saw the place.

Lewis's route roughly parallels Montana 200 from Missoula to Great Falls, a distance of about 170 miles. Lewis and Clark Pass may be visited in a fairly long day trip from Helena, Great Falls, or Missoula. Helena is closest, so we'll explore the route from there.

Driving north from Helena, take Exit 200 (Lincoln Road) off I-15. Turn onto County Road 279 and head west. This road crests at Flesher Pass and a spectacular view before descending to Montana 200.

Turn left on Montana 200 and look for Forest Road 293 (Alice Creek) about one mile west. This is the turnoff, but it might be wise to drive

Near Lewis and Clark Pass in the Helena National Forest.

American white pelicans on the Missouri River.

eight miles farther west to Lincoln for a stop at the Helena National Forest ranger station, where forest personnel can offer more detailed directions and a map to the site. The ranger station phone number is (406) 362-4265.

Return to Forest Road 293 and head north. Five miles in, there's a historical sign that notes Lewis and his party stopped in the vicinity for dinner on July 7, 1806. From here, the Indian trail they followed closely parallels the forest road. Ten miles from Montana 200, the traveler comes to a fork in the road. The right fork, now gated, is the way to the pass. A trail of about 1.5 miles leads in a northwesterly direction to the Continental Divide. Elevation at the pass is 6,421 feet.

Lewis and Clark Pass is rarely seen on Montana highway maps. Today, traffic is routed over the divide at Rogers Pass—elevation 5,610 feet—about six miles to the southeast. A sign on Montana 200 notes that the coldest official temperature ever recorded in the continental United States occurred at a mining camp near Rogers Pass on January 20, 1954, when the mercury hit seventy degrees below zero.

Had Lewis and Clark known heading west what they learned at Traveler's Rest, they could have saved themselves many weeks of tough travel. It took the expedition about two months to cover the route between Great Falls and Traveler's Rest on the outbound trek in 1805;

Lewis made the trip in just eight days using the shortcut the following summer, and Indians told the captains it could be done in as few as four days! But perhaps they would not have used the shortcut going westbound even if they'd known about it. After all, President Jefferson had instructed the corps to find the headwaters of the Missouri—a task they would not have accomplished had they followed the more direct route west from Great Falls.

THREE FORKS OF THE MISSOURI

As they moved up the Missouri past the Gates of the Mountains, Lewis and his party suddenly had reason to celebrate. Sacagawea recognized the land through which they were passing! "This piece of information has cheered the spirits of the party who...console themselves with the anticipation of shortly seeing the head of the Missouri yet unknown to the civilized world," Lewis wrote.

Clark and his contingent reached the Three Forks of the Missouri first, on July 25, and explored the surrounding area while waiting for Lewis. They looked everywhere for Indians, but there were still none to be seen. The rest of the party arrived July 27, and the expedition camped in the area through July 30, 1805, largely to allow time for rest. Clark in particular was well worn out, his feet throbbing painfully from the many miles of overland travel over prickly pear cactus. More than ever, the expedition realized its need for horses. But again, Sacagawea offered reason for hope, recognizing this as the place of her kidnapping some five years earlier. She had been camped at the forks with her Shoshoni family when the band was attacked by Hidatsa Indians, killing four men and taking a number of prisoners, "though I cannot discover that she shows any emotion of sorrow in recollecting this event, or of joy in being restored to her native country," Lewis wrote.

The captains also had to decide which of the three forks would lead them toward the Continental Divide and the Pacific watershed. Although the streams were roughly similar in size, it wasn't an especially tough puzzle. They soon settled on the westernmost of the rivers, which they named the Jefferson in honor of "the author of our enterprise," as Lewis put it. The middle fork was named for then-Secretary of State James Madison, and the easternmost stream honored Albert Gallatin, Jefferson's Secretary of the Treasury (and a strong supporter of the Louisiana Purchase).

Missouri Headwaters State Park now commemorates the expedition's arrival, as well as the area's importance to Indians, trappers, traders, and settlers. The park is located six miles northeast of the town of Three Forks on Montana Secondary Route 285. Within the park, a short trail leads to the riverbank and a sign marking the headwaters.

An excellent interpretive display elsewhere in the park tells about the many aspects of Three Forks history. The visitor learns, for example,

Near the Three Forks of the Missouri River headwaters.

that the headwaters later served as the setting for a dramatic episode involving two former members of the expedition, John Colter and John Potts. In 1808, the two men were trapping on the Jefferson River. A band of Blackfeet, angered by previous encounters with whites, attacked both men.

Potts was killed right away, but Colter's fate seemed even worse: He was stripped and told to run for his life. Colter tore barefoot across the cactus-laden plains, outrunning all but one of his pursuers for about six miles. Despite his exhaustion, Colter turned on the Indian and killed him. He continued on into the Jefferson River and hid under a snag, eluding the other Blackfeet. Later, naked and weaponless, Colter headed for Manuel Lisa's fort on the Big Horn River. He made the 200-mile trip in seven days.

In 1810, Lisa, of the Missouri Fur Company, sent thirty-two trappers to establish a post at the headwaters. They found good beaver trapping, but grizzly bears and Blackfeet killed several of the frontiersmen, including George Drouillard, another Lewis and Clark alumnus. "Popular history has surrounded the mountain man with glory and adventure," one interpretive panel reads. "But reality was often short rations, bitter cold, boredom and even sudden death." The idea of a permanent post was soon abandoned, although trappers continued to work the headwaters region until the 1840s. By that time, the beaver had nearly become extinct, and silk had replaced fur as the hat material of choice.

As Sacagawea would attest, the Three Forks area had long been an important hunting ground for the region's Indians. An 1855 treaty between the natives and whites declared the headwaters region to be a common hunting ground for ninety-nine years, supposedly guaranteeing all people "equal and uninterrupted privileges" in the area. But rapid settlement by the whites brought the treaty to its knees less than a decade later.

Native vegetation in the park remains much the same as when Lewis and Clark visited. Plants include buckwheat brush, big sagebrush, pincushion cactus, saltbrush, prickly pear cactus, and bluebunch wheatgrass. A short trail leads to an overlook that points out key features of the landscape in all directions, including the Tobacco Root, Madison, and Gallatin mountain ranges.

Missouri Headwaters State Park has a small but appealing campground, with a handful of choice secluded sites. There are no showers, but RV'ers will find a dump station available for use. Day-use visitors and campers alike enjoy facilities for picnicking, as well as fishing and boating access to the three rivers.

Three Forks is an interesting little town in a picturesque setting. Visitors can shoot a round at the scenic Headwaters Public Golf Course or hire a river guide for a day of fly-fishing or river running. Major events include a rodeo the third weekend of July and a Lewis and Clark pageant held every few years, also late in July.

The Headwaters Heritage Museum at the corner of Main and Cedar pays extensive homage to Sacagawea, albeit with the generally discredited story that she deserted Charbonneau, married a Comanche named Jerk Meat, lived to a ripe old age, and was buried at Fort Washakie on the Wind River Indian Reservation in Wyoming. As we noted in Chapter Four, this likely wasn't the case; an 1812 journal entry at Fort Manuel in North Dakota documented her death. Exhibits there also promote the debatable idea that Sacagawea and Clark were romantically involved. Certainly, the two shared a mutual admiration and respect, but no one has ever proven the relationship went beyond that.

From Three Forks, proceed west on Montana 2 and keep going west when US 287 swings south to Ennis—unless you want to visit Yellowstone Park, that is: It's about a two-hour drive from Three Forks to the park entrance at West Yellowstone.

SIDE TRIP: YELLOWSTONE NATIONAL PARK AND NEARBY ATTRACTIONS

Although only a sliver of Yellowstone National Park lies in Montana, the Treasure State claims three of the park's five entrances. The choices are West Yellowstone, south of Bozeman on US 191 or south of Three Forks via US 287; Gardiner, south of Livingston by way of US 89; and Cooke City/Silver Gate, reached by way of the famous Bear Tooth Highway, US 212, southwest from Laurel near Billings.

Yellowstone was the world's first national park, so declared by an act of Congress in 1872. Known for its geysers, waterfalls, and wildlife (not to mention the 1988 fires that burned more than a third of the park), Yellowstone is among the most frequently visited national parks, so it can be crowded. Still, Yellowstone is a big place, with more than a thousand miles of trails. Solitude is available for those who seek it out.

Yellowstone boasts so many spectacular sights that it's hard to know where to begin. Artist Point and Inspiration Point offer vistas of the Grand Canyon of the Yellowstone River and its famous falls. Old Faithful is but one example of the park's intense thermal activity, all triggered by an immense volcanic eruption 600,000 years ago. Norris Geyser Basin and the Fountain Paint Pots area offer the park's most concentrated displays of these steaming, gurgling natural features.

Sightseeing is definitely the main attraction at Yellowstone. But other opportunities available include fishing (it's free, but a permit is required), backcountry camping and hiking, and canoeing (especially on Shoshone Lake). Power boaters are permitted on Yellowstone and Lewis lakes.

While at Yellowstone, don't forget its less-famous but equally scenic sister park, Grand Teton National Park. Few people forget their first sight of the Tetons, which are among the youngest mountains in North America. These soaring, craggy peaks provide the setting for some of the greatest hiking in the world.

The Cascade Canyon Trail is among the most popular Teton treks, and the hikes to Hermitage Point or on the Paintbrush Trail often reward visitors with wildlife views. Mountain climbing instruction and guides are available. It's difficult to pull your gaze away from the mountains, but the lakes and the Snake River are lovely, too. Activities include scenic boat trips, boat rentals, sailboarding on Jackson Lake, and floats down the Snake. Horseback riding, fishing, and camping offer still more pleasures.

The town of Jackson sits south of Grand Teton National Park. Like other mountain resort towns, Jackson has gone through a lot of changes in recent decades. It no longer qualifies as a "typical" Western town, but it certainly is a fun place to visit. Jackson crackles with energy, from its creative restaurants to its lively nightlife (don't miss the famous Million

Dollar Cowboy Bar on the main square downtown), varied recreational menu, and active arts scene.

Another northwest Wyoming town, Cody, is famous for the Buffalo Bill Historical Center, widely considered to be the best overall Western museum in the United States. The four-part complex includes the Buffalo Bill Museum, which documents Colonel William Cody's colorful life; the Whitney Gallery of Western Art, featuring original works by such famous names as Russell and Remington; the Plains Indian Museum, with extensive displays on the life and times of the region's great tribes; and the Winchester Gun Museum, which actually includes firearms from throughout history. Cody is eighty miles east of the Fishing Bridge junction at Yellowstone National Park.

For more information, contact Grand Teton National Park at (307) 733-2880; Yellowstone National Park at (307) 344-7381; the Jackson Hole Area Chamber of Commerce at (307) 733-3316; or the Cody Country Chamber at (307) 587-2297.

*Denotes town on Lewis's explorations of the Marias River region in 1806.

**Denotes town on Lewis's return route over the Continental Divide in 1806.

LODGING

LOMA, MONTANA

Loma Motel, (406) 739-4252.

Virgelle Mercantile, (800) 426-2926. Cabins and bed & breakfast accommodations.

FORT BENTON, MONTANA

Cottonwood Bed & Breakfast, (406) 622-5675, 1104 16th St. $40-$60.

Fort Motel, (406) 622-3312, 1809 St. Charles. $40-$60.

Pioneer Lodge, (406) 622-5441, 1700 Front St. Under $40.

*CONRAD, MONTANA

Conrad Motel, (406) 278-7544, 210 N. Main. Under $40.

Conrad Super 8/TownHouse Inn, (800) 442-4667, 215 N. Main. $41-$43.

*SHELBY, MONTANA

Crossroads Inn, (406) 434-5134, US 2. $45.

O'Haire Manor Motel, (800) 541-5809, 204 2nd St. S. $36.

*CUT BANK, MONTANA

Corner Motel, (406) 473-5588, 201 E. Main St. under $40.

Glacier Gateway Inn, (406) 873-5544, 1121 E. Railroad St. $44.

Northern Motor Inn, (406) 873-5662, 609 W. Main. $44.

*BROWNING, MONTANA

Glacier Motel, (406) 338-7004, US 2. $40-$60.

Western Motel, (406) 338-7572, 121 Central Ave. E. Under $40.

GREAT FALLS, MONTANA

Best Western Heritage Inn, (800) 548-0361, 1700 Fox Farm Rd. $62-$68.

Edelweiss Motor Inn, (406) 452-9503, 626 Central Ave. W. $32.

O'Haire Motor Inn, (800) 332-9819, 7th St. and 1st Ave. S. $50-$60.

The Great Falls Inn, (800) 454-6010, 1400 28th St. S. $45-$55.

Three Pheasant Inn Bed & Breakfast, (406) 453-0519, 626 5th Ave. N. $40-$60.

Triple Crown Motor Inn, (800) 722-8300 (in state) or (406) 727-8300. $38-$43.

CASCADE, MONTANA

Badger Motel, (406) 468-9330, 132 1st St. N. Under $40.

Fly Fisher's Inn, (406) 468-2529, 2629 Old Hwy. 91. Lodging and guide service.

WOLF CREEK, MONTANA

Frenchy's Motel, (406) 235-4251. Under $40.

Holter Lake Lodge, (406) 235-4331, Beartooth Rd. $40-$60.

Montana River Outfitters, (406) 235-4350, cabins. Under $40.

HELENA, MONTANA

Econo Lodge, (406) 442-0600, 524 N. Last Chance Gulch. $40.

Jorgenson's Holiday Motel, (800) 272-1770 (in state) or (800) 521-2743, 1714 11th Ave. $39-$61.

King's Rest Motel, (406) 442-6384, 1831 Euclid. $35.

Shilo Inn, (800) 222-2244, 2020 Prospect Ave. $57.

Park Plaza Hotel, (800) 332-2290 (in state) or (406) 443-2200, 22 N. Last Chance Gulch. $55-$60.

The Sanders - Helena's Bed & Breakfast, (406) 442-3309, 328 N. Ewing. $65-$90.

**LINCOLN, MONTANA

Leeper's Motel, (406) 362-4333, MT 200, $33 and up.

TOWNSEND, MONTANA

The Bedford Inn Bed & Breakfast, (406) 266-3629, 7408 US 287. $40-$60.

Lake Townsend Motel, (406) 266-3461, 413 N. Pine. $30-$40.

Mustang Motel, (406) 266-3491, 412 N. Front. $30-$40.

THREE FORKS, MONTANA

Broken Spur Motel, (406) 285-3237, MT 2. $38.

Fort Three Forks Motel, (406) 285-3233, I-90 at US 287. $38.

Lewis and Clark Motel, (406) 285-3454, 510 Main St.

Sacagawea Inn, (800) 821-7326, 5 N. Main St. $55-$65.

CAMPING

BIG SANDY, MONTANA

Coalbanks Landing, eleven miles south on US 87, then south at sign for Upper Missouri Wild and Scenic River. Primitive sites.

Judith Landing, forty-four miles southeast on Secondary Route 236, on the Upper Missouri Wild and Scenic River. Primitive sites.

FORT BENTON, MONTANA

Benton RV Park, (406) (406) 622-5015, north side of town.

*CONRAD, MONTANA

Sunrise Trailer Court, (406) 278-5901, 4 blocks east of stoplight.

*SHELBY, MONTANA

Lake Sheloole Park, (406) 434-5222, 0.5 mile south on I-15 business bypass.

Lewis and Clark RV Court, (406) 434-2710, I-15 Exit 364, 131 9th Ave. N.

*CUT BANK, MONTANA

Shady Grove Campground, (406) 336-2475, six miles west on US 2.

*BROWNING, MONTANA

Aspenwood Camp, (406) 338-7911, nine miles west on US 89.

GREAT FALLS, MONTANA

Dick's RV Park, (406) 452-0333, I-15 Exit 278, west of river on 10th Ave. S.

Great Falls KOA, (406) 727-3191, 1500 51st St. S.

CASCADE, MONTANA

Atkinson Park, (406) 468-2808, adjacent to I-15 in town.

Cascade Trailer Park, (406) 468-2254, I-15 Exit 254.

WOLF CREEK, MONTANA

Holter Lake, (406) 235-4314, I-15 Exit 226, left three miles to lake. Primitive sites.

HELENA, MONTANA

Branding Iron Campground, (406) 443-9703, I-15 Exit 193.

Canyon Ferry State Park, (406) 444-4475, ten miles east on US 12/87, then twelve miles north on County Rd. 284.

Helena KOA, (406) 458-5110, 5820 N. Montana Ave.

Kim's Marina and RV Park, (406) 475-3723, ten east on US 12/87, then ten miles north on County Rd. 284.

Stewart's RV Park, (406) 227-5718, 4.5 miles east from I-15 Exit 192.

**LINCOLN, MONTANA

Aspen Grove, (406) 362-4265, seven miles east on MT 200. Primitive sites.

Copper Creek, (406) 362-4265, 6.5 miles east on MT 200, then 8.5 miles northwest on Forest Rd. 330.

TOWNSEND, MONTANA

Silos RV Park, (406) 266-3100, seven miles north on US 12/87, then east on Silos Rd.

THREE FORKS, MONTANA

Missouri Headwaters State Park, six miles northeast on Secondary Rd. 286. Primitive sites.

Three Forks KOA, (406) 285-3611, one mile south of I-90 Exit 274.

(See also Three Forks, Montana, in Chapter Six.)

RESTAURANTS

FORT BENTON, MONTANA

The Banque Club, 1318 Front St.

C-J's Diner, (406) 622-5035, 1402 Front St.

3-Way Cafe, (406) 622-5681, 2300 St. Charles.

*SHELBY, MONTANA

Capital Cafe, (406) 434-2991, 248 Main St.

Hong Kong Chan's, (406) 434-2646, 200 Front St. (at Division). Chinese food in casual atmosphere.

*CUT BANK, MONTANA

Big Sky Cafe, (406) 873-2542, 13 W. Main.

Village Dining and Lounge, (406) 873-5005, Northern Village Shopping Center.

*BROWNING, MONTANA

Browning Cafe. Open 24 hours.

GREAT FALLS, MONTANA

Bert and Ernie's Saloon and Eatery, (406) 453-0601, 300 1st Ave. S. Charbroiled burgers, big selection of imported draft beer. Also in Helena.

Borrie's, (406) 761-0300, 1800 Smelter Ave. (Black Eagle). Italian-American.

Charlotte's Web, (406) 453-5292, 600 Central Plaza. Breakfast and lunch with twenty kinds of homemade pie.

Mama Cassie's, (406) 454-3354, 319 1st Ave. N. Italian restaurant.

3D International, (406) 453-6561, 1825 Smelter Ave. (Black Eagle). Wide menu and big salad bar; restaurant overlooks Missouri River.

CASCADE, MONTANA

Badger Cafe, (406) 468-2777, 132 1st St. N. Homemade specialties.

Osterman's Missouri Inn, (406) 468-9884, 2474 Old Hwy. 91.

WOLF CREEK, MONTANA

Holter Lake Lodge, (406) 235-4331, on Holter Lake.

Oasis Bar and Cafe, (406) 235-9992.

HELENA, MONTANA

Yacht Basin Restaurant, (406) 475-3125, 7035 Canyon Ferry Rd. Steaks, seafood, and chicken with a view of Canyon Ferry Lake.

Frontier Town, (406) 442-4560, fifteen miles west on US 12. Dinner daily atop the Continental Divide.

Next to Hap's Cafe, (406) 443-9890, 1507 Railroad Ave. Another Dayton Duncan favorite from *Out West.*

The Rialto, (406) 442-1890, 52 N. Last Chance Gulch. Famous burgers.

The Stonehouse Restaurant, (406) 449-2552, 120 Reeder's Alley. Wide, imaginative menu.

The Windbag Saloon, (406) 443-9669, 19 S. Last Chance Gulch. Burgers, steaks, and colorful atmosphere.

TOWNSEND, MONTANA

Fireside Restaurant, (406) 266-3516, US 12. Beef and seafood.

Rosario's Italian Restaurant and Pizzeria, (406) 266-3603, 316 N. Front St. Authentic Italian cuisine featuring veal, chicken, and pasta.

Yummies Cafe and Bakery, (406) 266-3210, 321 Broadway. Specialties include burgers and Saturday breakfast buffet.

THREE FORKS, MONTANA

Blue Willow Inn, (406) 285-6660, six miles south of town in Willow Creek.

Sacagawea Inn, (406) 285-6934, 5 N. Main. Gourmet dining.

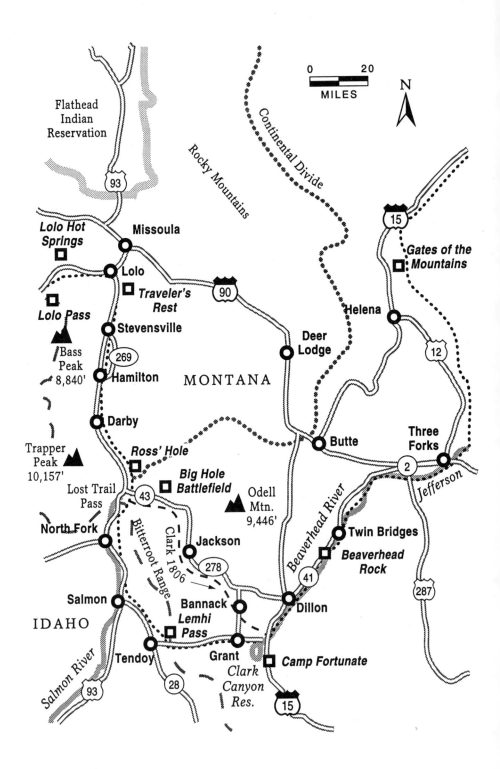

Flathead
Indian
Reservation

Rocky Mountains

Continental Divide

0   20
MILES

N

93

15

Lolo Hot Springs

Missoula

Gates of the Mountains

Lolo

Traveler's Rest

90

Helena

12

Lolo Pass

Stevensville

Deer Lodge

Bass Peak 8,840'

269

Hamilton

MONTANA

Darby

Butte

Three Forks

Trapper Peak 10,157'

Ross' Hole

2

Jefferson

Lost Trail Pass

43

Big Hole Battlefield

Odell Mtn. 9,446'

Beaverhead River

North Fork

Bitterroot Range

Clark 1806

Jackson

278

Twin Bridges

Beaverhead Rock

41

287

Salmon

Bannack

Lemhi Pass

Dillon

IDAHO

Salmon River

Tendoy

93

28

Grant

Clark Canyon Res.

Camp Fortunate

15

174

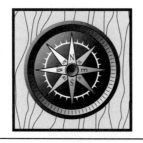

CHAPTER SEVEN

WESTERN MONTANA AND IDAHO

I have been wet and as cold in every part as I ever was in my life, indeed I was at one time fearful my feet would freeze in the thin moccasins I wore.
- William Clark, Sept. 16, 1805,
on the Lolo Trail in present-day Idaho.

THE JEFFERSON AND BEAVERHEAD VALLEYS

From the Three Forks area, follow Montana Highway 2/U.S. Highway 287. When US 287 branches off south toward Yellowstone, stay on the Lewis and Clark Trail by continuing west on Montana 2.

The entrance to Lewis and Clark Caverns State Park is just west of this junction. This was Montana's first state park, but before that it was a national monument, and President Theodore Roosevelt is credited with naming the park in honor of the captains. It's true the corps followed the Jefferson River right through this area, but there is no evidence the captains were aware of the caverns' existence.

The caverns, considered among the best in the Northwest, are reached by a steep, winding, three-mile road leading from the highway. Trailers may be left in the lower parking lot at their owners' discretion, but park staff say all sorts of big rigs have made the drive with no trouble. Two-hour guided tours of the caverns are available May 1 through September 30. The visitor center has additional information and displays, and food and gifts are offered for sale during summer months. The scenic road also winds past two shady picnic areas and an overlook of the Jefferson River valley.

Aside from cavern connoisseurs, Lewis and Clark State Park draws its share of cyclists, anglers, hikers, canoeists, and wildlife watchers.

Those who want to stay overnight have their choice of camping or cabins; the latter are available by reservation year-round. For more information, call (406) 287-3541.

From the park, continue west on Montana 2. North of Three Forks, travelers will recall, the landscape was wide open with mountains in the distance. Here, the canyon is not much wider than the river, with impressive cliffs towering on each side.

After leaving Three Forks, Lewis and three other men set out in advance to resume the search for Sacagawea's people. On August 1, they came upon a herd of elk near what is now the tiny town of La Hood and killed two for lunch before moving on, leaving most of the meat for Clark and the rest of the party. The rear guard reached the site later in the day and made camp. Today's travelers have it a lot easier: La Hood's Lewis and Clark Restaurant and Lounge offers ready-made meals and free RV camping with a dinner purchase.

At Whitehall, take Montana 55 south to its junction with Montana 41, which leads all the way into Dillon. About ten miles south of Whitehall, Montana 55 passes through three counties—Jefferson, Silver Bow, and Madison—within the space of about a mile.

At Twin Bridges, the Jefferson River splits into two forks, the right fork being the Big Hole River and the main stem becoming the Beaverhead (the Ruby River, meanwhile, branches off to the southeast a few more miles south). Concluding after a day's exploration that the main stem was still the correct route, Lewis left a note for Clark on a green willow pole and proceeded down the Beaverhead. This method of communication had worked before with no problem, but this time, a beaver gnawed down the willow and made off with the note. Confused, the Clark contingent set off down the Big Hole—a swift and dangerous stream. One canoe turned over and two others filled with water, resulting in the loss of some trade goods and gunpowder and an injury to Private Whitehouse. The party was finally turned back to the Jefferson by Drouillard.

Twin Bridges is a good jumping-off spot for Virginia City and Nevada City, two famous Montana mining towns. Both are accessible via Montana 287. Virginia City harbored ten thousand prospectors in the 1860s, and the town soon became a hotbed of lawlessness. A local group of vigilantes eventually took matters in their own hands, hanging the outlaws (along with the scofflaws' leader, the sheriff). Today, Virginia City has a population of only 150 or so, but it's still the seat of Madison County and a big hit with the tourists. Nevada City, one mile downriver, has nearly 100 buildings restored to preserve the air of an early mining camp.

Twin Bridges has a small riverside park. There's no camping, but a display board posts several large Forest Service maps. It's a good place to get your bearings and plot the rest of the day's travels. Twin Bridges is also home to the Madison County Fair each August. From here, continue south toward Dillon.

Seeing Beaverhead Rock from Montana 41, the traveler's first thought is, "Boy, those Shoshoni Indians must have had vivid imaginations." Supposedly, the rock resembles the head of a swimming beaver, and Sacagawea had no trouble recognizing the landmark when the corps arrived in the area. A historical marker about 0.5 mile south of the Beaverhead County line tells the tale: August 10, 1805, members of the Lewis and Clark expedition sighted what Clark called a "remarkable cliff" to the west. Both Lewis and Clark agreed on the resemblance and noted it in their journals, adding that Sacagawea said it meant her homeland was on a river just over the mountains to the southwest. About nine miles south of the rock, the expedition reached its three thousand-mile mark.

Area historians say Beaverhead Rock looks most like its namesake from the east, backlit by a setting sun. But there is some controversy in southwest Montana over which rock is the Beaverhead Rock. Most folks agree it is the one north of Dillon, but some feel it is an area otherwise referred to in the journals as Rattlesnake Cliffs—an area located south of Dillon at I-15's Exit 56. From the modern highway angle, however, Rattlesnake Cliffs looks a lot like a buffalo, not a beaver's head. In its brochure, Dillon Flying Service promises passengers a look at "both Beaverhead Rocks—you decide which one Sacagawea identified as her tribe's landmark."

Dillon is a major trade center for southwest Montana, as well as the home of Western Montana College. The Beaverhead County Historical Museum sits next to the visitor center on the west side of downtown. The museum has an extremely helpful staff and several items of Lewis and Clark lore including a splendid woodcutting of Sacagawea meeting her brother, Chief Cameahwait, an incident we shall soon relive.

By now, you've probably noticed many Montana towns mark their communities by painting letters on a nearby hillside. In Dillon, the letter is "B," which might seem strange until you learn it can stand for either Beaverhead or the Bulldogs of Western Montana College. Dillon has an excellent variety of stores for a town its size. It's a good place to get fuel or stock up for a trip over Lemhi Pass or into the Big Hole country. This is also major fly-fishing country, with many outfitters available to guide a trip on the Big Hole or Beaverhead rivers.

Clark's Lookout, just northwest of Dillon, is locally known as Lover's Leap. Clark—again bringing up the rear after Lewis and party had gone on ahead—reportedly ascended this bluff to survey the surrounding country and get his bearings before moving on. To get there, turn west at the sign for the Frontage Road/Old U.S. 91 north. (It's at the big Town Pump truck stop on Dillon's north side.) After about 0.3 mile, the road goes underneath the overpass to the interstate. At 0.6 mile, it crosses the

Beaverhead. After the bridge, turn left and cross a set of railroad tracks. Clark's Lookout is on the right.

The area is under the state parks department's jurisdiction, but it has not been developed. The only way to know you're in the right place is by the small sign on the log fence, noting that the site is property of the Montana Department of Fish, Wildlife and Parks. Perch atop the lookout for a picnic, then head for the interstate to continue following the explorers' trail.

County Road 278 (at Exit 59, Dillon) is the gateway to the Big Hole Valley, as well as a shortcut over the Divide for motorists unwilling to try Lemhi Pass. County Road 278 gives access to the ghost town of Bannack (Montana's first capital), the quintessentially Montanan ranching towns of Jackson and Wisdom, the Big Hole National Battlefield, and the Bitterroot Valley via Chief Joseph Pass. William Clark followed this route east on his trip home in 1806; highlights will be described in a separate section ("Homeward Bound: Clark Explores the Big Hole") later in this chapter.

CAMP FORTUNATE AND LEMHI PASS

Once back on Interstate 15, drive south to Exit 44 (Clark Canyon Dam).

Camp Fortunate was inundated by the reservoir, but a lookout on the lake's west side offers an approximate view of this important site. It was here the expedition was assured of help in its passage across the Continental Divide, and here that Sacagawea's presence proved especially beneficial.

Lewis arrived in the area first, coming to a fork at the head of the Jefferson River on August 10, 1805. He and the advance party decided to follow the right fork, although geographers later determined that the left fork—Red Rock Creek—led to the *true* Missouri River headwaters. Nevertheless, Lewis's instincts proved correct, as we shall soon see.

The next day, Lewis spotted a Shoshoni on horseback—the first Indian the expedition had seen in the whole of what is now Montana. Thrilled, he moved toward the Indian, shouting "*tab-ba-bone.*" Earlier, Lewis had asked Sacagawea the Shoshoni word for "white man." She must have misunderstood, however, for the word "*tab-ba-bone*" actually meant "stranger." To make matters worse, John Shields continued moving toward the Indian, who—frightened by Lewis's calls and Shields's action—took off into the mountains, "and with him vanished all my hopes of obtaining horses for the present," Lewis wrote. "I now felt quite as much mortification and disappointment as I had pleasure and expectation at the first sight of this Indian." Lewis fixed an American flag to a pole as a symbol of peace, and his party spent the rest of the day trying to track the Indians, but to no avail.

Clark Canyon Reservoir, site of Camp Fortunate and the meeting with the Shoshoni Indians.

On August 12, the party moved on up into the mountains, following what Lewis called a "large and plain Indian road.... I therefore did not despair of shortly finding a passage over the mountains and of tasting the waters of the great Columbia this evening." Another four miles on, Lewis and his men reached a stream he dubbed "the most distant fountain of the mighty Missouri in search of which we have spent so many toilsome days and restless nights. Thus far I had accomplished one of those great objects on which my mind has been unalterably fixed for many years." With great gusto, Lewis drank the water. Meanwhile, Private Hugh McNeal "had exultingly stood with a foot on each side of this little rivulet and thanked his god that he had lived to bestride the mighty and heretofore deemed endless Missouri."

Plenty of excitement for one day, but there was more to come, and a bit of disappointment, too. "After refreshing ourselves we proceeded on to the top of the dividing ridge"—Lemhi Pass—"from which I discovered immense ranges of high mountains still to the West of us with their tops partially covered with snow," Lewis continued. "I now descended the mountain about three-quarters of a mile which I found much steeper than on the opposite side, to a handsome bold running creek of cold clear water. Here I first tasted the water of the great Columbia River."

Lewis had crossed the divide, but the sight of those "immense ranges of mountains" made it clear there was still no easy way to the Columbia. It was already mid-August, and who knew how far they had to go? The men made their first camp in what is now Idaho, determined to contact the Shoshonis the next day—which is exactly what happened.

On August 13, the advance party made its way into the valley and finally, about a mile ahead, saw two women, a man, and some dogs. Lewis and his men kept walking as the Shoshonis stood still; when they came within a half-mile, Lewis asked the others to wait as he moved ahead, unfurling the flag and still calling out *tab-ba-bone*. These Indians soon disappeared, but a mile down the road, the white men saw three more women. Giving them presents and painting their cheeks with vermillion, a sign of peace, Lewis asked them to alert their village that the white men came in peace. "We had marched on about two miles when we met a party of about sixty warriors mounted on excellent horses who came in nearly full speed," Lewis wrote. "The chief and two others who were a little in advance of the main body spoke to the women, and they informed them who we were and exultingly showed the presents which had been given them. These men then advanced and embraced me very affectionately...both parties now advanced and we were all caressed and besmeared with their grease and paint til I was heartily tired of the national hug. I now had the pipe lit and gave them smoke."

Lewis' next task was to convince the Shoshonis to accompany him back over the divide. He told how Clark and the others were waiting over the mountains with their baggage, and that they needed horses to make the trip. At first, Lewis's pleas were met with resistance, for some of the Shoshoni feared the white men might be in league with their enemies, the Pahkees. But Lewis finally convinced Cameahwait, the Shoshoni chief, and a number of others to go with him. They arrived back at the forks of the Jefferson, with Clark nowhere to be found. Lewis feared the Indians, feeling tricked, would leave. But most stayed, and Clark and his contingent arrived the next day, August 17.

Nicholas Biddle, in his 1814 history of the expedition, related the meeting this way: "On setting out at 7 o'clock, Captain Clark with Charbonneau and his wife walked on shore, but they had not gone more than a mile before Clark saw Sacagawea, who was with her husband 100 yards ahead, begin to dance and show every mark of the most extravagant joy." As the parties drew closer, "a woman made her way through the crowd toward Sacagawea, and recognizing each other, they embraced with the most tender affection." The two women, it turned out, had been childhood friends, both kidnapped at the Three Forks and comforting each other in captivity, until the other woman escaped.

The captains and Indians exchanged greetings and made preparations for council. Sacagawea was set to help interpret the Shoshoni message. "She came into the tent, sat down, and was beginning to interpret, when in the person of Cameahwait she recognized her brother," Biddle wrote. "She instantly jumped up, and ran and embraced him, throwing over him her blanket and weeping profusely. The chief was himself moved, though not in the same degree. After some conversation between them, she returned to her seat, and attempted to interpret, but her new situation seemed to overpower her, and she was frequently interrupted by tears."

Despite her emotion, Sacagawea was successful in helping the expedition negotiate for horses. Here at the newly named Camp Fortunate, the corps also cached canoes and supplies for the return trip, and prepared to begin their overland journey.

Today, just about any vehicle can travel over Lemhi Pass in the summertime, although the Idaho side (more steep and narrow than the Montana side, as Lewis noted) isn't recommended for large motor homes or vehicles towing trailers. The turnoff for Lemhi Pass is twenty-two miles from Clark Canyon Dam and about nine miles past the small settlement of Grant. Coming from Clark Canyon, turn right at the second of two Forest Service access signs. From the turn, it is twelve miles to the pass. The route is marked by a Lewis and Clark Trail sign.

The road crosses through the Bar Double T ranch about six miles in. Keep going. Past the ranch houses, the road can be a bit boggy and rutted, but still passable. A few miles farther, the road forks left to Frying Pan Road. Stay on the main way; it's just three miles to the pass.

Although the marker at Lemhi Pass lists its elevation at 7,339, most maps put it at 7,373 feet. In either case, this marked the high spot on the Lewis and Clark Trail. Today, it is a most splendid place to watch a sunset and perhaps spend the night. As dusk falls, the skies may turn purple, pink, or orange, shadows falling over one mountain ridge after another. A small campground, Sacagawea Memorial Camp, rests just below the pass on the Montana side. This area is known as an elk calving ground, and lucky visitors may see elk or their tracks and other signs.

From Lemhi Pass, it is thirteen miles to Tendoy and Idaho 28. A sign about two miles down the mountain marks the corps' first Idaho campsite. Other signs explain later facets of area history. If you think modern vehicles have it tough, imagine what this route must have been like for the Red Rock Stage, which ran the 125 miles between Salmon, Idaho, and Red Rock, Montana, daily from 1866 until 1910. Several holdups occurred near Lemhi Pass, and it wasn't unusual for a stage to overturn on the treacherous road.

The area also saw some mining activity, most notably at the Copper Queen Mine, which operated sporadically from 1883 to 1940. There's another small campground about 7.5 miles from the summit. This one, a BLM site called Agency Creek, has a toilet and picnic tables.

Eleven miles west of Lemhi Pass, a sign on the left-hand side notes the nearby grave of Chief Tendoy, who was a well-respected and influential Indian leader. The site is sacred to Native Americans and visitation by the general public is not considered appropriate. At twelve miles, the traveler comes to a "T" in the road. Turn right, then left to get to the hamlet of Tendoy. A small store sells gas and food.

From Tendoy, it's a quick and scenic twenty-two miles north to Salmon, the major town in these parts. Somewhere along this stretch Meriwether Lewis unfurled the American flag for the first time west of the Continental Divide. This was also Sacagawea's true homeland, the area in which she was born and grew up until that ill-fated trip to the Three Forks.

Salmon is a prime launching point for pack and float trips into the Central Idaho Rockies. The Lemhi County Historical Museum at 210 Main St. displays pioneer and Indian artifacts, along with antique treasures from the Far East. Stop by the visitor center at 200 Main St. for more information on the many recreational opportunities close to Salmon. The Salmon River, which originates in central Idaho not far from Sun Valley, is the longest American river running entirely within one state. It parallels US 93 north and south of Salmon, and numerous fishing and recreation points dot the way.

Near what is now North Fork, Idaho, Clark and an advance party—including his newly hired Shoshoni guide, Toby—explored the Salmon River several miles downstream to see if it might provide the hoped-for route to the Pacific. But it soon became apparent this waterway—often called "the River of No Return"—would not be passable. Clark sent Lewis a message outlining three possible options.

The first involved obtaining one horse for each man and, using Toby as a guide, proceeding by land to a navigable river. The second plan would divide the men into two groups. One party would attempt to navigate the Salmon River, while the other would travel by horseback. The third idea also involved splitting the corps into two parties, with one going over the mountains to the north while the other returned to Great Falls for supplies that had been cached there before traveling, via the Sun River to the land of the Flatheads near present-day Missoula.

Clark recommended the first, noting that if the Indians and their women and children could make it, it would be a snap for his trail-hardened men. When Lewis received the message, however, he had learned the Shoshoni didn't have enough horses to spare one for each of the white men. Lewis wrote back and asked Clark to come anyway, and get the twenty-two horses he had been able to buy. Clark negotiated for another two animals. Reunited, the parties started their ascent toward Lost Trail Pass.

HOMEWARD BOUND: CLARK EXPLORES THE BIG HOLE

On his return trip in 1806, Clark explored what is now one of Montana's most isolated and beautiful areas: the Big Hole. To follow his footsteps today, head east on Montana 43 at Lost Trail Pass. Clark, coming from the north, actually traversed Gibbons Pass, also nearby. This way is navigable, but the road is not much better than the one Clark found almost two hundred years ago. An interpretive marker between mileposts 12 and 13 on Montana 43 mentions that Clark passed through the area in July 1806.

From the pass, Clark and his party traveled down into the Big Hole, southeast toward what is now Jackson, to Bannack, and to the Beaverhead River at what would become Armstead, a town now inundated by Clark Canyon Reservoir. From there, they followed the Beaverhead and Jefferson rivers to the Three Forks. Sacagawea, familiar with all this country, continued to help find the way.

Big Hole National Battlefield, ten miles west of Wisdom, is definitely worth a stop. Start in the visitor center, where a slide show is projected on a screen just above a panoramic window that looks out on the battlefield. The presentation explains just why and how the Nez Perce War of 1877 got started, while other exhibits tell of key Indian and white players in the battle. Many of the photos are accompanied by quotes.

Big Hole Battlefield National Monument near Wisdom, Montana.

Before the war, the Nez Perce prided themselves on never killing a white settler. In fact, the tribe was instrumental in helping Lewis and Clark complete their journey, as we shall see. By 1855, the Nez Perce were convinced to move onto a reservation, albeit one that preserved most of their original homelands. But with the discovery of gold on the reservation in 1860, whites wanted to redraw the boundaries to exclude the mining lands. In 1863, the U.S. government proposed a reservation just one-tenth the size originally agreed on. President Andrew Johnson signed the treaty in 1867, and the government started a campaign to get the Nez Perce onto the new reservation.

Some agreed to the move, but others did not. By 1877, the non-treaty Nez Perce were told they would be forcibly moved to the reservation if they did not go on their own. The major band of non-treaty Nez Perce lived in Oregon under Old Joseph—but Old Joseph's son, Young Joseph, wanted a peaceful solution and prepared to move the band to the reservation by the June 14 deadline. On June 13, however, three young Nez Perce men, angered by the forced move and seeking revenge for the murder of one of their fathers by a white man, killed four settlers. Over the next two days, the group—joined by seventeen others—killed fourteen or fifteen whites. The Nez Perce War was on.

By the time they reached the Big Hole, Chief Joseph and the Nez Perce had fought several battles in Idaho—one, a crushing defeat of General Oliver O. Howard at White Bird Canyon, and others that proved inconclusive. Chief Joseph decided to take five non-treaty bands of some eight hundred people and two thousand horses into Montana and on, they hoped, to refuge at the Canadian border. They arrived at the Big Hole August 7, sure they were far ahead of Howard and his troops. They did not know, however, that a second force led by Colonel John Gibbon had joined the chase and was closing in. The battle of August 9-10, 1877, resulted in the deaths of some sixty to ninety Nez Perce, only thirty of whom were warriors, the rest women and children, and twenty-nine U.S. soldiers.

Three short hikes from a lower parking lot lead to key sites in the battle. The trails aren't long, but they are largely out in the open, so sunscreen and water are advised. It's 1.5 miles to the Nez Perce camp, 0.75 miles along a level trail to the siege area and 0.75 miles uphill to the howitzer site. (The original howitzer sits just outside the visitor center.) Picnic tables are available at the lower parking lot.

Country star Hank Williams Jr., who has ranches in the area, recently put up the funding for an archaeological study of the battlefield. Metal detecting for artifacts began in the 1950s, but the detectors were large and unwieldy, and the surveys found very little. Techniques gradually improved, but lack of money prevented a large-scale survey until "Bochephus" came along in the fall of 1990. Many artifacts found in the subsequent dig are now on display, along with photos of Williams taking part in the project.

Memorial observances take place on the battlefield every year on the weekend closest to the battle anniversary. The white casualties are usually mourned Saturday, while the Nez Perce conduct a memorial on Sunday. Both are open to the public, but no picture taking is permitted.

Clark camped within a mile-and-a-half of the battlefield, but no one is exactly sure where. Big Hole Battlefield itself has no campground, but May Creek Campground—about eight miles east of Chief Joseph Pass—attracts many park visitors. Park service staff sometimes conduct interpretive campfire programs there on summer evenings.

Big Hole National Battlefield is open 8 a.m. to 8 p.m. late May through Labor Day and 8 a.m. to 5 p.m. the rest of the year. Admission is $3 per vehicle during the summer and free otherwise. For more information, call (406) 689-3155.

The Big Hole is just as its name implies: wide 360-degree views rimmed everywhere you look by towering mountains. This is the haystack capital of the world—"valley of 10,000 haystacks," many call it. Wisdom and Jackson, ten and thirty miles, respectively, east of Big Hole National Battlefield, are the area's two major towns (although each is actually quite tiny). Although it is home to just 175 people, Wisdom boasts the noted Wisdom River Gallery, specializing in Western and wildlife art. Jackson, meanwhile, is best known for its hot springs—Clark and company not only soaked their weary bones here in 1806; they also cooked dinner in the water! These days, boiling meat is probably off limits in the pools at Jackson Hot Springs Resort, but you can still get a home-cooked meal, along with a comfy cabin.

Bannack State Park commemorates another famous Montana ghost town (and seat of the first territorial capital). You can reach Bannack either from County Road 278 west of Dillon, or via sixteen miles of good gravel road from Grant on the route to Lemhi Pass. Remains of several original buildings may be viewed, along with a visitor center that offers more information and photos on the nineteenth century mining boom in Bannack.

LOST TRAIL PASS AND THE BITTERROOT VALLEY

The Corps of Discovery had one heck of a time getting over Lost Trail Pass—largely because their hapless guide, Toby, lost the trail to the pass. On September 2, 1805, Clark wrote: "We were obliged to cut a road over rock hillsides where our horses were in...danger of slipping to their certain destruction." Several horses fell. One was crippled and two gave out.

Toby led the explorers over a trail more than a thousand feet higher than the current route, US 93, which generally follows the path of least resistance. Still, modern travelers may also encounter some difficulty traversing the pass, which was due to be under road construction at least

U.S. Highway 93 and the Bitterroot Mountains near Darby, Montana.

through the fall of 1994, with traffic only allowed through several times a day. Contact the Idaho or Montana highway department for the latest information, or watch for signs posted in nearby towns.

An interpretive panel at Lost Trail Pass shows the historic routes through the area, from Lewis and Clark's trek to those taken by the Nez Perce and Generals Howard and Gibbon to the Battle of the Big Hole. From the pass, it is thirty-one miles to Darby, the first sizable town along US 93 in Montana's booming Bitterroot Valley.

Once they negotiated the mountains, the explorers had a relatively easy time of it in the Bitterroot Valley. Soon after descending, they came upon an area later known as Ross' Hole for Alexander Ross of the Hudson Bay Company, who ranged far and wide over these parts. He camped here with fifty-five Indian and white trappers, eighty-nine women and children, and 392 horses in 1824 en route from Spokane to the Snake River. They spent nearly a month trying to break across the pass to the Big Hole, and Ross wound up naming the basin "the valley of troubles." For Lewis and Clark, however, this area brought their first meeting with the Flathead Indians and an opportunity to trade for more horses.

Sula has a small store, a campground and cabins. A sign welcoming visitors to the Bitterroot Valley must be pretty old: It lists Darby's population as 415 and Stevensville's at 772; as of the 1990 Census, they had climbed to 625 and 1,221, respectively, and the figures are probably a lot higher now.

Montana's Bitterroot Valley is one of the nation's fastest-growing areas. The boom is most evident in the towns nearest Missoula, but even the smaller settlements have been converted from sleepy little timber towns to bustling burgs complete with espresso machines and offbeat shops. A taste of the past isn't impossible to find, however. The Sula Ranger Station rents out its historic East Fork Guard Station, sixteen miles east of town, on a year-round basis. Stop by the ranger station weekdays or call (406) 821-3201 for more information.

Lewis and Clark camped about two miles downstream from the present-day Spring Gulch Campground north of Sula, and everyone went to bed wet and hungry. Clark wrote: "It rained this evening. Nothing to eat but berries. Our flour out and but little corn. The hunters killed two pheasants only."

US 93 parallels the East Fork Bitterroot River, which runs along the highway from Sula to Conner, picking up the main stem there. The Bitterroot is noted for its rainbow and cutthroat trout. Several fishing access points are easily accessible near the road. Conner is also the access point to Trapper Peak, at 10,157 feet the highest in the Bitterroots.

The Bitterroot National Forest ranger station in Darby doubles as a historic center offering displays and books. Five miles north of town, watch for the road to Lake Como. This popular and beautiful lake offers another great view of Trapper Peak, along with fishing, boating, camping, and hiking.

Hamilton—about half-way to Missoula from Lost Trail Pass—is the main trade center for the Bitterroot Valley. This was home to the Rocky Mountain Laboratory, which researched Rocky Mountain Spotted Fever, first detected here in 1873. "Neither cause nor cure was known and mortality was high," a historic marker reads. By 1906, scientists realized the disease was spread by a tick and were finally able to prevent and treat the fever via vaccinations and medicine. A modern federal laboratory has replaced the tents, log cabins, woodsheds, and abandoned schoolhouse that served the first researchers, and the center still studies infectious diseases.

At Hamilton, it's possible to get off the beaten path of US 93 and tool along on the Eastside Highway (also known as Montana 269). Simply turn east instead of west at the signs for Hamilton's city center. The famous Daly Mansion is the back road's first landmark. Marcus Daly came to America from Ireland as a poor immigrant. He liked mining and was soon attracted to camps of the West, where he quickly learned the trade. He rapidly grew rich and was a powerful force in Montana business and politics for many years.

A splendid Georgian Revival-style dwelling, also called Riverside, served as the summer home for the Daly family. Its forty-two rooms are filled with exquisite furnishings. Privately held for many years, Riverside was acquired by the state in 1987 and is now open for tours. Cost is $5 for adults and $3 for students ages 5 through 14. Visitors may tour just the grounds for $1 per person. Hours are 11 a.m. to 4 p.m. daily.

The Lee Metcalf National Wildlife Refuge, north of Stevensville, offers a close-by oasis of calm in the bustling Bitterroot Valley. The refuge is primarily a home for birds and waterfowl, including blue-winged teal, osprey, Canada geese, and many others. For another great hiking opportunity, try the Bass Creek Trail into the Bitterroot range. To get there, drive north from Stevensville on US 93 and watch for a sign on the west side of the road marking the turnoff to the Charles Waters Campground and Recreation Site. There's good fishing along the Bitterroot, too, although the stretch from Tucker Crossing to Florence Bridge is catch-and-release only. Look for other regulations posted near the many fishing access spots.

The Lewis and Clark expedition camped at what is now the town of Lolo on September 9 and 10, 1805, and named the site Traveler's Rest. No signs remain of the camp, now surrounded by light industry and housing developments, but historians believe it was close to where the Mormon church now stands.

It was here the captains learned they could have taken a shortcut west from the Great Falls, rather than the arduous route they had just completed. That was disappointing news, especially now, with still more mountains to cross and winter quickly drawing nigh. There was little time to waste, and on September 11, the party started up the Lolo Trail—a march that would prove the most taxing part of the entire twenty-eight-month trip.

SIDE TRIP: MISSOULA AND ENVIRONS

Missoula, just eleven miles north from Traveler's Rest and Lolo, is indisputably one of the Rocky Mountain region's most interesting, lively towns. This city of about 45,000 people makes a fine place to overnight and re-supply before heading out over the Lolo Trail.

Five valleys converge in the Missoula area, so it's not surprising this has long been a way-station for travelers. Lewis and party camped at the confluence of the Rattlesnake and Clark's Fork rivers on July 3, 1806, before leaving east on their shortcut across the Great Divide. Before that, Indians used the area as a thoroughfare to hunting grounds east of the mountains.

The valley floor here was once covered by glacial Lake Missoula to a depth of two thousand feet, about five hundred feet higher than the "M" above the University of Montana campus. Formed about fifteen thousand years ago during the most recent Ice Age, geologists reckon the lake filled and drained at least six times during its existence. The big valley makes for a fairly moderate climate (for Montana, at least), but the topography also tends to make Missoula susceptible to air inversions and pollution—again, at least by Big Sky standards.

The Historical Museum at Fort Missoula is the city's most interesting relic from the past. Federal troops arrived at the site in 1877, just in time to try stopping Chief Joseph and the Nez Perce from traveling down Lolo Creek. Failing that, they joined Colonel Gibbon at the Battle of the Big Hole. The fort's buildings were built soon after, and three of the original structures still remain. Later, the fort was home to an unusual experiment in American military history: a bicycle corps. (Missoula remains a big cycling community, home of the national Bikecentennial organization and bike shops galore.)

The fort grounds is now home to a historical museum with permanent exhibits on Missoula history and changing displays on other aspects of early settlement in the area. Military reserve units and the U.S. Forest Service also have offices here. Don't miss climbing the fire lookout. Fort Missoula is open 10 a.m. to 5 p.m. Tuesday through Saturday and noon to 5 p.m. Sundays, Memorial Day through Labor Day. The rest of the year, the museum is open noon to 5 p.m. Tuesday through Sunday. It is closed Mondays year-round. Admission is by donation.

Missoula is perhaps best known as home of the University of Montana, not to mention a primary cultural capital between Minneapolis and

Seattle. In recent years, Missoula has become a real writers' and readers' center, with an abundance of fine bookstores and an active literary community. Don't miss the University bookstore, or Freddy's Feed and Read, among others. The city also has active theatrical and visual arts scenes, not to mention fourteen movie screens—a heck of a lot for a city this size.

Needless to say, the recreation-minded have it made in Missoula. Aside from the city's own network of riverside trails and the ever-popular hike to the "M" (a 1.5-mile round trip), residents and visitors can take their pick of the Rattlesnake National Recreation Area and Wilderness to the north, Patee Canyon Recreation Area to the southeast, and Blue Mountain Recreation Area to the southwest, all within a few miles from downtown.

Missoula has a full calendar of special events, especially during the summer. The city's big Fourth of July bash takes place out at Fort Missoula. In town, people go "Out to Lunch at Caras Park" on the riverfront every Wednesday June through August. Other regular events include an active farmers market (Tuesday evenings and Saturday mornings) and Wednesday-night band concerts at Bonner Park July through mid-August. For more information on Missoula, call (406) 543-6623 or stop by the Visitors Bureau office on the downtown side of the Van Buren Street footbridge.

U.S. HIGHWAY 12

Lewis and Clark expected to cross one mountain range in the Bitterroots. Instead, they found ridge after ridge. By the time the expedition arrived in what is now northern Idaho, corps members were a hardened, gristled lot—mountain men, really. Still, nothing could have prepared them for what they encountered on the Lolo Trail.

Patrick Gass, who would survive longer than any other expedition member, called the Idaho Bitterroots "the most terrible mountains I ever beheld." For his part, Captain Clark—at thirty-five one of the oldest members of the corps—had long lived the military life, and wasn't one to complain. But over and over as his men crossed these mountains, he said he'd never been colder, never been wetter.

Today's travelers have a choice of routes across this rugged land. US 12 winds through the Lochsa-Clearwater canyon at the base of the Bitterroots. It's a good, scenic route officially marked as the Lewis and Clark Trail, but the corps followed only a tiny portion of it. Most of the time, they were high on the ridge to the north: the real Lolo Trail. The canyon below—which had to be extensively blasted just to make room for the two-lane US 12—was far too narrow in 1805-1806 to allow passage by land, and the rivers were unnavigable. US 12 itself wasn't even completed until 1962, which gives some indication of just how rough things were.

Which route to take? Both have plenty to offer. US 12 is the best route for enjoying the scenery and for making time, but the Lolo Motorway (Forest Road 500) gives the traveler a much better feel for the hardships the expedition endured. The best possible trip might combine parts of each, jumping off for the Lolo Motorway at Parachute Hill Road (Forest Road 569) and returning to US 12 via Saddle Camp Road (Forest Road 107). We'll look at US 12 first, then examine the Lolo Motorway.

Tank up with plenty of gasoline no matter which route you take. There's no fuel on US 12 west of Lolo for fifty miles, and only one station (at Powell) in the next 115 miles! Allow plenty of time, too: a half-day to travel US 12 between Lolo, Montana, and Lewiston, Idaho, and at least a full day if you plan to take any part of the actual Lolo Trail (two days if you intend to drive the whole route).

From Lolo, US 12 follows Lolo Creek west. A few miles out of town, the traveler reaches Fort Fizzle, erected by the Army to try to prevent Chief Joseph and the Nez Perce from crossing Lolo Creek. It's now a Forest Service Historic Site.

The Forest Service has named a campground for our heroes on the south side of Lolo Creek, 15.5 miles from Lolo. Interpretive panels on the bridge leading to the campsites explain the presence of tiny migratory songbirds that nest in bushes along the creek each summer. Birds to look for include Swainson's Thrush, Greenish Willow Flycatcher, and Yellow

Lolo Pass Visitor Center on the Montana-Idaho border.

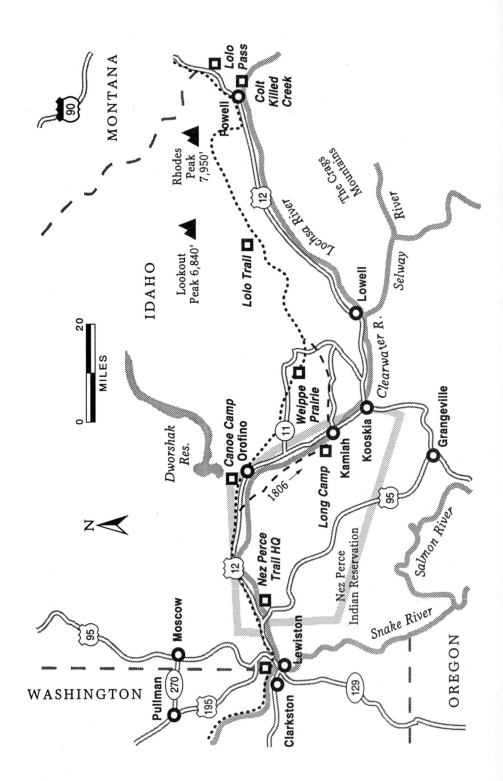

192

Warbler. Trails lead down to the creekbed on either side of this bridge. Altogether, Lewis and Clark Campground has eighteen sites, a few of them pull-throughs. It's a pleasant and handy place to spend the night.

Alas, Lewis and Clark did not camp in the immediate vicinity. The corps kept mostly to the open, north side of the creek as it moved westward. Howard Creek Trail, accessed off the north side of US 12, is one place visitors still can follow closely in the steps of the expedition. The trailhead is accompanied by a picnic area.

US 12 continues its steady climb, soon arriving at Lolo Hot Springs Resort. "I tasted this water and found it hot and not bad tasting," Clark wrote. "I put my finger in the water and at first could not bear it for a second." Today, the resort offers a pool, restaurant, casino, campground, tepee rentals, and a hotel, all surrounded by intriguing rock formations. Visitors can also enjoy horseback trail rides, offered seven days a week every hour-and-a-half starting at 9 a.m., or a trail ride and steak dinner held seven nights a week. For more information, call (406) 273-2290.

From Lolo Hot Springs, it is seven miles to the Idaho border. West of the resort, a sign reads: "Winding road next 77 miles." More than any other highway along the trail, motorists need to be alert while traveling US 12. It's curvy, it's narrow, it's heavily used by logging and grain trucks, and it's one long deer-crossing zone.

The highway traverses the Montana-Idaho border and the Mountain-Pacific time zone line at Lolo Pass, elevation 5,233 feet. A visitor center here is open Memorial Day through the end of summer. The area is especially pretty in early June, when nearby Packer Meadows turn purple with blooming camas. The expedition crossed the Lolo divide about a mile east of the present pass and camped in the Packer Meadows area that night.

A picnic area near milepost 165 on US 12 is of more than passing interest to avid Lewis and Clark buffs. This is the DeVoto Memorial Cedar Grove, a cool green cathedral named in honor of Bernard DeVoto, noted writer, historian, and editor of the Lewis and Clark journals. DeVoto used to camp here among the western red cedar while preparing his edition of the journals. Some say DeVoto's spirit still lingers in the area—his ashes were scattered over the grove after his death in 1955.

On September 14, the party reached what is now the Powell Ranger Station. Toby, their guide, had mistakenly left the main Lolo Trail and descended to the Lochsa—or *Koos Koos Kee*—River. By now, nearly all their food supplies were exhausted, and game was nowhere to be seen. Lewis broke out his food of last resort, an experimental "portable soup" he had obtained from the Army as emergency rations. It was barely edible, and the corps was forced to more extreme measures. "Here we were compelled to kill a colt for our men and selves to eat for the want of meat and we named the south fork Colt Killed Creek," Clark wrote. "The

DeVoto Memorial Cedar Grove along U.S. Highway 12, Idaho.

mountains which we passed today (were) much worse than yesterday...our men and horses much fatigued."

The Powell Ranger Station and nearby Lochsa Lodge are the last real outposts of civilization on US 12 until Lowell about fifty miles west. Aside from gasoline, Lochsa Lodge offers several cabins and motel-type rooms and a restaurant with a big fireplace. A company called Lewis & Clark Trail Adventures uses the lodge as a base for trips along the Lolo Trail; three-day, seventy-five-mile mountain biking treks and single-day drive-hiking tours are available. Mountain bikes can be rented at the Lochsa Lodge. For more information on the tours, call (406) 728-7609, or write Lewis & Clark Trail Adventures, P.O. Box 9051, Missoula, MT 59801.

Aside from being a good source of information, the Powell Ranger Station serves as home to the local post office and the Powell Public Library—two cardboard boxes filled with books. Colt Killed Creek—now White Sand Creek—runs nearby. Forest Road 569—Parachute Hill Road—is located on the north side of US 12 just east of the Powell Ranger Station road. This is probably the best access road to the eastern half of the Lolo Motorway.

On September 15, the corps trudged another four miles down the Lochsa River. Toby had finally figured out he had lost the trail, and he determined the party should climb a steep ridge to regain the route. So the party started up Wendover Ridge, located across US 12 from the present-day Wendover-Whitehouse campgrounds (the latter named for expedition member Joseph Whitehouse). It was no picnic, particularly for the horses. "Several horses slipped and rolled down steep hills which hurt them very much. The one which carried my desk and small trunk turned over and rolled down a mountain for forty yards," Clark wrote. The field desk was smashed, but the horse managed to survive "and appeared but little hurt," according to Clark. After a rest of two hours, the party continued on to the Lolo Trail, where they found snow but no water. There, the men supped on the portable soup, made a bit more palatable with some leftover colt. "From this mountain I could observe high rugged mountains in every direction as far as I could see," Clark added.

It's possible to hike part of the Wendover Ridge today, from US 12 to the Wendover-Badger Road. It takes a moderately fit person about forty minutes to hike from the highway to the road, and about a half-hour to come back. From the Wendover-Badger Road, the trail continues, but it becomes faint and the air gets thin. The second leg goes to Wendover Ridge Rest Site, and the third to the snowbank camp.

Colgate Licks and Jerry Johnson Hot Springs, both located not far west of the Wendover-Whitehouse campgrounds, are among the most popular stops along US 12. At Colgate Licks, deer, elk, and other animals are attracted to the springs by their salty content. A loop trail winds from the parking lot past the springs. Jerry Johnson springs are accessed by a mile-long trail up Warm Springs Creek.

West of the hot springs, the traveler can make a little better time while enjoying the river canyon scenery. That's not to say the distractions fade completely, however: the Lochsa Historical Ranger Station has one of the West's best collections of Forest Service memorabilia. The ranger station, located across US 12 from the Wilderness Gateway campground, is staffed by Forest Service retirees all summer. Forest Road 107—the Saddle Camp Road and another good access point to and from the Lolo Motorway—is located midway between Colgate Licks and the Lochsa Ranger Station.

Twenty-five miles west of the historical station, US 12 finally reaches Lowell and, just beyond it, Syringa. Lowell serves as gateway to the Selway River; together, the Selway and Lochsa become the Clearwater River west of here. A twenty-three-mile back road parallels the Selway, a river well known to whitewater enthusiasts. In fact, the Lochsa, Selway, and Clearwater all present challenging rafting and kayaking opportunities. Area businesses can provide more information, as can the Idaho Outfitters and Guides Association at (208) 342-1438.

From Lowell, it's twenty-three miles to Kooskia (pronounced KOO-skee), a pretty little town surrounded by hills. The Kooskia National Fish Hatchery near the junction of US 12 and Idaho 13 raises more than one million salmon each year. Kamiah (KAM-ee-eye), a slightly larger town with good visitor services, is seven miles north on US 12.

As we've already seen, the history of the Nez Perce people is closely intertwined with that of the Lewis and Clark Trail, and we're now entering an area offering many opportunities to explore this tribe's history and present. The Nez Perce sites are well worth visiting, both because of the tribe's important contributions to the expedition and the Nez Perces' own proud history.

One such site is a basaltic formation on the outskirts of Kamiah that for centuries has been known as the "Heart of the Monster." According to Nez Perce legend, Coyote slew a great monster near here. The Nez Perce and other tribes sprang forth, each from where parts of the monster fell. The site is located across the road from the Lewis-Clark Resort RV park and motel just south of Kamiah on US 12.

On their return trip east in 1806, Lewis and Clark spent twenty-seven days camped in the Kamiah area while waiting for snow to melt along the Lolo Trail. Here, the expedition members hunted, fished, and learned more about the Nez Perce, with whom the whites had become good friends. "Those people have shown much greater acts of hospitality than we have witnessed from any nation or tribe since we have passed the Rocky Mountains," Clark wrote. The site of the Long Camp, also sometimes called Camp Chopunnish, is noted with a state historical marker on US 12 not far from the Heart of the Monster.

Kamiah has a vaguely Victorian flavor and a full calendar of annual events. The Nez Perce celebrate Mata-Lyma, a root feast and powwow,

Heart of the Monster Nez Perce site near Kamiah, Idaho.

the third weekend each May and Chief Looking Glass Days the third weekend in August. The local business community throws a free barbecue over Labor Day Weekend, complete with dances, games, and the crowning of the Barbecue Queen. Kamiah's Riverfront Park has a boat ramp and free RV camping for no more than forty-eight hours. The town is also the western gateway to the Lolo Motorway; stop by Kamiah's Clearwater National Forest office for more information and a map.

From Kamiah, it's twenty-three miles northwest on US 12 to Orofino, site of the expedition's Canoe Camp. But before we proceed, let's take a better look at the Lolo Motorway, the difficult but rewarding alternate route across the Bitterroot Mountains, and the Weippe Prairie, where the Corps of Discovery finally descended from the mountains in the fall of 1805.

THE LOLO MOTORWAY

Indians, trappers, military men, and settlers have used what is now known as the Lolo Trail as the main way across northern Idaho. But the corps were almost certainly the first white men to travel it. Much of their route is paralleled by present-day Forest Road 500, the Lolo Motorway. The "motorway" designation may conjure up images of men in snappy driving caps and women in smart scarves breezing through the countryside in a convertible, but don't be misled: *This* motorway is no joyride.

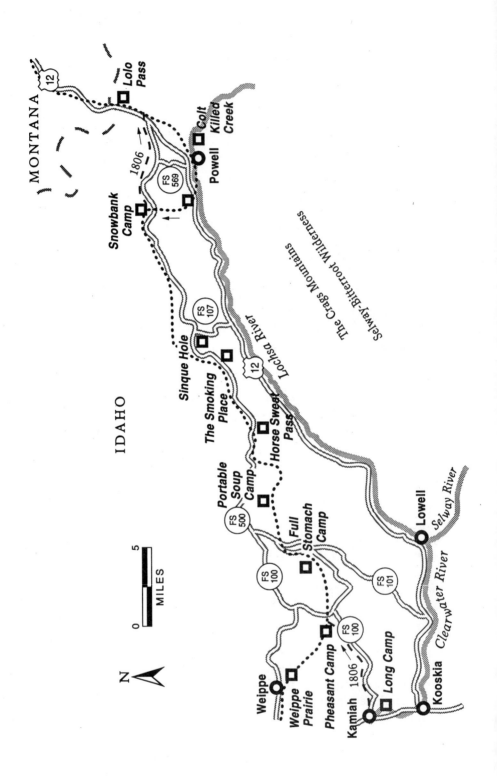

Campground entrance on U.S. Highway 12.

US 12 is open year round, but the Lolo Motorway is typically accessible only from mid-July through mid-September. Four-wheel drive isn't essential, but good clearance is advised. Make sure tires, belts, etc. are in good shape (and carry spares). Needless to say, there are no services of any kind.

Check with the Forest Service on current conditions before setting out. It's not even a bad idea to carry an axe (or chain saw) and shovel, since downed trees and isolated patches of snow aren't uncommon on the motorway even in high summer. Finally, have a good, detailed forest map (available at the Lolo Pass Visitors Center or Powell Ranger Station) before attempting exploration of the back roads.

As an alternative to driving, you might want to explore the Lolo Trail on horseback. Harlan and Barbara Opdahl of Triple "O" Outfitters offer weeklong Lewis and Clark trail adventures at a cost of $1,500 per person. For information, call (208) 464-2349 or (208) 464-2761, or write Triple "O" Outfitters, P.O. Box 217, Pierce, ID 83546.

A few Forest Service signs along the Lolo Trail are slightly off kilter, either on the wrong side of the road or some distance from the actual sites they describe. But it's important to remember that the Lewis and Clark Trail isn't something you can follow exactly. The corps passed through only briefly and left scant evidence of its visit. Rather than dwelling on locating the exact campsites—a sure recipe for frustration— enjoy the spirit of the place and the scenery.

After they climbed the Wendover Ridge and regained the Lolo Trail September 15, Lewis, Clark, and company camped at what is now referred to as the Snowbank Camp. The next morning, they awoke to find their beds covered with four inches of fresh snow. All day, the snow kept falling, obscuring the trail and making everyone miserable. It was this day Clark pronounced he was "wet and as cold" as he'd ever been in his life. And on this night, the party had to kill yet another colt to keep from starving. Clark had tried to shoot a deer—one of very few the men saw in this area—but his gun apparently misfired.

The next day, September 17, the party passed a landmark known as Indian Post Office, several rock cairns marking the highest point on the Lolo Trail at 7,033 feet. A short spur, Forest Road 500E, leads to the Indian Post Office, and views in the vicinity are quite scenic.

Past the Indian Post Office, the corps left the main ridge and followed a more northerly route for about twelve miles. The trails converge again past Forest Road 107, and although that road is a good one back to US 12, travelers may want to proceed on a bit farther before backtracking, particularly if they can manage a stay at Castle Butte Lookout, the ideal base camp for explorations on the Lolo Trail.

Castle Butte, a former working fire lookout now available for rent, is about fifteen feet square, perched on a stone foundation about twenty feet high. A catwalk extends around the lookout, and lightning rods at each corner give visitors a feeling of vulnerability and safety at the same

Castle Butte fire lookout on the Lolo Trail, Idaho.

time. Sweeping vistas are impressive in all directions, but especially to the south where the Selway-Bitterroot Wilderness—among the largest in the continental United States—lies sprawled beyond the Lochsa River. The river, for its part, may barely be seen, a slim and silvery ribbon far below your feet.

The lookout is furnished with a double bed, single cot, table with two chairs looking out toward the west (perfect for sunset dinners), propane stove, and several chests of drawers. A looseleaf-bound visitors' guide logs past renters' reactions, which range from deeply religious ("Thank you God for your marvelous creation") to anger at government policies that endanger the surrounding wild country. ("It would be a shame to come back to Castle Butte in five years to be surrounded by clearcuts," one guest wrote in 1992.)

Castle Butte is a marvelous place to nap, write, paint, make music, learn to use the firefinder, or read: The visitors' book also contains a copy of "The Smokechaser," a memoir by Carl A. Weholt, who tells of his days in the fire lookout and of the many colorful characters he met during his Forest Service career. It's also fun to rummage through items left by past occupants: On a 1993 visit, the author found an October 1965 *Reader's Digest*, a deck of cards, a Western novel, and lots of matches. For information on how to rent Castle Butte, contact the Clearwater Na-

Rock cairns mark the Smoking Place on the Lolo Trail, Idaho.

tional Forest's Lochsa Ranger District office, Route 1, Box 398, Kooskia, ID 83539, or call (208) 926-4275.

Several Lolo Trail landmarks are a short drive (or hike) from Castle Butte. To the east are the Sinque Hole camp of September 17, 1805, and the Smoking Place of June 27, 1806, where the returning expedition stopped to share a pipe with its Nez Perce guides. To the west, the Dry Camp of September 18, 1805, marks the spot where Captain Clark moved ahead with six hunters to look for game. Left behind, Lewis and the rest suffered a particularly toilsome night. There was scant water, and supper consisted once again of leftover colt, portable soup, "a little bears oil and about twenty pounds of candles from our stock of provisions." Candles! Could matters possibly get worse?

From here, however, things finally looked up—literally. From nearby Sherman Peak, first Captain Clark and later Captain Lewis glimpsed a wide, inviting plain, the Weippe Prairie. True, the plain was still about forty miles off, but the end of the mountains was finally in sight. The corps called this place Spirit Revival Ridge.

At Horse Sweat Pass, the Lewis and Clark Trail again leaves the main divide, regaining it twelve miles to the west. Travelers can either backtrack from here to Forest Road 107 and US 12 or proceed on across the motorway past Rocky Ridge Lake and Weitas Meadows, a pleasant picnic and hiking spot. At Boundary Junction, travelers can head west on Forest Road 103, a steep road heavily used by logging traffic, or continue on the motorway to the Lolo Campground, the motorway's western terminus. From there, follow Forest Road 100 either north to Weippe (via the gravel road at Petersons Corners) or south to Kamiah.

WEIPPE PRAIRIE

An Indian had told Lewis and Clark the Lolo Trail crossing could be made in five days. It had taken the corps twice that. But on September 20, 1805, Clark and his advance party of six other men finally stumbled out of the Bitterroots and onto the Weippe Prairie.

As he and his men walked across the open plain, Clark saw three Nez Perce boys at a slight distance. Frightened, the boys hid in the grass as the white men approached. Clark found two of them and, after reassuring them, asked the boys to lead him and the others to their village.

Once again, many of the village leaders were away on a hunt. The nearest one, Twisted Hair, was at a fishing camp twenty miles down the Clearwater. Clark decided to go meet the chief the next day, but in the meantime bartered for some dried salmon, berries, and camas roots for his party and for the starving men still back in the mountains. He then dispatched Reuben Field and a Nez Perce guide to bring food back to Lewis and the others, who arrived at the Nez Perce camps on September 22.

Weippe Prairie, Idaho, where the expedition first met the Nez Perce Indians.

Within a day, all the white men were sick as dogs. The reason, all thought, was the sudden change in diet from near-starvation rations to the rich salmon and camas roots. Yet despite the rampant illness, the mood was generally joyful. All had survived the mountain crossing, and few obstacles remained between the expedition and its goal, the Pacific Ocean.

The site where expedition members first met the Nez Perce may be viewed southeast of Weippe, about three miles from the historical marker on Idaho 11 west of Weippe. To get there, turn south on 4th Street South 100 (just east of the elementary school, but on the opposite side of the road). Drive south and turn left (or east) about 0.4 mile past the Weippe Cemetery. The site is another 0.4 mile east on the south side.

Weippe Prairie is a designated National Historic Landmark. A historical marker here notes that, "For the Nez Perce, this meeting meant the beginning of change for their way of life. For the members of the Lewis and Clark Expedition, it meant survival." Once again, native people had saved the Corps of Discovery from bitter defeat.

Weippe is a small town with minimal visitor services, but it does offer a great pizza parlor and a couple of places to buy gas. From Weippe, head west on Idaho 11 to return to US 12 and the Clearwater corridor. En route, motorists are treated to dazzling views while descending a magnificent, winding grade. At US 12, turn right to proceed west toward Orofino.

THE CANOE CAMP AND THE CLEARWATER

After more than a month's search, Lewis and Clark had finally found a westward river to take them to the Pacific Ocean. Their next task was finding a campsite where they could make new canoes. They found the spot just west of what is now Orofino, Idaho, now a roadside park along US 12.

Interpretive panels at Canoe Camp recap the expedition's route through the Bitterroots and its meeting with the Nez Perce, as well as their labors at the Canoe Camp. They arrived in the area on September 26, 1805, and camped on the river's south side. Just days before, the men had been freezing in the mountains. Now, the weather was hot, and it sapped the men's already frail health. But by October 6, the party had built five new canoes to complete the run to the Pacific. The following day, the corps proceeded downriver with two new guides: Twisted Hair and Tetoharsky, both Nez Perce chieftains.

Look northeast across the river from Canoe Camp to see Dworshak Dam. This mighty structure is the highest straight-axis concrete dam in the West. Completed in 1973, it rises 717 feet and backs up a popular fifty-three-mile long reservoir with some of Idaho's best steelhead fishing. Dworshak Reservoir is also known for its boat-accessed mini-camps:

Canoe Camp along the Clearwater River, Orofino, Idaho.

80 scenic spots scattered along the shoreline that together provide 125 sites for camping and day use. To visit the dam or the town of Orofino proper, backtrack east from the Canoe Camp site and take the bridge across the Clearwater.

The Clearwater National Forest supervisor's office is just east of the Canoe Camp park, on the opposite side of US 12. Stop by for recreation information or a look at the displays, which include a wildlife diorama and an interesting relief map of the region.

Going upriver as they did east of the Rockies, Lewis and Clark frequently traveled as few as fifteen miles a day. But now the current was with them, and it wasn't unusual to complete thirty or forty miles in a day. In many places, however, the party encountered dangerous rapids—on October 8, Sergeant Gass's canoe struck a rock and sank, necessitating a day's stop for repairs.

US 12 hugs the Clearwater from Orofino all the way to Lewiston. On the way, watch the terrain change from forested river canyon to the grassy steppes of the Inland Northwest. For the next 200 miles, this arid landscape of velvety, undulating green-and-gold hills will be the dominant visual feature along the Lewis and Clark route.

This also remains the heart of the Nez Perce country, and a visitor center at Spalding serves as headquarters for the various units of Nez Perce National Park. The center is reached via a short jog south from US 12 on US 95. Lapwai, three miles south of Spalding, serves as Nez Perce tribal headquarters.

Spalding is named for the Presbyterian missionary Henry Spalding, who sincerely believed it was his duty to Christianize the Indians. "What is done for the poor Indians of this Western world must be done soon," he said. "The only thing that can save them from annihilation is the introduction of civilization."

The Nez Perce visitor center chronicles and exhibits many of the changes—good and bad—this philosophy brought to the Indians. A Book of Matthew printed in Nez Perce is among the items on display in the center. Other exhibits include a case full of beautiful beadwork, as well as a silk ribbon and silver friendship medal presented to the Nez Perce from Lewis and Clark. The center is also a good spot to find out about the Nez Perce of today. A scrapbook of news clippings has items ranging from the latest historical research on Chief Joseph to a profile of a Native American rap group.

The large factory on the south side of the Clearwater River near Lewiston is the Potlatch paper mill. Lewiston has its share of industry (and occasionally fragrant air to match), but it is also an educational center and major retail hub. Stop by the visitor center just north of the Clearwater River bridge to get local information or play with the interactive Idaho tourism computer terminal.

Lewiston is blessed with a mild climate most of the year (although summer days can be scorchers). Because of that, local residents enjoy some recreational pursuits other Idahoans cannot: golfing twelve months a year, for example. Lewiston and its sister city, Clarkston, also have more than fifteen miles of paths for joggers, cyclists, walkers, and strollers. Many of these trails are on the Lewiston Levee, which was constructed by the U.S. Army Corps of Engineers to protect Lewiston after the completion of Lower Granite Dam downriver.

Lewiston has two major attractions for history buffs. The first is an interpretive shelter overlooking the confluence of the Clearwater and Snake rivers. To get there, park at the Lewiston Levee Parkways Center on the northwest side of downtown (on D Street) and walk over the footbridge. The center's entrance is graced with the sculpture *"Tsceminicum,"* meaning "meeting of the waters" in Nez Perce. Designed by Nancy N. Dreher, the artwork depicts a variety of wildlife and the symbolic Earth Mother.

Displays in the shelter note that when Lewis and Clark arrived here, they thought they'd found the Columbia River. Six days later, after a difficult journey across the eastern Washington desert, they actually did reach the Columbia. While here, the corps camped on the north bank of what was then named Lewis's River—the Snake—on October 10, 1805.

Lewiston's historical center, the Luna House Museum, also has some exhibits of interest to Lewis and Clark buffs. One recent installation fea-

Near the confluence of the Clearwater and Snake rivers, Lewiston-Clarkston, Idaho-Washington.

tured a Lewis and Clark exhibit designed by California eighth-graders which won the National History Day contest. Another exhibit worth a look is a series of portraits of Chief Joseph by artist Dan Piel. The haunting paintings show the Nez Perce leader in his youth, maturity, and old age. The Luna House Museum is located at 3rd and C streets and is open from 9 a.m. to 5 p.m. Tuesday through Saturday.

Lewiston/Clarkston is also the unofficial headquarters for Hells Canyon, the deepest gorge in North America (deeper than the Grand Canyon because the Snake River runs smack dab against Idaho's towering Seven Devils mountain range). The Hells Canyon National Recreation Area straddles the Snake River south of Lewiston and includes parts of the Wallowa Whitman National Forest in Oregon and the Nez Perce and Payette national forests of Idaho.

When Congress created the recreation area in 1975, it saved some of the best whitewater rapids in the United States by protecting sixty-seven miles of the Snake River. Congress also set aside 215,000 acres as the Hells Canyon Wilderness, with an outstanding network of trails open only to hikers and horseback riders.

Abundant in fish, wildlife, and geologic splendor, Hells Canyon is a sight to see. Sturgeon up to twelve feet long swim the depths of the Snake River. Elk, mule deer, bighorn sheep, cougar, bobcat, bear, and smaller mammals patrol the mountainsides. More than thirty outfitters offer float, jet boat, or whitewater trips through the canyon. For a list, contact the Hells Canyon National Recreation Area headquarters in Clarkston at (509) 758-0616. (The number for boat trip reservations is (509) 758-1957.) Private rafters and jet-boaters may also ply the area, but a Forest Service permit is required before launching.

From Lewiston, continue west on US 12 into Clarkston and Washington state. It's all downriver from here.

*Denotes town on Clark's return route through the Big Hole, 1806

LODGING

WHITEHALL, MONTANA

Chief Motel, (406) 287-3921, 303 E. Legion. $40-$60.

Rice Motel, (406) 287-3895, 7 N. A St. Under $40.

TWIN BRIDGES, MONTANA

Kings Motel, (800) 222-5510, 307 S. Main St. Under $40.

Stardust Country Inn, (406) 684-5648, 409 N. Main St. Under $40.

DILLON, MONTANA

Best Western Paradise Inn, (800) 528-1234, 650 N. Montana St. $42-$48.

Creston Motel, (406) 683-2341, 335 S. Atlantic. $29.

Sacagawea Motel, (406) 683-2381, 775 N. Montana. Under $40.

Sundowner Motel, (800) 524-9746, 500 N. Montana St. $32-$33.

TownHouse Inns of Dillon, (800) 442-4667, 450 N. Interchange. $42-$46.

SALMON, IDAHO

Heritage Inn Bed & Breakfast, (208) 756-3174, 510 Lena St. $24-$35.

Stagecoach Inn, (208) 756-4251, US 93 North. $45-$67.

Suncrest Motel, (208) 756-2294, 705 Challis St. $32.

Wagons West Motel, (208) 756-4281, US 93 North. $31-$54.

NORTH FORK, IDAHO

North Fork Motel, (208) 865-2412, US 93. Under $40.

River's Fork Inn, (208) 865-2301, US 93.

GIBBONSVILLE, IDAHO

Broken Arrow, (208) 856-2241, US 93.

Lost Trail Inn, (208) 865-2222, US 93.

*WISDOM, MONTANA

Nez Perce Motel, (406) 689-3254. Under $30.

Sandman Motel, (406) 689-2689. Under $30.

*JACKSON, MONTANA

Jackson Hot Springs Lodge, (406) 834-3151. $24 and up.

SULA, MONTANA

Broad Axe Lodge, (406) 821-3878, 1237 East Fork Rd.

Camp Creek Inn Bed & Breakfast, (406) 821-3508. US 93, $40-$60.

CONNER, MONTANA

Rocky Knob Lodge, (406) 821-3520, US 93. Under $40.

DARBY, MONTANA

Bud & Shirley's Motel, (406) 821-3401. $40-$60.

Honey's Motel, (406) 821-3111, US 93. Under $40.

Triple Creek Guest Ranch, (406) 821-4664, West Fork State Route.

Wilderness Motel, (406) 821-3405, 308 S. Main St. Under $40.

HAMILTON, MONTANA

Best Western Hamilton Inn, (800) 528-1234, US 93. $46.

Bitterroot Motel, (406) 363-1142, US 93. Under $40.

Deer Crossing Bed & Breakfast, (406) 363-2232, 396 Hayes Creek Rd. $50-$75.

TownHouse Inn, (800) 442-4667, US 93. $49-$57.

LOLO, MONTANA

Piney Woods Motel, (406) 273-6993, US 12. $40-$60.

MISSOULA, MONTANA

BelAire Motel, (800) 543-3184, 300 E. Broadway. $40-$45.

City Center Motel, (406) 543-3193, 338 E. Broadway. $32.

4-B's Inn South, (800) 272-9500, US 93. $43.

Goldsmith's Inn Bed & Breakfast, (406) 721-6732, 809 E. Front St. $65-$95.

Holiday Inn-Missoula Parkside, (800) HOLIDAY, 200 S. Patee St. $64-$73.

Traveler's Inn Motel, (406) 728-8330, 4850 N. Reserve St. $34.

LOLO HOT SPRINGS, MONTANA

Fort Lolo Hot Springs Motel, (406) 273-2290, US 12. $50-$60.

POWELL, IDAHO

Lochsa Lodge, (208) 942-3405, US 12. $28-$38.

LOWELL, IDAHO

Ryan's Wilderness Inn, (208) 926-4706, US 12. $30-$35.

Three Rivers Resort, (208) 926-4430, US 12.

KOOSKIA, IDAHO

Bear Hollow Bed & Breakfast, (800) 831-3713, US 12. $55-$85.

Ida-Lee Motel, (208) 926-0166. Under $30.

Looking Glass Lodge Bed & Breakfast, (208) 926-0855, US 12. $60.

KAMIAH, IDAHO

Clearwater Motel, (208) 935-2671, US 12. $30.

Lewis-Clark Resort, (208) 935-2556, US 12.

Snooky's Carriage Inn, (208) 935-2531, US 12. $25-$35.

OROFINO, IDAHO

Riverside Motel, (208) 476-5711, US 12. Under $40.

Vacation Land Motel, (208) 476-4012, US 12.

White Pine Motel, (208) 476-7093, 222 Brown Ave. $36.

LENORE, IDAHO

Harper's Bend River Inn Bed & Breakfast, (208) 486-6666, US 12. $65-$75.

LEWISTON, IDAHO

Carriage House Bed & Breakfast, (208) 746-4506, 611 5th St. $65-$85.

El Rancho Motel, (208) 743-8517, 2240 3rd Ave. N. $30-$35.

Ramada Inn, (800) 228-2828, 621 21st St. $66-$94.

Sacajawea Motor Inn, (800) 333-1393, 1824 Main St. $48-$52.

Super 8, (800) 800-8000, 3120 N. South Highway. $48.

Tapadera Motor Inn, (800) 722-TAPS, 1325 Main St. $40-$55.

CAMPING

THREE FORKS, MONTANA

Lewis & Clark Caverns State Park, (406) 287-3541, west on MT 2. Campground and cabins.

WHITEHALL, MONTANA

Pipestone Campground, (406) 287-5224, 41 Bluebird Lane (I-90 Exit 241, six miles west of town).

TWIN BRIDGES, MONTANA

Jefferson River Camp, (406) 684-5262, MT 41 between Silver Star and Twin Bridges.

Stardust Country Inn RV Park, (406) 684-5648, 409 N. Main St.

DILLON, MONTANA

Armstead Campground, (406) 683-6674, I-15 Exit 44, at Clark Canyon Reservoir.

Clark Canyon Reservoir, I-15 Exit 44.

Dillon KOA, (406) 683-2749, 735 W. Park St.

Southside RV Park, (406) 683-2244, I-15 Exit 62, then right on Poindexter.

SALMON, IDAHO

Century II Campground, (208) 756-2063, US 93.

Salmon Meadows Campground, (208) 756-2640, US 93 at St. Charles St.

NORTH FORK, IDAHO

North Fork Campground, (208) 865-2412, US 93.

GIBBONSVILLE, IDAHO

Broken Arrow Campground, (208) 865-2241, US 93.

Twin Creek, (208) 865-2383, US 93. Primitive sites.

*WISDOM, MONTANA

May Creek, (406) 689-2431, west of Big Hole National Battlefield on MT 43.

Trails Rest, (406) 689-3149, west of Big Hole National Battlefield.

*JACKSON, MONTANA

Jackson Hot Springs Lodge, (406) 834-3151, on County Rd. 278.

*BANNACK, MONTANA

Bannack State Park, (406) 834-3413, four miles south of County Rd. 278.

SULA, MONTANA

Lost Trail Hot Springs Resort, (406) 821-3574, US 93 south of Sula.

Moosehead Campground, (406) 821-3327, US 93.

Spring Gulch Campground, north of Sula on US 93. Primitive sites.

Sula Store & Campground, (406) 821-3364, US 93.

HAMILTON, MONTANA

Angler's Roost RV Park, (406) 363-1268, four miles south on US 93.

KOA-Bitterroot, (406) 363-2430, nine miles south on US 93.

Lick Creek Campground, (406) 821-3840, twelve miles south on US 93.

Riverside RV Park, (406) 363-3744, 1.5 miles north on US 93.

LOLO, MONTANA

Bitterroot Gateway RV Park, (406) 273-6034, US 93.

Lee Creek, (406) 329-3750, twenty-six miles west on US 12. Primitive sites.

Lewis and Clark Campground, (406) 329-3750, fifteen miles west on US 12. Primitive sites.

MISSOULA, MONTANA

El Mar KOA, (406) 549-0881, Reserve St. to Tina Ave.

Outpost Family Campground, (406) 549-2016, north of town on US 93.

LOLO HOT SPRINGS, MONTANA

Lolo Hot Springs RV Park & Campground, (406) 273-2290, US 12.

POWELL, IDAHO

Jerry Johnson, (208) 942-3113, west on US 12. Primitive sites.

Wendover-Whitehouse, (208) 942-3113, west on US 12. Primitive sites.

LOWELL, IDAHO

Apgar, (208) 926-4275, east on US 12. Primitive sites.

Knife Edge, (208) 926-4275, east on US 12. Primitive sites.

Three Rivers Resort, (208) 926-4430, US 12.

Wild Goose, (208) 926-4275, east on US 12. Primitive sites.

Wilderness Gateway, (208) 926-4275, east on US 12. Primitive sites.

KAMIAH, IDAHO

Lewis-Clark Resort RV Park, (208) 935-2556, US 12.

OROFINO, IDAHO

Hidden Village, (208) 476-3416, west on US 12.

Vacation Land RV Park, (208) 476-4012, west on US 12.

LENORE, IDAHO

Dworshak State Park, (208) 476-5994, one mile north of town to Cavendish, then ten miles east.

LEWISTON, IDAHO

Hells Gate State Park, (208) 743-2363, four miles south on Snake River Ave.

RESTAURANTS

LA HOOD, MONTANA

Lewis and Clark Restaurant and Lounge, MT 2. Offers free RV camping with dinner purchase.

WHITEHALL, MONTANA

Land of Magic Too Supper Club, (406) 287-5252, 27 W. Legion. Steaks and seafood.

SILVER STAR, MONTANA

Barkell Hot Springs Supper Club and Lounge, just south of town on MT 41.

Star Bar, (406) 287-3648. Lunch and dinner.

TWIN BRIDGES, MONTANA

Blue Anchor Bar and Cafe, (406) 684-5655, 102 N. Main.

DILLON, MONTANA

Anna's Oven, (406) 683-5766. 120 S. Montana. Homemade food, lunches to go.

Bannack House, (406) 638-5088, 33 E. Bannack St. Italian food.

Crosswinds Restaurant, (406) 683-6370, 1008 S. Atlantic. Breakfast all day, prime rib on weekends.

Papa T's, (406) 683-6432, 10 N. Montana. Family-oriented restaurant featuring burgers, pizza.

Western Wok, (406) 683-2356, 17 E. Bannack. Chinese and American food.

SALMON, IDAHO

Granny's Steakhouse, (208) 756-2309, 1403 E. Main St. Burgers, pies, cinnamon rolls.

Shady Nook Restaurant, (208) 756-4182, US 93. Specialties include prime rib and seafood.

Union Avenue Depot, (208) 756-2095, 720 Union Ave. Steaks and pasta.

NORTH FORK, IDAHO

North Fork Cafe, (208) 865-2412, US 93. Hearty food popular with river rats.

River's Fork Inn, (208) 865-2301. Riverside dining featuring steaks and seafood.

GIBBONSVILLE, IDAHO

Broken Arrow, (208) 856-2241, US 93. Mexican food.

*WISDOM, MONTANA

Fetty's Bar & Cafe, (406) 689-3260. Specialties include shakes and burgers.

Pioneer Mountain Restaurant, (406) 689-3800. Home cooking.

*JACKSON, MONTANA

Jackson Hot Springs Lodge, (406) 834-3151.

Rose's Cantina Cafe, (406) 834-3100. Breakfast, lunch, and dinner.

SULA, MONTANA

La Fiesta Mexican Restaurant, (406) 821-3574, US 93. Indoor/outdoor dining.

CONNER, MONTANA

Rocky Knob Restaurant, (406) 821-3520, between Sula and Conner on US 93. Hickory-smoked ribs.

DARBY, MONTANA

Outpost Restaurant, (406) 821-3388. Between Sula and Darby on US 93.

Trapper's Family Restaurant, (406) 821-4465, 561 Main.

HAMILTON, MONTANA

Coffee Cup Cafe, (406) 363-3822, 500 S. 1st. Popular for breakfast.

The Grubstake, (406) 363-3068, 1017 Grubstake Rd. Mountainside dining with a wide menu.
Stavers Tavern, (406) 363-4433, 163 S. 2nd. Steaks, seafood, fine beer, and ales on tap.
Wanda's Wagon Wheel Steak House, (406) 363-1434, US 93. Hand-carved steaks to order.

VICTOR, MONTANA

Cantina La Cocina, (406) 642-3192, US 93. Homemade Mexican food.

STEVENSVILLE, MONTANA

Fort Owen Inn, (406) 777-3483, US 93. Steaks and beef.
Marie's Italian Cafe, (406) 777-3681, US 93.
Sam's Deli and Pizza, (406) 777-3500, 514 Main.

FLORENCE, MONTANA

Glenn's Cafe, (406) 273-2534, US 93. Famous for pie.

LOLO, MONTANA

Guy's Lolo Creek Steakhouse, (406) 273-2622, US 12. Western-style steaks, chicken.
Lolo Trail Cafe, (406) 273-6580, US 93.
P.J.'s Pizza and Pasta, (406) 273-0777, 6555 US 12.

MISSOULA, MONTANA

The Depot, (406) 728-7007, Railroad & Ryman. Steaks, salad bar, desserts.
Dos Lobos Restaurant, (406) 728-7092, 130 E. Broadway. Mexican-American food.
Mammyth Bakery Cafe, (406) 549-5542, 131 W. Main. Breakfast, lunch, baked goods galore.
The Mustard Seed, (406) 728-7825, 419 W. Front. Oriental and vegetarian food.
Old Town Cafe, (406) 728-9742, 127 W. Alder. Great breakfasts in funky atmosphere.
The Shack, (406) 549-9903, 222 W. Main. Another breakfast favorite, patio dining.
Zimarino's, (406) 549-7434, 424 N. Higgins. Popular for pizza and pasta.

LOLO HOT SPRINGS, MONTANA

Lolo Hot Springs, (406) 273-2290, US 12.

POWELL, IDAHO

Lochsa Lodge, (208) 942-3405, US 12. Fireside dining.

LOWELL, IDAHO

Three Rivers Resort, (208) 926-4430, US 12. Wide menu three meals a day.

SYRINGA, IDAHO

Syringa Cafe, US 12. Huckleberry pie heaven.

KOOSKIA, IDAHO

Rivers Cafe, (208) 926-4450, North Main.

KAMIAH, IDAHO

Jilinda's, (208) 935-0014, US 12. Family dining with great view of the Clearwater River.
Kamiah Cafe, (208) 935-2563, US 12. Homemade food.
Syringa Lounge & Steak House, (208) 935-0960, Idaho & 4th. Steaks and salad bar.

WEIPPE, IDAHO

Weippe Pizza & Cafe, (208) 435-4823, 118 N. Main. Creative pizzas and more. Closed Mondays and Tuesdays.

OROFINO, IDAHO

Konkol's Steakhouse, (208) 476-4312, 2000 Konkolville Rd. Steaks, seafood, lobster.

Lewis & Clark Trail Cafe, (208) 476-7548, 10290 US 12.

LEWISTON, IDAHO

Effie's Tavern, (208) 746-1889, 1120 Main St. Huge burgers.

Italian Gardens Cafe, (208) 743-7632, 1st Ave. and W. 22nd N. Sandwiches, pasta, seafood.

Jonathan's, (208) 746-3438, 301 D St. Wide menu including Mexican and Cajun fare.

Meriwether's Restaurant, (208) 799-1000, in the Ramada Inn. Fine dining.

Mighty Potato, (208) 746-7783. Idaho's specialty, prepared many ways.

Waffles N' More, (208) 743-5189, 1421 Main. Popular for breakfast, close to motels.

Zany Graze, (208) 746-8131, 2006 19th Ave. Sandwiches and barbecue in fun atmosphere.

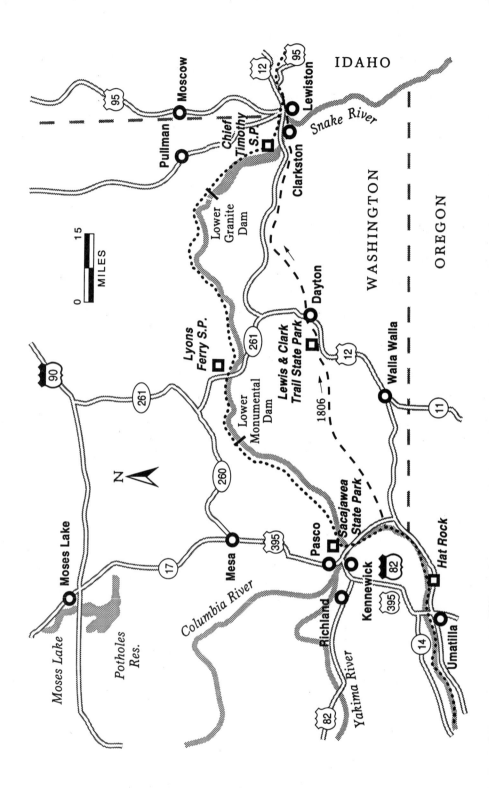

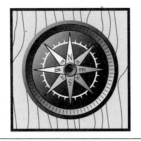

CHAPTER EIGHT

WASHINGTON AND OREGON

Men appear much satisfied with their trip, beholding with astonishment the high waves dashing against the rocks and this immense ocean.

- William Clark, November 18, 1805,
on the Pacific coast.

THE SNAKE RIVER

When most travelers think of the Northwest, they think of evergreen forests, snow-capped Cascade peaks, and copious amounts of rain. All those qualities are true of western Washington and Oregon, but the Inland Northwest could not be more different. East of the Cascades, Washington is dominated by arid, rolling hills and bisected by deep river canyons. It was this land Lewis and Clark floated through during the week of October 10-16, 1805, on their way to the Columbia River.

In Clarkston, Washington, a Lewis and Clark Timeline can be found at Hells Canyon Resort, 1550 Port Drive. Growing numbers of small-ship cruises ply these waters, too. Ask a travel agent about the "Spirit of Columbia" from Alaska Sightseeing Cruise West and "In the Wake of Lewis and Clark" from Special Expeditions.

The Snake River here is actually Lower Granite Lake, backed up by the Lower Granite Dam, which was the eighth and final dam built on the Columbia and Lower Snake rivers by the U.S. Army Corps of Engineers. Chief Timothy State Park, eight miles west of Clarkston on U.S. Highway 12, offers an excellent beach and pleasant camping. The park is also home to the Alpowai Interpretive Center, which includes information on the Lewis and Clark expedition. Unfortunately, its hours of operation have been curtailed in recent years due to state budget cutbacks.

Chief Timothy State Park was built near the site of Alpowai, a major Nez Perce settlement at the junction of Alpowa Creek and the Snake

River. The town was led by Chief Timothy and Chief Red Wolf, who—like many Washingtonians after him—ran an apple orchard. In the 1860s, when the second treaty with the U.S. government drastically reduced the size of the Nez Perce reservation, Alpowai found itself outside the reservation boundaries. White settlers flowed into the area, and by the late 1880s the small town of Silcott overshadowed Alpowai, only to deteriorate by the 1920s and eventually disappear. In 1975, Lower Granite Dam's gates were closed, and water covered the Nez Perce village site.

After a steep climb up US 12, the panorama shifts again, this time to rolling fields of grain. This is the edge of the Palouse, one of the nation's most beautiful and productive wheat-growing areas. An interpretive sign mentions that on their way home May 3, 1806, the Lewis and Clark expedition camped at a grove of cottonwoods near the highway after a tedious twenty-eight-mile journey up Pataha Creek. Supper that night included scant rations of dried meat and dog. Throughout their travels in the Northwest, the party turned frequently to dog meat to help extend their rations—a phenomenon that had to unnerve Lewis's steadfast companion, Seaman, at least a little. The next morning, they followed a branch of the Indian trail they had followed up the creek. The trail can still be faintly seen on the north side of the highway across from the historic marker.

By now, today's traveler has lost the river Lewis and Clark worked so hard to find. Mayview Road, located past the rest areas east of Pataha, provides access to Lower Granite Dam and a backroad that follows the Snake River and the Lewis and Clark route of 1805. US 12 runs parallel at a distance, following more closely the return route of 1806.

Pomeroy is a major agricultural hub for Garfield County. The city park has a pool, lots of shade, and even a small golf course. Centennial Boulevard, planted for the one hundredth anniversary of Washington's statehood, boasts a lovely garden.

Twenty-two miles west of Pomeroy, Washington Highway 261 leads to Lyons Ferry State Park, nestled at the confluence of the Snake and Palouse rivers. The expedition had earlier named the Palouse River for George Drouillard, misspelling it as usual "Drewyer." Throughout the journals, Drouillard was praised as a hunter, scout, and interpreter. He was a good friend to Lewis and is considered one of the two or three most valuable members of the expedition.

Like Chief Timothy State Park, Lyons Ferry has a superb little beach area, perfect for cooling off on a blazing summer day. (Temperatures in Eastern Washington frequently exceed one hundred degrees Fahrenheit. in the summer, so travelers should take advantage of any available means to keep cool.) Nearby Palouse Falls State Park is also worth the drive, largely because it seems entirely out of place in this denuded landscape. You're driving through a landscape with no water in sight when suddenly a gorge opens up and a 190-foot waterfall plunges majestically

Historical marker at Lyons Ferry State Park, Washington.

into a small pond. There's no easy way down to the pool, but some folks make the hike anyway.

Camping is available at both parks. From there it's possible to follow the Snake River's north side on backroads; take Washington 261 and 260 west of US 395, which then heads south to the Tri-Cities, or backtrack to US 12. The last option is preferable for anyone wishing a look at Lewis and Clark Trail State Park.

The park is just west of Dayton, another agricultural center and the seat of Columbia County. The site's heavy woodsiness is in extreme contrast to many of southeastern Washington's other state parks. The preserve sits on both sides of US 12, with the campground located on the northwest side and a day-use picnic area (and Lewis and Clark marker) situated on the southeast. The marker explains how, in this area, the corps ate cow parsnip and dog for lack of better food. Again, they were on their way home, and camped west of present-day Dayton on May 1, 1806, and east of town May 2.

Waitsburg is a small community at the junction of US 12 and Washington 124. It is one of only a few towns whose welcome sign trumpets its location on the Lewis and Clark Trail—a rare sight sure to change as the expedition nears its bicentennial in 2004-2006. From here, it's possible to bypass the Tri-Cities and follow the corps' homeward trek and

Palouse Falls, Washington.

Campsite marker along Snake River, Lewiston , Idaho.

take a shortcut to the Columbia through Walla Walla on US 12. To stay
on the westward trail, follow Washington 124 west to the Tri-Cities.

MEETING THE COLUMBIA

Travelers approaching the Tri-Cities on Washington 124 will find a
wealth of camping opportunities along the lower reaches of the Snake
River. These mostly come courtesy of the U.S. Army Corps of Engineers.
Areas include Fishhook, Charbonneau, and Hood parks, each boasting a
swimming beach, boat launch, and trailer dump station. As with other
public campgrounds in eastern Washington, lawns at these parks are irri-
gated on a daily or nightly basis. Tenters should take care to make sure
their shelter is placed far from sprinkler heads.

Sacajawea State Park near Pasco has no camping, but it is home to a
fine, small interpretive center. This site has fared better than the
Alpowai Center at Chief Timothy State Park; in recent summers, the
park has established a corps of volunteer park hosts who've been able to
keep the center open for visitors.

The center was built by the Work Projects Administration in 1939
and renovated in 1978. The park uses the spelling "Sacajawea" which, although considered inaccurate by many scholars, is definitely the most

common spelling popularly used in the Northwest. A plaque notes that Sacagawea is now the preferred scholarly spelling, and that is the one used in most of the center's displays.

Sacagawea's contributions to the expedition are extensively and accurately explained. Other exhibits praise the pairing of Lewis and Clark. "Both men were experienced leaders and seasoned wilderness travelers. Lewis had commanded a frontier fort; Clark had dealt extensively with Indians. The skills one man lacked, the other possessed," one display reads. "In temperament, this was also true. Lewis was intellectual, speculative, and moody. Clark was pragmatic, extroverted, and even-tempered. Most important of all, Lewis and Clark worked together so harmoniously that it is difficult to believe the expedition actually had two individual leaders."

Viewed from the center, the Snake River is on the left and the Columbia River is on the right. The corps arrived in the area October 16, 1805, to a most hearty welcome from the Columbia River Indians—mostly Wanapums and Yakimas. Clark wrote: "After we had our camped fixed and fires made a chief came at the head of about 200 men singing and beating on their drums. They formed a half-circle around us and sung for some time. We gave them all smoke and spoke to their chief as well as we could by signs." By that night, the Corps of Discovery had logged 3,714 miles from Camp Wood.

The explorers had become used to the sight and taste of salmon long before this point, but they were astounded at the spectacle they met at the junction of the Snake and Columbia. They arrived at the height of fall chinook runs, and the men wrote of the immense quantities of salmon jumping from the rivers. Clark seemed frustrated at being unable to describe the spectacle. The corps was also confused by the vast numbers of dead salmon on the riverbanks. They didn't yet know that Pacific salmon, unlike Atlantic varieties, die after spawning, so they spurned the natives' offer of fish in favor of purchasing still more dogs.

The expedition camped at the confluence two nights, during which time the men made celestial observations, updated their journals, mended clothes, and bought at least forty dogs. Clark also explored the Columbia several miles upstream, during which time he met with more Indians and was shown the mouth of the Yakima—or Tapteel—River. On October 18, a council was held and in the afternoon, the expedition at long last moved onto the Columbia River.

Sacajawea State Park is open April through September from 6:30 a.m. to dusk, and the interpretive center is open from 1 p.m. to 5 p.m. Friday through Tuesday, May through September. To get to the park from Washington 124, turn right at the intersection for US 12. Immediately after crossing the Snake River, get into the left-hand lane. Signs point to the park, which is two miles from the intersection. For more information or the latest operating schedule, call (509) 545-2361.

A colorful railroad town, Ainsworth, once occupied land near the confluence of the Snake and Columbia. The town was founded in 1879 when a railroad bridge was being built over the Snake River. A historical marker at the turnoff for Sacajawea State Park notes "it was a wild and lusty town, noted for brawls, gunfights, and hangings."

From the park, Lewis and Clark's route is most closely followed by taking US 12 south to Wallula, where the traveler picks up US 730 southwest to Umatilla, Oregon. This is the route we will follow next. It's also possible to spend the night in Washington's Tri-Cities—Kennewick, Pasco, and Richland—and take Interstate 82 south from Kennewick. In this event, it will be necessary to backtrack east about seven miles from Umatilla on US 730 to reach Hat Rock, the next major trail landmark.

Travelers who love wine might want to take an optional route from the Tri-Cities to the Columbia River Gorge. I-82 west of the Tri-Cities travels through the Yakima Valley, an area filled with more than a dozen wineries, numerous fruit stands, and a vital mix of Anglo-Hispanic-Native American culture. The Yakima Valley Highway, a scenic two-laner, parallels the interstate much of the way. Head south to Oregon on US 97 at Toppenish, a town full of murals and the excellent Yakima Nation cultural center. From Toppenish, the Columbia River Gorge is just sixty miles over Satus Pass. Either route totals about 125 miles from the Tri-Cities.

The Tri-Cities have a combined population of close to 100,000. For years, the Tri-Cities have had a roller-coaster economy heavily dependent on nuclear energy and the infamous Hanford Works—a way of life explained via videotapes and hands-on exhibits at the U.S. Department of Energy's Hanford Science Center, 825 Jadwin in Richland. But recent years have seen some change, notably a trend toward research on how to contain (and clean up after) the nuclear genie. As a result, the Tri-Cities economy seems to be chugging mightily along, with one of the highest home-appreciation rates of any metropolitan area in the nation: values shot up twenty percent in one recent year.

With three rivers at their disposal, Tri-Cities residents enjoy all kinds of water sports, from boating and fishing to swimming and water-skiing. If the rivers seem too intimidating, there's always the Oasis Waterworks at 6321 W. Canal Drive, Kennewick, a nine-acre amusement park with waterslides, a river ride, swimming pool, batting cages, picnic grounds, and more. For additional information on the Tri-Cities, call (800) 666-1929.

HOMEWARD BOUND: THE LAND ROUTE

On their way back east in the spring of 1806, Lewis and Clark decided to try an overland shortcut from the mouth of the Walla Walla River northeast to the confluence of the Clearwater and Snake and the

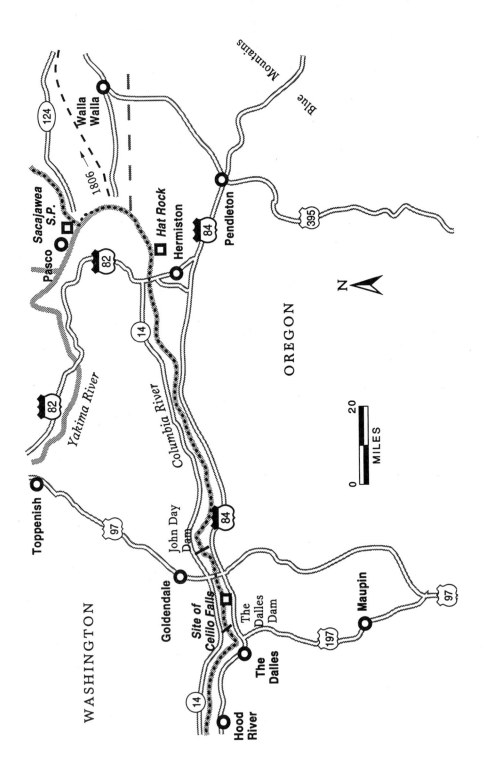

land of the Nez Perce—a trek roughly followed by US 12 through Walla Walla, Waitsburg, and Dayton.

The jumping-off spot was present-day Wallula, a small town south of the Tri-Cities best known for the large Boise Cascade plant on the outskirts of town. Near here, the Corps of Discovery spent three days camped with the friendly Walla Walla Indians and their leader, Chief Yellept, whom they had met on the way west and promised to visit again. "He appeared much gratified at seeing us return, invited us to remain at his village three or four days, and assured us that we should be furnished with a plenty of such food as they had themselves, and some horses to assist us on our journey," Lewis wrote.

Madam Dorian Memorial Park is located just north of the junction of US 12 and US 730, with camping, picnicking, fishing access, and an RV dump station. The park is named for Marie Dorian, an Iowa Indian who—if it weren't for Sacagawea's amazing adventures—may have become the most famous Native American woman in history.

Dorian traveled west with the Wilson Price Hunt party of Astorians in 1811. The Astorians had left Missouri to establish trading posts along the Columbia and arrived at Wallula in January 1812. Later, members of the Dorian party trekked to the Snake River country to trap. There, the men were killed by Bannack Indians. Remarkably, Marie and her two young children survived the winter hiding in the Blue Mountains. She managed to get her children to safety in the spring, and lived the rest of her years in Walla Walla and the Willamette Valley.

From Wallula, it's a half-hour drive east on US 12 to the town so nice they named it twice. Walla Walla, meaning "many waters" or "small rapid stream," is best known as home of the Whitman Mission National Historic Site, a crucial outpost in the history of U.S. westward expansion.

In November 1834, the Reverend Samuel Parker traveled around New York State asking for missionaries to go west with him the following spring. Marcus Whitman, a country doctor from Wheeling, N.Y., agreed to make the trip. Together, Parker and Whitman got as far as the Green River, where Whitman decided to return to the States to prepare for a trip the following year—a trip designed to establish the Whitman Mission.

The next spring, Whitman set off anew. With him were two things that would forever alter the course of American history: A wagon, which he was determined to take all the way west, and his bride, Narcissa Prentiss Whitman. She, too, had heard Parker's speech two autumns before and had yearned to make the trip. Narcissa made it all the way, and with Eliza Spalding—another missionary's wife—was the first white woman to cross the continent overland. The wagon was converted to a cart in Idaho and later traveled as far as Fort Boise, farther than any other wheeled vehicle before it. These successes inspired many frontier families to try the trip themselves.

Together, the Whitmans founded Waiilatpu, "Place of the Rye Grass," on the banks of the Walla Walla River. For the next decade, they would serve as missionaries, teachers, and friends to the Cayuse. Their efforts brought only limited success and were destined to end in tragedy. In the meantime, however, the mission served as an important station on the Oregon Trail during the emigration's first few years. Travelers stopped for rest, supplies, medical treatment, and the Whitmans' hospitality.

Whitman thought that for his mission to succeed he needed to change the Cayuse's nomadic ways. He encouraged them to farm, but few went along. The Cayuse were also indifferent to religious books, worship, and school. By 1842, reports of the mission's troubles caused Methodist officials back in the United States to order Waiilatpu closed. But Whitman, convinced the mission should stay open, made a midwinter ride back east to plead his case. Impressed by his commitment, the officials changed their minds.

Still, the cultural differences remained and—with the coming of ever more whites—deepened. In 1847, emigrants brought a measles epidemic that spread rapidly among the Cayuse, who had no resistance to the disease. Soon, half the tribe was dead. When Dr. Whitman's medicine helped whites but not Indians, many Cayuse believed they were being poisoned to make way for the pioneers. On November 29, 1847, a band of Cayuse attacked the mission and killed the Whitmans and eleven others.

Through its exhibits, the Whitman Mission clearly shows the collision between the native people of the West and those who pursued religious zeal and America's "manifest destiny." A small interpretive center tells the sad story from both sides. Other sites at the Whitman Mission include a great grave in which the massacre victims were buried and an excavated area where early mission buildings are outlined. Visitors can get a good view of the entire grounds by taking the short, steep walk to the Whitman Memorial Shaft. From the top, you can see all of Waiilaptu, as well as the Blue Mountains. Living history demonstrations featuring pioneer and Indian crafts are given on summer weekends.

Whitman Mission is located seven miles west of Walla Walla on US 12. The site is open daily from 8 a.m. to 6 p.m. June through August and from 8 a.m. to 4:30 p.m. the rest of the year. The cost of admission is $2 per person, or $4 per family group. Call (509) 522-6360 for more information.

Although primarily an agricultural and regional retail and service center, Walla Walla and its neighbor, College Place, are home to three colleges: Whitman College and Walla Walla College (both four-year schools) and the two-year Walla Walla Community College. From Walla Walla, US 12 arcs northeast to Waitsburg and Dayton. For more information on these towns, see the "Snake River" section at the beginning of this chapter.

THE COLUMBIA PLATEAU AND THE DALLES

US 730 starts its run alongside the Columbia River at the Wallula Gap just a few miles north of the Oregon state line. From here, the highway hugs the Columbia, offering splendid vistas. A turnout about two miles south of the US 12 junction tells the Cayuse legend of "Two Sisters," who may still be seen in rock on the cliffs above the road.

Lewis and Clark didn't mention the Two Sisters in their journals, but they did write of Hat Rock; Clark, in fact, is credited with giving the landmark its name. The Hat Rock State Park entrance is just west of the junction of US 730 and Oregon 37. The road that leads east of the rock winds up in a private subdivision; the road to the left leads to an absolutely gorgeous little park area with big shade trees, picnic tables, and a pond filled with ducks and geese eager for handouts.

Looking south across the Columbia River with The Dalles and Mount Hood in the background.

View of the Columbia River near The Dalles, Oregon.

The Lewis and Clark historical marker is located at the upper parking lot. It notes the captains passed and named this point on October 19, 1805. Clark climbed to the top of the landmark and said that, from its summit, a snow-covered mountain could be seen to the northwest. He first thought it was Mount Saint Helens, but it was really Mount Adams, Washington's second-highest peak at 12,307 feet. Homeward bound, the expedition passed Hat Rock again on April 27, 1806.

There is no camping in the park itself, but a private campground is located just outside the site boundaries. Other activities include swimming and boating. Climbing Hat Rock is no longer permitted.

From Hat Rock, continue west on US 730 to Umatilla, home of McNary Dam, the first of four on the Oregon-Washington border. Two highways parallel the Columbia River the length of the Washington-Oregon border from Umatilla west. Washington 14 is a two-lane road that generally sits higher above the river with better views, while I-84 allows the traveler to really make some time.

Washington 14 has no services between I-82 and the junction with US 97 some eighty-two miles west, but camping is available in two places. Crow Butte State Park, on an island accessible by causeway, is near the Lewis and Clark campsites of October 20, 1805, and April 25, 1806. Maryhill State Park near the US 97 intersection is a popular oasis for camping and sailboarding.

Hat Rock along the Columbia River near Umatilla, Oregon.

Other landmarks near Maryhill State Park include the Maryhill Museum of Art and a replica of Britain's Stonehenge. Both were built by the somewhat eccentric railroad magnate Sam Hill. He wanted Stonehenge to serve as a monument to peace. Maryhill Museum, meanwhile, is sometimes called the nation's most isolated art museum. Its priceless collection includes many Rodin sculptures, Indian artifacts, Russian icons, antique chess sets, and personal possessions donated by Queen Marie of Romania, all showcased in a lovely, lonely building overlooking the Gorge.

People traveling the Washington side may want to take a short side trip to the town of Goldendale, Washington, eleven miles up US 97, if for no other reason than to see the splendid mountain panorama on the plateau above the river gorge. If the weather is clear, the mountains may be "out," which is Pacific Northwest lingo for the peaks being visible. From south to north they are Mount Hood (elevation 11,245 feet), Mount Saint Helens (8,365 feet), Mount Adams (12,307 feet), and Mount Rainier (14,410 feet). Goldendale has the full range of visitor services, as well as the nation's largest telescope open to the general public at Goldendale Observatory State Park.

Horsethief Lake State Park is a satellite area of Maryhill State Park, and it is famous for its excellent Indian petroglyphs, including "She Who Watches," perhaps the most famous native drawing in the Northwest. Sadly, the rock art area was closed to the public after vandalism during the summer of 1993. Tours are still available by reservation on Friday and Saturday at 10 a.m. For information, contact the park staff or call (509) 767-1159.

On the Oregon side, the Columbia takes the starring role, even though it is little more than a lake. As has the Missouri River, the Columbia River has been greatly changed by the dams along its length. It's scarcely possible to imagine the raging, churning Columbia encountered by Lewis and Clark in 1805-1806. On the plus side, however, the U.S. Army Corps of Engineers provides abundant visitor facilities and recreational access at all its locations. The centers downriver at the Bonneville Dam are probably the most popular, but visitors may also want to visit the McNary Dam at Umatilla, John Day Dam (with the world's highest lock lift, 110 feet) at Rufus, and The Dalles Dam near the town of the same name.

On the Columbia Plateau, the traveler joins another historic route in addition to the one taken by Lewis and Clark. During the mid-nineteenth century, tens of thousands of Americans passed this way on the last leg of their journey to the fertile river valleys of western Oregon. Remnants of the Oregon Trail may still be seen in several locations near I-84, the most notable near the town of Biggs at Exit 104. Drive west from Biggs on US 30 and watch for the Oregon Trail marker on the road's south side.

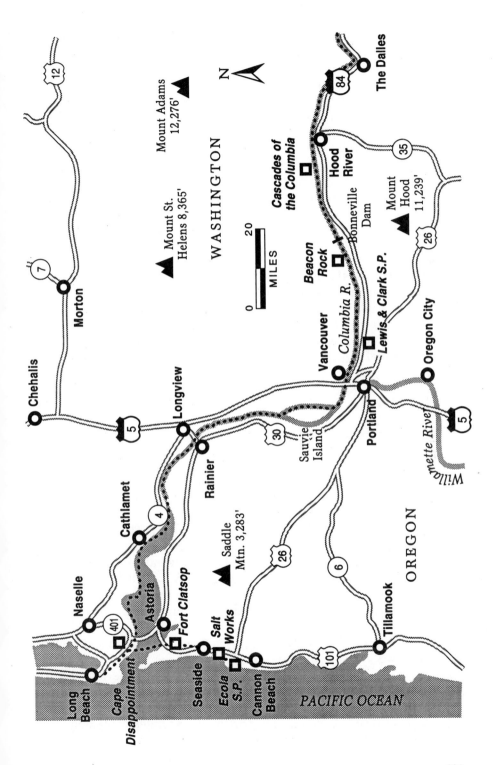

A bit farther west, the traveler comes to a small settlement called Celilo. This was once the greatest fishing area and gathering point along the Columbia River and a place revered by the Indians who called this river gorge home. Lewis and Clark reached a falls—the first of four major obstacles they encountered on the Columbia—on October 22, 1805, and spent two days negotiating the barrier.

At Celilo, the Columbia swept into several narrow channels and dropped a total of thirty-eight feet. The men had to portage around the greatest drop of twenty feet, and found themselves besieged with fleas. "Every man of the party was obliged to strip naked during the time of taking over the canoes, that they might have an opportunity of brushing the fleas off their legs and bodies," Clark wrote. Celilo Falls were inundated by the waters of The Dalles Dam in 1957, changing the Indians' way of life forever. Travelers who have been proceeding west on I-84 will also get their first view of Mount Hood around this area.

No sooner had Lewis and Clark made it through Celilo Falls than the corps was faced with The Dalles, where the river again narrowed and spilled over a great series of rapids. Here, the white men amazed the local Indians by riding their canoes and much of the cargo straight through the Short Narrows. Three miles farther downriver, the party reached the Long Narrows and again shot the rapids. The exhausted corps then camped several nights at the "Rock Fort" site now buried amid The Dalles's riverfront industrial area.

THE COLUMBIA RIVER GORGE

The Dalles marks the traveler's entrance into the Columbia River Gorge National Scenic Area, the first region so designated in the United States. Quite simply, the Gorge is an area of sublime scenic splendor and recreational choices so abundant it would take weeks to exhaust the possibilities.

Once they passed the Short and Long Narrows of The Dalles, Lewis and Clark had just one major obstacle remaining: the Cascades of the Columbia. On the way there, the party enjoyed several days of relatively calm waters between The Dalles and Hood River. But although the water was placid, relations with the region's Indians were not; in fact, tensions rose higher here than in any place since the Teton Sioux country back in South Dakota.

Unlike the friendly bands at the confluence of the Snake and Columbia, many of the Indians farther downriver partook in thievery, deception, and begging, perhaps influenced by their past experiences with early white traders near the mouth of the Columbia. (It was in the mid-Columbia region that Lewis and Clark first saw wool clothing and blankets, powder flasks, and guns, all signs of other whites preceding them from the west.) Moreover, many of the Columbia River people were dirty and infested with fleas or lice, afflictions they passed on to the newcomers. As the corps moved through the Celilo-Dalles stretch, either Twisted Hair or Tetoharsky of the Nez Perce heard a rumor that one of the local tribes planned to massacre the white men. This story may have sprung from the Nez Perce's own mistrust of the Columbia River tribes—both men decided to leave the corps and return home after the passage through The Dalles—but the captains decided not to take any chances. With the local Indians watching, the men made a great show of examining their stores of weapons and ammunition, making sure all were in proper working order.

The Corps of Discovery successfully made it through the last water barrier, the Cascades of the Columbia, on November 1-2, 1805. The rapids here were known as the Upper and Lower Cascades; Clark came to call the Upper rapids "the Great Chute." The baggage was portaged through this area, but the empty canoes once again made it through the rapids unscathed. Soon after the passage, Clark noted in his journal the presence of "a remarkable high rock...about 800 feet high and 400 yards round." He named it Beacon Rock, and it is indeed the world's second-largest freestanding rock monolith, second only to Gibraltar.

Once again, the traveler has a choice of driving Oregon's I-84 or Washington 14 through the Gorge (with the US 197 bridge at The Dalles offering the last free river crossing until the Portland-Vancouver metropolitan area). Both sides have plenty to offer. We'll look at I-84 first.

The Dalles is home to the new Columbia George Discovery Center, featuring varied exhibits, a "river gallery," a multimedia theater, and a living history park with Lewis and Clark interpretation. The center is open from 10 a.m. to 6 p.m. daily March 15 through November 15 and Thursday through Sunday the rest of the year. Admission is $6.50 for adults, $5.50 for senior citizens, and $3 for ages 6 to 16. (Children age 5 and under are free.) A cafe and store are available, too. For more information, call (541) 296-8600.

Hood River is unofficial Gorge headquarters, and a town that has changed dramatically with the influx of sailboarders, rock climbers, bungee jumpers, and other (mostly) youthful adventurers. Hood River plays host to some of the world's premiere sailboarding competitions (notably the High Wind Classic in late June), as well as a full calendar of festivals such as the Apple Jam, a music festival held in late August. Hood River also serves as a gateway to Mount Hood, with Oregon 35 south of town traversing the south shoulder of Oregon's highest peak.

Cascade Locks is home port for the Sternwheeler *Columbia Gorge*, a pleasure boat that offers a narrated Lewis and Clark cruise every day during the summer. Another daily sailing focuses on the Oregon Trail. No matter what the topic, the sternwheeler is a good way to get to know the Gorge, or at least a small part of it. For more information on sailing times, call (503) 223-3928.

At one time, a natural bridge spanned the Columbia River near what is now Cascade Locks. Indian legend traces this "Bridge of the Gods" to Ka'nax, a chief who ruled the tribes on both sides of the Columbia. Ka'nax used the bridge to carry on love affairs with two different princesses: Wy'east (Mount Hood) and Pahto (Mount Adams). Ultimately, the gods of these two mountains destroyed the natural bridge, ending both the romances and Ka'nax's reign. Scientists explain it a bit differently, but with similar results. Around A.D. 1100, a massive landslide crumbled the bridge and created several sets of rapids within a five-mile stretch of the Columbia River—the same rapids that slowed Lewis and Clark's passage in 1805.

If you visit only one dam on your Lewis and Clark journey, Bonneville Dam is probably the best choice. It has a visitor's facility on both the Washington and Oregon sides, and each tells the important role hydropower plays in the Northwest economy. The fish ladders may be Bonneville Dam's most popular exhibit. Children especially enjoy watching salmon swim through the maze-like structures that have been erected to help fish past the dams. Here, people employed as fish counters sit by a window all day and keep tabs on how many fish swim by. This close to the Pacific, the numbers are high. But the salmon have many more dams to pass before they reach their spawning grounds upriver. For wild salmon, life in the Columbia River is more than ever an uphill struggle for survival.

A new lock was recently built at Bonneville Dam. The original lock, completed in 1938, was the first and smallest of eight ultimately constructed along the Columbia-Snake river system. Only two standard 42-foot by 220-foot barges could be locked through Bonneville at any one time, so any groups of three or more had to be separated, and lockages at Bonneville took up to six times as long as those upriver. It was a waste of water, too: Each lockage uses about seventeen million gallons of water, enough to supply electricity to a Northwest home for about a year.

Moreover, Bonneville is the busiest of the eight locks. In 1991, more than nine million tons of shippage passed through here, more than any of the locks upstream. Petroleum products are the primary products shipped upstream, and logs and grain are the major commodities moving downriver. The new lock increases Bonneville's shipping capacity to thirty million tons annually, with the average passage time through the locks slated to decrease from more than twelve hours to less than two hours. A viewing area was expected to open by late spring 1994.

Just west of Bonneville, I-84 travelers have the opportunity to leave the freeway and drive the Columbia River Scenic Highway, a twenty-two-mile masterpiece of engineering that provides close-up access to the famous Gorge waterfalls, as well as to Crown Point, a promontory 733 feet above the river.

Each set of falls has its own character and beauty. Horsetail Falls unfurls like a banner, while Wahkeena Falls cascades in a mass of curlicues. Multnomah Falls is world-famous and easily accessed from the interstate, as is Bridal Veil Falls. And that's just the start. Other falls can be reached by trails. The Gorge is a hiking paradise, with a multitude of paths snaking through shady side canyons and up mountain grades. For hiking information, stop by any Forest Service office or the Crown Point Visitor Center on the historic river route, where a computer is programmed to match trails with hikers' interests and abilities. A few favorites include the Eagle Creek Trail to Punch Bowl Falls (Exit 41); Dog Mountain Trail, a challenging hike that starts between Bingen and Stevenson on the Washington side; and the Oneonta Gorge.

The scenic route ends at Troutdale just east of Portland. Nearby is Lewis and Clark State Park, where a self-guiding nature trail showcases the local plants chronicled by the expedition. The small state park is near the Sandy River, where the expedition stopped November 3 on their final push to the Pacific. They found the river silty and shallow, and when Clark tried to wade across, he found the bottom like quicksand. So the captains named the waterway "Quicksand River" and explored along its shore for about a mile-and-a-half before returning to make camp on Government Island in the Columbia. On the trip home, the corps again camped near the mouth of the Sandy and several men explored about six miles up the river. They learned from local Indians they had already passed the major tributary of the Columbia they had been seeking: the Willamette River, so Clark and several men backtracked to explore ten miles up the Willamette from modern-day Portland.

On the Washington side, Washington 14 remains an absolute delight, dominated by interesting little towns and stupendous views of Mount Hood. The Cascades are strikingly different from the Rocky Mountains, and they must have seemed strange to Lewis and Clark. The corps had grown used to the jagged, sawtooth contours of the Rockies, which frequently stretched out one ridge after another. The Cascade peaks, on the other hand, stand alone. These snowy sentinels seem to almost hover in mid-air, dwarfing everything around them. (Remember the average elevation in the valleys here is less than 100 feet above sea level, unlike the high valleys of the Rockies where towns sit at 3,000 to 5,000 feet.) Mount Hood and its Cascade cousins are, of course, volcanic in nature, thus their conical shapes and isolated placement.

If the Columbia River Gorge is the nation's top sailboarding area, then Doug's Beach State Park east of Lyle, Washington, is the sport's epicenter. Hood River, the hip town downriver, may be where people work, eat, and sleep, but Doug's Beach is where they play. People interested in learning sailboarding will find several Gorge-area businesses eager to

Horsetail Falls, Columbia River Gorge.

Native American fishing platforms along the Columbia River.

help. And although Doug's Beach is the place to see and be seen, many other less-crowded areas are better bets for novice sailboarders as well as for people who crave a more solitary sailing experience.

The twin towns of Bingen and White Salmon sit right across the river (and a toll bridge) from Hood River. Bingen has a winery, Mont Elise, with tours and tastings. The White Salmon River is popular for rafting, kayaking, and fishing. Both towns boast a number of German-style buildings, including the Glockenspiel Tower in White Salmon.

Carson is the gateway to Mount Saint Helens, as well as the site of Carson Hot Springs. Here, visitors are treated to hot mineral baths, massages, and towel wraps. Lodging, meals, and RV hookups are available, too. The best time to visit is on a weekday; folks from Portland and even Seattle crowd in on the weekends.

At Stevenson, plan a stop at the Columbia Gorge Interpretive Center, where you might catch storyteller Merna DeBolt portraying Meriwether Lewis' mother. (Call ahead to find out when she will be performing.) Hours are 10 a.m. to 5 p.m. except New Year's Day, Thanksgiving, and Christmas. Admission is $6 for adults, $5 for students, and senior citizens, and $4 for children ages 6-12. Call (509) 427-8211 for more information.

Bonneville Dam's Washington-side visitor center is situated between Stevenson and North Bonneville. The latter is a planned community in every sense of the word: The entire town was moved to its present location before construction began on Bonneville Dam's second powerhouse. The new town was dedicated in 1978.

Beacon Rock, just west of Bonneville Dam, is truly immense, to use one of the captains' favorite words. It was here Lewis and Clark first saw the effects of the tide as it rolled in from the Pacific. They didn't yet know they were still 142 river miles from the coast!

The remnants of a volcanic core, Beacon Rock is composed of basalt and has been eroded for years by the river. As the Oregon territory was settled, the 848-foot monolith was for years known as Castle Rock, but it has reclaimed its previous name. Interestingly enough, the rock was once owned by Henry J. Biddle, a descendant of Nicholas Biddle, early editor of the Lewis and Clark journals. Biddle built the first trail to its top, completing it in 1918 after two years of work.

Today's trail is 4,500 feet long with a fifteen percent grade and handrails lining most of the way. It's possible to hike to the top in about a half-hour, but the trek isn't recommended for people wary of heights. Advanced rock climbers are also welcome to try an ascent off the trail, but all climbers must register. Required equipment for climbers includes a hard hat, two 150-foot climbing ropes, clothes for any change in the weather, a standard rack for fifth-class climbing, rappelling equipment, proper footwear, and a headlamp for the longer routes.

Beacon Rock in the Columbia River Gorge.

Beacon Rock State Park actually overlooks the rock from the north side of Washington 14. It has a small campground and picnic facilities, as well as several hiking trailheads. The picnic area just down the road from the campground affords a good view of Beacon Rock, particularly at sunrise and sunset.

For more information on activities and attractions in the Columbia River Gorge, call (509) 427-8911 (Skamania County, Washington); (800) 366-3530 (Hood River); or (800) 255-3385 (The Dalles). From Beacon Rock, continue west on Washington 14 or backtrack to Stevenson, cross the Bridge of the Gods, and proceed west via I-84 or the Columbia River Scenic Route.

SIDE TRIP: PORTLAND AND VANCOUVER

The Lewis and Clark Trail is anchored by two great metropolitan areas: St. Louis, Gateway to the West, and Portland, Gateway to the Pacific. Oregon's largest city is growing by leaps and bounds but still manages to preserve the Northwest outpost character that so endears it to residents and visitors alike.

Several Portland sights are of special interest to the Lewis and Clark aficionado. A striking statue of Sacagawea by sculptress Alice Cooper sits in the city's Washington Park. A trompe l'oeil mural at the Oregon Historical Society, corner of Park and Madison in downtown Portland, depicts an almost-lifelike Lewis, Clark, York, Sacagawea, Pomp, and Seaman. Inside, the Historical Society offers permanent and changing exhibits on Northwest history. Finally, the lobby of the newly renovated Governor Hotel at 611 S.W. Tenth downtown features several murals honoring the Lewis and Clark Expedition.

Naturally, many Portlanders spend their free time fleeing town to the slopes of Mount Hood or the beaches of the windswept Oregon Coast. But anyone deciding to stay and explore the city itself has plenty of options from which to choose. Portland is a city of parks, with 4,700-acre Forest Park on the west side leading the way. This beauty spot boasts hiking trails and picnic grounds with spectacular views of the city. It is also close to Washington Park, home of the Metro Washington Park Zoo, the World Forestry Center, and an impressive Japanese Garden.

Weekends between March and December, the Portland Saturday Market beneath the Burnside Bridge offers wares from more than 250 artists, craftspeople, and fresh produce sellers. Food to eat on the premises and a wide array of entertainment are also available, and the market is open Sundays as well as Saturdays. Families flock to the acclaimed Oregon Museum of Science and Industry (OMSI) at 1945 S.E. Water Avenue for its interactive exhibits, planetarium presentations, and OMNIMAX Theater shows.

Lewis and Clark mural at the Oregon Historical Society in Portland.

Special events in Portland include the Rose Festival, which takes place annually each June and lasts several weeks. Activities include parades, an air show, a hot air balloon festival, and more. Downtown Portland is known for its public gathering places and eclectic architecture. Northwest 23rd Avenue is another interesting area, full of shops and strolling people. For more information on Portland-area attractions, call the Portland/Oregon Visitors Association at (800) 345-3214 (or (503) 222-2223 inside Oregon). The state also maintains an "Oregon Welcome Center" at Exit 308 off of I-5 near the Oregon-Washington border.

Vancouver, the oldest city in Washington State, has a population of about 47,000. It sits right across the river from Portland, offering its residents what may be the best of both worlds: life in a large metropolitan area combined with Vancouver's lingering small-town feel and easy access to recreation. Because of these attributes, Vancouver has twice been named an "All-American City." The Clark County Fair, held early each August, is one of the nation's ten largest.

In the years following Lewis and Clark's explorations, Fort Vancouver became an important way station for trappers, traders, and emigrants on their way to the Oregon country. The fort was established by the Hudson's Bay Company in 1824, which hoped to secure Britain's claim to Oregon by moving its Northwest headquarters inland from the mouth of the Columbia. But by 1846, Britain's hopes of claiming Oregon were dashed when the Northwest territory was divided along the 49th parallel (the current United States-Canada boundary), not the Columbia River, as the British had hoped.

Fort Vancouver is now a national historic site. Its stockade and several major buildings have been reconstructed on their original locations. Visitors are welcome from 9 a.m. to 5 p.m. daily Memorial Day through Labor Day and from 8 a.m. to 4 p.m. the rest of the year. Admission is $1 per person or $3 for a family. This is the site of a gala Fourth of July celebration often cited as one of the Northwest's best. For more information on Vancouver, contact the Vancouver/Clark County Visitor and Convention Bureau at (206) 693-1313.

TO THE PACIFIC

From Vancouver or Portland, the traveler has three major options for getting to the Washington and Oregon coasts, final destination of our heroes. The fastest choice by far is US 26—the Sunset Highway—best accessed via the I-405 beltway around downtown Portland. This route strays the farthest from Lewis and Clark's river route, but it is the best option if time is of the essence. US 30 out of northwest Portland stays close to the river on a two-lane crawl through heavy forests and small towns, winding up in Astoria. Washington routes 4 and 401 also take their time meandering along the river west from Longview/Kelso to the

Long Beach Peninsula, although travelers choosing this option get a jump on things by taking I-5 north from Vancouver to Longview.

For travelers desiring a scenic approach or the closest route to that of Lewis and Clark, the best approach is probably a hybrid of the slower options: I-5 to Washington 432 (at Exit 36), then west to Washington 433 (Oregon Way), which crosses the Columbia to US 30 at Rainier, Oregon. Whichever way you choose, try to preserve historical order in your coastal explorations by starting on the Washington side, as the Corps of Discovery did.

As the Corps of Discovery pressed down the last stretch of the Columbia River, the captains noted more sightings of Indians who already possessed white men's trade goods. They also marveled at the natives' large, ornate, and high-prowed canoes, much more suited to the turbulent Columbia than the explorers' dugouts. But most of all, they spoke and wrote of unceasing rain—a phenomenon that would prove the hallmark of the corps' winter on the coast.

On November 7, 1805, the party camped near Pillar Rock, a site just east of the small modern-day town of Altoona, Washington. "Great joy in camp," Clark reported. "We are in view of the ocean, this great Pacific Ocean which we have been so long anxious to see, and the roaring or noise made by the waves breaking on the rocky shores (as I suppose) may be heard distinctly." Clark wasn't quite right. As historian David Lavender explained in *The Way to the Western Sea*, "Those waves were breaking on the steep shores of Gray's Bay, and the ocean was still about twenty direct-line miles away. And yet psychologically, Clark was right.

"Gray's Bay had been named for the American ship captain Robert Gray, who, on the bright spring morning of May 11, 1792, had entered the mouth of the Columbia and a little later had anchored in that bay, the first white man to do so. On entering that same bay from the east, the first whites to do so, the Corps of Discovery was finally tying the middle section of North America together."

From the the bay, progress down the river was slow, no doubt much slower than the captains would have liked. On November 8, the corps pulled over to shore after finding the waves so high "that we thought it imprudent to proceed," Clark wrote. The next day, "monstrous trees" set afloat by a high afternoon tide nearly smashed the party's beached canoes. On November 10, the corps made all of two miles before high winds returned, compelling them to once again make camp. And so on. "We are all wet as usual and our situation is truly a disagreeable one," Clark wrote on November 11. On November 15, noting the eleventh straight day of rain, Clark railed: "...the most disagreeable time I have ever experienced.... I can neither get out to hunt, return to a better situation, or proceed on."

Yet later that same day, the winds abated and the party pressed on. Again, the captains made but a few miles, but it was far enough. Now, there was no doubt: they had reached the Pacific Ocean. Noting the sweeping tide and immense waves, "I concluded to form a camp on the highest spot I could find in the marshy bottom, and proceed no further by water as the coast becomes very dangerous for crafts of the size of our canoes," Clark wrote, adding that "the ocean is immediately in front and gives us an extensive view of it from Cape Disappointment to Point Adams." Camp was made, and the corps stayed put November 15-24, 1805, while various parties went off to explore the coast.

This first coastal campsite is now marked at a roadside picnic area about two miles south of Chinook, Washington, on US 101. (The roadside area is immediately west of the bridge from Astoria.) The area includes a large statue of the captains looking out to sea.

US 101 proceeds through the towns of Chinook and Ilwaco before looping back east for its journey up the coast. At Ilwaco, Washington 103 heads up the Long Beach Peninsula, while a spur route provides access to Fort Canby State Park and its Lewis and Clark Interpretive Center on Cape Disappointment.

Overall, this is one of the best Lewis and Clark interpretive centers in the nation, with exhibits detailing the entire expedition in photos, journals, and sketches. The only shortcoming is the lack of place identification on the scenic photos; a map pinpointing the location of events discussed would help, too. Nevertheless, especially informative displays include those on map-making techniques, weapons, frontier diplomacy, and members of the Corps of Discovery. One of the best is about Patrick Gass, including such items as his family Bible, expense account journal, metal flask, and a razor box believed to been carved and given to Gass by Sacagawea. The culmination of the exhibits is real: A picture-perfect, floor-to-ceiling window view of the Columbia River Bar and the Pacific Ocean beyond. It was likely near this spot that Clark stood with his men on November 18, 1805, and viewed with wonder "the high waves dashing against the rocks and this immense ocean." Lewis and a separate party explored the area earlier, and probably also saw this exact view.

The interpretive center is open from 10 a.m. to 5 p.m. daily from early May through September and 10 a.m. to 3 p.m. Saturdays and Sundays the rest of the year. Admission is free. For more information, call (360) 642-3029.

Following a tour of the center, be sure to explore more of the grounds. Cape Disappointment was named by British sea captain and fur trader John Meares, who visited the area in 1788 in an attempt to confirm the presence of a large river in the vicinity. Failing to do so, he named the promontory Cape Disappointment. Although others had speculated on the river's existence, it took Robert Gray, the American, four more years to cross the Columbia River Bar and explore nearly 100 miles upriver.

Secluded beach at Cape Disappointment, Fort Canby State Park, Washington.

A trail leads to the Cape Disappointment Lighthouse, built in 1856 and the oldest one remaining in use along the West Coast. The lighthouse isn't generally open to the public, but it's easy to look in, and personnel on duty are happy to step out and answer visitors' questions. Ask about the treacherous Columbia Bar or the Coast Guard's Motor Lifeboat School, where students learn to conduct rescue operations on the world's most predictably rough surf. Another commonly asked question is: "Where does the river stop and the ocean begin?" The truth is, the river current is detected several miles out into the ocean at a spot the Coast Guard calls Buoy 2, while brackish seawater is often found upriver all the way past Cathlamet, so pinpointing a precise dividing line is just about impossible.

The lighthouse vicinity also affords a good view of the rest of Cape Disappointment, including the bluff on which the visitor center sits and the Pacific Ocean beyond. It makes a fine picture from this angle. The lighthouse trail also boasts a short, steep side trail leading to a scenic beach tucked in a tiny bay—a perfect place for a picnic.

Fort Canby State Park has a large campground with about 250 sites, but it is dwarfed by Fort Stevens State Park across the Columbia in Oregon, which has more than 600 sites. Despite these parks' gargantuan proportions, visitors can forget about just driving in and finding a site during summer. In fact, it's essential to make reservations for any state park campgrounds on the Pacific coast well before peak vacation season. Private campgrounds will still have spaces in most instances, but it's still wise to call and secure a spot in advance. Nehalem Bay State Park in Oregon is first-come, first-served, no reservations, but at twenty miles south of Cannon Beach, it's also pretty far off the beaten path from where Lewis and Clark camped. For more information on reserving a campsite on the coast, call (206) 642-3078 (for Washington) or (503) 731-3411 (for Oregon).

Washington's Long Beach Peninsula is heavily oriented to tourists. Visitors will find plenty of restaurant choices and legions of motels and campgrounds, although many will be full on summer weekends. The town of Long Beach has a pleasant beach area and boardwalk. The highway was once right on the beach, and freight moved by stagecoach. These days, some parts of the beach may be driven upon even in peak season; others are closed to vehicular traffic. Exhibits along the boardwalk explain the many shipwrecks that have occurred along the Columbia River Bar, where clouds, sandbars, and ceaseless drizzle all wreak havoc with navigation. In all, about two thousand boats have been wrecked or sunk and some seven hundred lives lost.

Watching the ocean is almost like gazing into a campfire—simply mesmerizing. Waves roll, crash, and fall...roll, crash, and fall, doubling in on themselves. It's no place to swim, but other activities may be enjoyed including kite-flying, beachcombing, clam-digging, whale-watching, and simple strolling.

FORT CLATSOP NATIONAL MEMORIAL

By late November, it had become clear that the corps would not be able to stay on the Washington side of the coast. There was little game, and the explorers were sick of eating salmon and roots—goods they had to purchase from the local Indians at a high price. Moreover, there was the interminable rain, rotting clothing, bedding, and spirits.

Lewis and Clark had heard game was more plentiful on the south shore of the Columbia, and hoped that a suitable camp might be established close to both a freshwater river, which they'd had difficulty finding on the north side, and a seawater source from which they could make salt. Moreover, by staying close to the ocean, they increased their chances of meeting any trading ships that pulled into the Columbia harbors. Jefferson had instructed Lewis to send two men and a copy of his notes back by sea if a suitable vessel could be found.

Still, many members of the expedition had other ideas. Sick of the damp weather, they talked of moving back up the Columbia to spend the winter in a drier climate. Eager to reach a consensus before winter, the

Historic interpretive program at Fort Clatsop National Memorial near Astoria, Oregon.

captains decided to put the matter to a vote, extending the franchise to York and Sacagawea as well as to the enlisted men. As Stephen Ambrose noted in *Undaunted Courage*, "It was the first time in American history that a black slave had voted, the first time a woman had voted." Based on scouting reports from Lewis, who'd gone over to examine the options, the party agreed to check out the south shore and stay there if enough game was available. The decision made, the party moved back to the vicinity of Pillar Rock and crossed to the south shore. Before they left, Clark carved his name in a tree, adding "December 3rd 1805. By Land. U. States in 1804-05."

The Corps of Discovery had a dangerous paddle across the Columbia to reach its new winter camp at the site of present-day Fort Clatsop National Memorial. Today, the trip is as easy as driving over the four-mile-long bridge from Megler, Washington, to Astoria, Oregon. To get to Fort Clatsop from Astoria, follow the signs for Warrenton and Seaside. Both US 101 and the 101 business loop lead there, and both routes are marked. (Motorists taking US 101 should get into the left-hand turn lane as soon as possible after crossing Youngs Bay from Astoria to Warrenton. Turn left onto Marlin Avenue, then left at the next stop sign.

Fort Clatsop is among the very best interpretive sites along the Lewis and Clark route. Exhibits and living history programs combine to give visitors a comprehensive picture of the expedition's winter on the Pacific coast. It's an especially interesting place for kids, who really delight in the summer living history programs (and are often invited to take part). Don't miss the fort replica, lovingly furnished in detail and staffed by National Park rangers who will answer any and all questions. Rangers are often asked whether the fort is original. It is not. In fact, the first Fort Clatsop rotted within ten to fifteen years of its occupancy, reclaimed by the soggy coastal climate.

In 1901, the Oregon Historical Society started searching for the original site. But it wasn't until the expedition's 150th anniversary in 1955 that the replica was built, its construction based on floor plan drawings and descriptions from the expedition journals. Archaeologists have not pinpointed the fort's exact location, but they are certain it was near the current replica. The wood in the replica is now treated every year to make sure the fort escapes the fate of its predecessor.

During most of the journey, the captains and their corps shared very similar conditions. Here at Fort Clatsop, however, rank had its privileges. The fort measured about fifty feet square, with two rows of huts separated by a parade ground. One row had three small rooms, two of which measured sixteen feet by fifteen feet, with the other fifteen feet by eighteen feet. These were the enlisted men's quarters, each housing eight men. The other row held four rooms, the largest of which was the captains' quarters. Charbonneau, Sacagawea, and Pomp had another

Dugout canoe replica at Fort Clatsop.

room for their own. An orderly room housed the sergeant of the guard and his three men, a rotating assignment. It's not known exactly where York lived, but he may have slept in the orderly room, too. The fourth room was used for smoking and storing meat.

There were also differences in the daily routine. After the voyage's original shakedown period, all the men generally pulled together, everyone more or less equal. But when they arrived at Fort Clatsop, the captains realized they would have to restore a level of military discipline. Sentries were always posted. Weapons were cleaned and inspected each day. Without some regimentation, the men would have likely started deserting to go live with the Indians after just a few weeks at their soggy outpost.

And it was rainy. In fact, it rained ninety-four days that winter, all but twelve days of their stay. Of the 106 days spent at the site, only six were sunny. The men spent their time in various ways: hunting, updating maps and journals (and plotting their return routes home), and sewing elk-hide moccasins for the trip home. Each man made about ten pairs of shoes during the winter's stay. That may sound like a lot of moccasins, but each pair typically only lasted ten days before wearing out.

There was game, but it was of dubious quality. On Christmas Day 1805, Clark wrote: "We would have spent this day the nativity of Christ in feasting, had we anything either to raise our spirits or even gratify our appetites. Our dinner consisted of poor elk, so much spoiled that we ate it through mere necessity, some spoiled pounded fish, and a few roots." Dogs, too, remained part of the diet.

All in all, it was a difficult winter. But again, the captains were able to gain information from the nearby Indians who, although reportedly prone to thievery, were friendly. And there were occasional diversions, such as the trip Clark and others made to see a beached whale on the ocean shore, and of other sorts, too: Lewis reported on January 27, "Goodrich has recovered from the Louis Veneri which he contracted from an amorous contact with a Chinook damsel. I cured him as I did Gibson last winter by the use of mercury."

Fort Clatsop has several great exhibits unlike those anywhere else. One, right by the visitor center entrance, describes exactly where the Corps of Discovery was in its voyage during any given day you might visit. Another explains in great detail the events leading up to the expedition, from early exploration of the Northwest coast to the Louisiana Purchase. Other features include a handsome sculpture called "The Arrival" by Stanley Wanlass, commissioned in 1980 to celebrate the expedition's 175th anniversary, and a slide show closed-captioned for the hearing-impaired.

One especially interesting display records the pay level of each expedition member, the roles each played in the mission, and comments from the captains on each. Drouillard was paid $833, Charbonneau earned $490, but Sacagawea received nothing. Most of the comments made about the men were complimentary, but Charbonneau proved an exception. "A man of no particular merit. Was useful as an interpreter only," Lewis wrote, perhaps remembering the near-disastrous episodes with the white pirogue on the Missouri River. Clark was more kind, saying: "You have conducted yourself in such a manner as to gain my friendship." Of Sacagawea, Clark added to Charbonneau, "Your woman on that long, dangerous, and fatiguing route deserved a better reward than we had in our power to give her." And of Pomp, he said, "As for your little son, my boy Pomp, you well know my fondness for him and my anxiety to take and raise him as my own child." Pomp was indeed adopted by Clark, educated in St. Louis and Europe, worked as a frontier interpreter and guide, and died in Oregon in 1866.

The corps originally planned to leave April 1, but hunting became difficult weeks earlier as the elk moved back to the mountains. Moreover, the warming temperatures gave the men a good case of spring fever, so they departed Fort Clatsop March 23, 1806. On that day, Clark wrote in his journal: "At this place we had wintered and remained from the 7th of December 1805 to this day and have lived as well as we had any right to expect."

Fort Clatsop is open daily from 8 a.m. to 6 p.m. mid-June through Labor Day and 8 a.m. to 5 p.m. daily the rest of the year. Admission is $2 per person with a maximum of $4 per family. Admission tickets are good for a week. For more information, call (503) 861-2471.

Astoria is a fascinating, historic town worth a look either before or after Fort Clatsop. The Astoria Column atop Coxcomb Hill pays tribute to Lewis and Clark and others who led American westward expansion. A 164-step circular stairway leads to the top of the 125-foot column and great views of the area. The drive to Coxcomb Hill gives visitors a good glimpse of the Victorian architecture of Astoria, the first American settlement in the Northwest. The Union Steam Baths, Finnish-style hot tubs at 285 W. Marine Drive, are another local institution.

The Columbia River Maritime Museum is one of the best of its kind. In addition to seeing exhibits on seafaring history, visitors can tour the lightship *Columbia*, which not so long ago was the last seagoing lighthouse on the West Coast. Union soldiers at nearby Fort Stevens guarded the mouth of the Columbia during the Civil War, and in 1942, Fort Stevens became the only American military installation in the continental United States to be fired upon by foreigners since the War of 1812. A Japanese submarine fired seventeen shells at the fort. There was no damage.

From Astoria or Fort Clatsop, continue south on US 101 to Seaside, home of the expedition's salt works, and the picturesque Oregon coastline of Cannon Beach.

SEASIDE AND ECOLA STATE PARK

By the time it reached the Pacific, the expedition had long since run out of salt for preserving and flavoring food, so shortly after the party's arrival at Fort Clatsop, Captain Lewis ordered that a salt cairn be established near the camp. After a search of five days, a suitable location was found in what is now the town of Seaside, about fourteen miles south of Fort Clatsop.

The operation was established on January 2, 1806, by the expedition's three saltmakers: Joseph Field, William Bratton, and George Gibson. They remained on the site until February 20 and were able to produce about four bushels of salt by boiling sea water day and night, laboriously walking back and forth the 100 paces to and from the ocean. Sampling an early batch on January 5, Lewis pronounced it "excellent, fine, strong, and white. This was a great treat to myself and most of the party...I say most of the party for my friend Captain Clark declares it to be a mere matter of indifference with him whether he uses it or not; for myself I must confess I felt a considerable inconvenience from the want of it."

A replica of the Salt Works remains in its original location. To get there, take Avenue G west off US 101 to South Beach Drive and follow the signs. The monument sits between two private homes—a site determined in 1900 by the Oregon Historical Society, based on the testimony of a Seaside woman, Jenny Michel, whose Clatsop Indian father remembered the white men boiling water. He pointed out the spot to her when she was young. The site is now officially part of Fort Clatsop National Memorial.

Seaside is the most commercial town on the north Oregon coast, with lots of shopping, several good restaurants, and all kinds of entertainment ranging from an aquarium to miniature golf to active nightlife. Surprisingly, however, morning may be the best time to explore the coastal towns of Oregon and Washington. The beaches and boardwalks are nearly empty, allowing perfect conditions for a leisurely stroll. Moreover, nearly every town has a great local bakery or coffee shop where you can pick up a good cup of espresso and a snack for the trip.

Seaside's main commercial drag ends near the beach at what is called "the turnaround." A statue of Lewis and Clark shows the captains gazing off at the ocean, an exhausted Seaman lying at their feet. Other scenes from the expedition circle the monument's base. This statue, like the one at Fort Clatsop, is by former Astoria artist Stanley Wanlass.

Like many communities along the Lewis and Clark Trail, Seaside and Astoria are gearing up for the expedition's upcoming bicentennial in 2003-2006 with the formation of a local bicentennial association. This local group, like others across the country, will be working with the National Lewis & Clark Bicentennial Council to plan observances marking

Saltworks at Seaside, Oregon.

End of the trail monument at Seaside, Oregon.

the anniversary. If you'd like to be involved in the national effort or find a group near you, contact the National Lewis & Clark Bicentennial Council, P.O. Box 9550, Seattle WA 98109-0550.

Midway through the winter, the corps heard of a great whale that had washed up on a nearby beach. Clark led a contingent of fifteen people (including Sacagawea and Pomp) to seek the whale, which was pretty well picked over by the local Indians by the time the visitors arrived. Nevertheless, Clark succeeded in negotiating for the purchase of some 300 pounds of blubber and a few gallons of whale oil. "Small as this stock is I prize it highly; and thank providence for directing the whale to us; and think him much more kind to us than he was to Jonah, having sent this monster to be swallowed by us instead of swallowing of us as Jonah's did."

It's possible to hike over the ocean headlands, following almost exactly in Clark's footsteps as he and his party pursued the whale. The Tillamook Head Trail begins in Seaside and can end at six miles (Ecola Point) or seven miles (Indian Beach). A fourteen-mile roundtrip would take the better part of a day to complete, but a few hiker-bike campsites are scattered along the way for folks who want to make an overnight of it.

If a long hike doesn't fit your schedule, simply drive to Ecola State Park, where short pathways lead to wonderful vistas of Haystack Rock and the rugged coastline. Just head south from Seaside on US 101 and watch for the Cannon Beach turn. (It's somewhat sudden on the right-hand side.) Follow the signs to Ecola State Park, and take care driving the winding entrance road. The park charges a small day-use fee.

Another Cannon Beach site, Les Shirley Park, offers further interpretation of the Lewis and Clark story. To get there, continue on the road into Cannon Beach instead of turning right toward Ecola State Park. The park is almost immediately on the left. Aside from another fine Haystack Rock view, the park has picnic grounds. Wherever you wind up, take time to savor the ocean sights and sounds and reflect on the journey of Lewis and Clark—one of the greatest adventures the world has ever known.

*Denotes town on Lewis and Clark's homeward route, 1806.

LODGING

CLARKSTON, WASHINGTON

Hacienda Lodge, (509) 758-5583, US 12.

Highland House Bed & Breakfast, (509) 758-3126, 707 Highland.

Nendel's Valu Inn, (509) 758-1631, 222 Bridge St. $42.

Quality Inn, (800) 221-2222, 700 Port Dr. $58-$85.

POMEROY, WASHINGTON

Pioneer Motel, (509) 843-9960, 1201 Main.

*DAYTON, WASHINGTON

Blue Mountain Motel, (509) 382-3040, 414 Main St.

Dayton Motel, (509) 382-4503, 111 S. Pine St.

*WAITSBURG, WASHINGTON

Lewis & Clark Motel, (509) 337-6412, 533 Preston.

Waitsburg Motel, (509) 337-8103, 711 Coppei.

TRI-CITIES, WASHINGTON

Columbia Center Dunes Motel, (800) 638-6168, 1751 Fowler St. (Richland). $33-$35.

DoubleTree Inn, (800) 547-8010, 2525 N. 20th Ave. (Pasco). $80-$90.

Hallmark Motel, (509) 547-7766, 720 W. Lewis St. (Pasco). $34.

Motel 6, (509) 546-2010, 1520 N. Oregon St. (Pasco). $31.

Quality Inn on Clover Island, (800) 221-2222, 435 Clover Island (Kennewick). $64-$68

Super 8, (800) 800-8000, 626 N. Columbia Center Blvd. (Kennewick). $46.

Val-U Inn, (800) 443-7777, 1800 W. Lewis St. (Pasco). $52-$57.

*WALLA WALLA, WASHINGTON

Capri Motel, (509) 525-1130, 2003 Melrose. Under $45.

Green Gables Inn Bed & Breakfast, (509) 525-5501. $75-$100.

Nendel's Whitman Inn, (509) 525-2200, 107 N. 2nd Ave. $49.

Walla Walla Travelodge, (509) 529-4940, 421 E. Main. $50.

UMATILLA, OREGON

Heather Inn, (541) 922-4871, 705 Willamette Ave. $51.

Tillicum Motor Inn, (541) 922-3236, 1481 6th St. $36-$45.

BOARDMAN, OREGON

Dodge City Motel, (541) 481-2451, 1st and Front St. $34-$37.

Nugget Inn, (800) 336-4485, 105 Front St. S.W. $40 and up.

THE DALLES, OREGON

Barretts of Harris Street Bed & Breakfast, (541) 296-2027, 100 Harris St. $40-$60.

Best Western Tapadera Motor Inn, (800) 528-1234, 112 W. Second (I-84 Exit 84). $52-$59.

Shamrock Motel, (541) 296-5464, 118 W. 4th St. $30-$35.

Shilo Inn, (541) 298-5502, 3223 N.E. Frontage Rd. $50-$99.

The Inn at The Dalles, (541) 296-1167, 3550 S.E. Frontage Rd. $32-$48.

HOOD RIVER, OREGON

Columbia Gorge Hotel, (541) 386-5566, 4000 Westcliff Dr. $175 and up.

Hood River Hotel, (541) 386-1900, 102 Oak St. $59-$95.

Love's Riverview Lodge, (541) 386-8719, 1505 Oak. $69.

Meredith Gorge Motel, (541) 386-1515, 4300 Westcliff Dr. $38-$43.

State Street Inn Bed & Breakfast, (541) 386-1899, 1005 State St. $55-$75.

Vagabond Lodge, (541) 386-2992, 4070 Westcliff Dr. (I-84 Exit 62). $40-$59.

WHITE SALMON, WASHINGTON

Inn of the White Salmon Bed & Breakfast, (800) 972-5226. $89-$115.

Llama Ranch, (800) 800-LAMA, 1980 Hwy. 141. $46-$75.

BINGEN, WASHINGTON

City Center Motel, (509) 493-2445, 208 W. Steuben.

STEVENSON, WASHINGTON

Econolodge (formerly the Riverview Motor Inn), (509) 427-5628, Frank-Johns Rd. $40-$42.

Skamania Lodge, (800) 221-7117, 1131 S.W. Skamania Lodge Dr. $95-$145.

CASCADE LOCKS, OREGON

Bridge of the Gods Motel, (541) 374-8628, US 30. $30-$50.

Shahala Bed & Breakfast, (541) 374-8222, 1280 N.E. Forest Ln. $45-$125.

Scandian Motor Lodge, (541) 374-8417, US 30. $43.

PORTLAND, OREGON

Cameo Motel, (503) 288-5981, 4111 N.E. 82nd Ave. $29-$32.

Governor Hotel, (503) 224-3400, 611 S.W. 10th. $155-$185.

Hartman's Hearth Bed & Breakfast, (503) 281-2182, 2937 N.E. 20th Ave. $50-$70.

DoubleTree Inn Columbia River, (800) 547-8010, I-5 Exit 308 (Hayden Island). $114-$134.

Holiday Inn-Downtown, (800) HOLIDAY, 1021 N.E. Grand Ave. $59-$108.

Imperial Hotel, (503) 228-7221, 400 S.W. Broadway. $60-$75.

Motel 6-Troutdale, (503) 665-2254, I-84 Exit 17 (Troutdale). $36.

Sauvie Island Bed & Breakfast, (503) 621-3214, 26504 N.W. Reeder Rd. $55-$80.

VANCOUVER, WASHINGTON

Comfort Inn, (800) 221-2222, 13207 N.E. 20th. $50-$70.

Fort Motel, (360) 694-3327, 500 E. 13th. Under $45.

Nendel's Suites, (800) 547-0106, 7001 N.E. Hwy. 99. $45-$48.

Salmon Creek Motel, (360) 573-0751, 11901 N.E. Hwy. 99. $40-$45.

KELSO/LONGVIEW, WASHINGTON

Comfort Inn, (800) 221-2222, 440 Three Rivers Dr. (Kelso). $53-$70.

Hudson Manor Motel, (360) 425-1100, 1616 Hudson St. (Longview). $32-$36.

Kelso Inn Motel, (360) 636-4610, 505 N. Pacific (Kelso). $34.

Lewis and Clark Motor Inn, (360) 423-6460, 838 15th Ave. (Longview). $35-$41.

ST. HELENS, OREGON

Hopkins House Bed & Breakfast, (503) 397-4676, 105 S. 1st St. $40-$60.

McCormick Hotel, (503) 397-4700, 293 1/2 S. 1st St. $25-$29.

RAINIER, OREGON

Rainier Motor Inn, (503) 556-4231, 120 A St. W.

CLATSKANIE, OREGON

Northwoods Inn Motel, (503) 728-4311, 945 E. Columbia River Hwy. $35-$55.

CATHLAMET, WASHINGTON

Cathlamet Hotel, (800) 446-0454, 69 Main.

Country Keeper Bed & Breakfast, (360) 795-3030, 61 Main St. $60-$80.

Nassa Point Motel, (360) 795-3941, 851 E. WA 4.

NASELLE, WASHINGTON

Hunter's Inn, (360) 484-9215, WA 4.

Naselle Village Inn Motel, (360) 484-9666, WA 4.

Sleepy Hollow Motel, (360) 484-3232, WA 4.

ILWACO, WASHINGTON

Heidi's Inn, (360) 642-2387, US 101. Under $45.

The Inn at Ilwaco, (360) 642-8686, 120 Williams St. N.E. $45-$75.

LONG BEACH, WASHINGTON

Fort Lewis and Clark Motel, (360) 642-8458, 700 N. Pacific Hwy. Under $45.

Nendel's Edgewater Inn, (800) 547-0106, 409 10th St. N.W. $55-$80.

Shaman Motel, (800) 753-3750, 115 3rd St. N.W. $49-$84.

The Shelburne Inn, (206) 642-2442, one mile south in Seaview. $85-$165.

Super 8 Motel, (800) 800-8000, 500 Ocean Beach Blvd. $58-$64.

ASTORIA, OREGON

Astoria Inn Bed & Breakfast, (503) 325-8153, 3391 Irving Ave. $65-$70.

Bayshore Motor Inn, (503) 325-2205, 555 Hamburg. $55.

Crest Motel, (800) 421-3141, 5366 Leif Erickson Dr. $45-$72.

Dunes Motel, (503) 325-325-7111, 288 W. Marine Dr. $52-$65.

Franklin Street Station Bed & Breakfast, (503) 325-4314, 1140 Franklin Ave. $63-$85.

Red Lion Inn, (800) 547-8010, 400 Industry St. $80-$85.

SEASIDE, OREGON

Best Western Ocean View Resort, (800) 582-1234, 414 N. Prom. $70-$180.

Ebb Tide Motel, (503) 738-8371, 300 N. Prom. $60-$125.

Gearhart Ocean Inn, (503) 738-7373, 67 N. Cottage St. $49-$79.

Huntley Inn, (503) 738-9581, 441 2nd Ave. $69.

Riverside Inn Bed & Breakfast, (503) 738-8254, 430 S. Holladay. $45-$85.

Royale Motel, (503) 738-9541, 531 Ave. A. $43-$55.

CANNON BEACH, OREGON

Blue Gull Inn Motel, (503) 436-2714, 487 S. Hemlock St. $45-$95.

Cannon Beach Hotel, (503) 436-1392, 1116 S. Hemlock. $50-$120.

Hallmark Resort, (800) 345-5676, 1400 S. Hemlock. $70-$170.

McBee Motel, (503) 436-2569, 888 S. Hemlock. $35-$80.

CAMPING

CLARKSTON, WASHINGTON

Chief Timothy State Park, (509) 758-9580, eight miles west on US 12.

STARBUCK, WASHINGTON

Lyons Ferry State Park, (509) 646-3252, WA 261.

Palouse Falls State Park, (509) 646-3252, WA 261. Primitive sites.

*DAYTON, WASHINGTON

Krose's Tuccannon RV Park, fifteen miles north on US 12.

Lewis and Clark Trail State Park, (509) 337-6457, four miles east on US 12.

*WAITSBURG, WASHINGTON

Meadowlark RV Park, (509) 337-8103, in center of town on US 12.

TRI-CITIES, WASHINGTON

Arrowhead Campground & RV Park, (509) 545-8206, 3120 Commercial (Pasco).

Charbonneau Park, (509) 547-7781, off of WA 124 east of Pasco.

Columbia Park Campground, (509) 783-3711, 6601 S.E. Columbia Dr. (Richland).

Fishhook Park, (509) 547-7781, off of WA 124 east of Pasco.

Hood Park, (509) 547-7781, three miles east of Pasco on Hwy. 12E.

Lloyd's Desert Gold Motel & RV Park, (509) 627-1000, Columbia Dr. west of I-182 Exit 3 (Richland).

*WALLA WALLA, WASHINGTON

Fort Walla Walla Campground, (509) 527-3770, west on Dalles Military Rd.

UMATILLA, OREGON

Hat Rock Campground, (541) 567-4188, east on US 730 opposite Hat Rock State Park.

Umatilla Marina and RV Park, (541) 922-3939, north of US 730. No tents.

GOLDENDALE, WASHINGTON

Horsethief Lake State Park, (509) 767-1159, west on WA 14. Primitive sites.

Maryhill State Park, (509) 773-5007, near junction of US 97 and WA 14.

THE DALLES, OREGON

Lone Pine Travel Park, (541) 296-9133, I-84 Exit 87.

Memaloose State Park, eleven miles west on I-84.

HOOD RIVER, OREGON

Viento State Park, (541) 874-8811, eight miles west on I-84.

CASCADE LOCKS, OREGON

Bridge of the Gods RV Park, (541) 374-8619, I-84 Exit 44.

Cascade Locks KOA, (541) 374-8668, US 30.

Cascade Locks Marine Park, (541) 374-8619, I-84 Exit 44.

STEVENSON, WASHINGTON

Hidden Coves Campground, (509) 427-8098, WA 14.

NORTH BONNEVILLE, WASHINGTON

Beacon Rock RV & Trailer Park, (509) 427-8473, west on WA 14.

Beacon Rock State Park, (509) 427-8265, three miles west on WA 14.

Lewis and Clark Campground, (509) 427-5982, west on WA 14.

GRESHAM, OREGON

Oxbow Park, (503) 663-4708, 3010 S.E. Oxbow Pkwy.

PORTLAND, OREGON

Jantzen Beach RV Park, (800) 443-7248, 1503 N. Hayden Island Dr. No tents.

Portland Fairview RV Park, (800) 336-1047, 21401 N.E. Sandy Blvd. (Troutdale). No tents.

RIDGEFIELD, WASHINGTON

Big Fir Campground, (800) 532-4397, I-15 Exit 14.

WOODLAND, WASHINGTON

Columbia Riverfront RV Park, (800) 845-9842, I-5 Exit 22.

Lewis River RV Park, (360) 225-9556, I-5 Exit 21.

Paradise Point State Park, (360) 263-2350, south via I-5.

KALAMA, WASHINGTON

Camp Kalama RV Park, (360) 673-2456, I-5 Exit 32.

KELSO/LONGVIEW, WASHINGTON

Brookhaven RV Park, (360) 577-6474, I-5 Exit 39 (Kelso).

The Cedars RV Park, (360) 274-7019, I-5 Exit 46 (Kelso).

CATHLAMET, WASHINGTON

County Line Park, East on WA 4 at the Cowlitz/Wahkiakum county line.

CHINOOK, WASHINGTON

Chinook County Park, (360) 777-8442, US 101.

Mauch's Sundown RV Park, (360) 777-8713, four miles east on US 101.

River's End Campground, (360) 777-8317, west of town on US 101.

ILWACO, WASHINGTON

Fort Canby State Park, (360) 642-3078, 2.5 miles southwest of US 101.

Ilwaco KOA, (360) 642-3292, two miles south on US 101.

LONG BEACH, WASHINGTON

Andersen's On the Ocean, (360) 642-2231, north on WA 103.

Driftwood RV Park, (360) 642-2711, north on WA 103.

Pegg's Oceanside RV Park, (360) 642-2451, north on WA 103.

Pioneer RV Park, (360) 642-3990, WA 103 and Pioneer Rd.

ASTORIA, OREGON

Astoria-Warrenton-Seaside KOA, (800) 762-3443, 1100 N.W. Ridge Rd. (Hammond).

Fort Stevens State Park, (503) 861-1671, ten miles west on US 101.

SEASIDE, OREGON

Circle Creek RV Park & Campground, (503) 738-6070, US 101.

Riverside Lake Resort RV Park, (503) 738-6779, US 101.

CANNON BEACH, OREGON

RV Resort at Cannon Beach, (503) 436-2231, Elk Creek Rd. No tents.

RESTAURANTS

CLARKSTON, WASHINGTON

Bamboo Gardens, (509) 758-8898, 907 6th St. Mandarin and Szechuan cuisine. Closed Mondays.

Bridge Street Connection, (509) 758-3141, US 12. Prime rib, daily specials, sports bar.

PATAHA, WASHINGTON

Eaton Place Cafe, (509) 843-1465, US 12.

POMEROY, WASHINGTON

Donna's Drive-In, (509) 843-1510, 14th and Main.

The Steakhouse, (509) 843-3501, 831 Main.

*DAYTON, WASHINGTON

Panhandler's Pizza & Pasta, (509) 382-4160, 404 W. Main.

Patit Creek Restaurant, (509) 382-2625, 725 E. Dayton. French cuisine.

*WAITSBURG, WASHINGTON

Farmer's Cafe, (509) 337-6845, 216 Main.

TRI-CITIES, WASHINGTON

Boulevard Bar & Grill, (509) 735-6575, 1250 Columbia Center Blvd. (Richland). Specializing
in seafood.

Clover Island Inn, (509) 586-0541, in the Quality Inn-Kennewick. Located near site where
Lewis and Clark met with local Indians.

Country Gentleman, (509) 547-6446, 1320 N. 20th (Pasco).

O'Callahan's Restaurant, (509) 946-9006, in the Shilo Inn-Richland. Prime rib, seafood, pasta.

Roy's Western Smorgy, (509) 735-8539, 1400 Columbia Center Blvd. (Kennewick). One-price
buffet. Also in Pasco.

*WALLA WALLA, WASHINGTON

The Homestead Restaurant, (509) 522-0345, 1528 Isaacs. Lunch and dinner specials daily.

Jacobi's Cafe, (509) 525-2677, 416 N.2nd. Wide menu, vegetarian dishes.

Pastime Cafe, (509) 525-0873, 215 W. Main. Italian and American food.

The Turf, (509) 522-9807, 10 N. 2nd. Sandwiches, Northwest microbrews.

THE DALLES, OREGON

Cousins, (541) 298-2771, at the Tillicum Inn. All-day breakfast, ribs, pot roast.

Lone Pine Restaurant, (541) 296-5333, I-84 at US 197. Family dining.

Marcella's Pizza, (541) 296-4567, 1455 W. 6th. Hand-thrown pizza, calzone, salads.

Tapadera Restaurant, (541) 296-5404, 112 W. 2nd. Steaks, prime rib, seafood.

Wasco House, (541) 296-5158, 515 Liberty. Seafood, steak, pasta.

HOOD RIVER, OREGON

Columbia River Court Dining Room, (541) 386-5566, in the Columbia Gorge Hotel. Elegant
dining and "famous farm breakfast."

The Mesquitery, (541) 386-2002, 1219 12th St. Gourmet grilling with mesquite wood.

Purple Rocks Art Bar & Cafe, (541) 386-6061, 606 Oak St. Favorite for breakfast and
lunch.

Sixth Street Bistro & Loft, (541) 386-7797, 6th & Cascade. Pasta and seafood featuring
local foods.

Stonehedge Inn, (541) 386-3940, 3405 Cascade Dr. Elegant dining amid wooded sur-
roundings.

Sundown Chinese Restaurant, (541) 386-5331, 2680 Old Columbia River Rd. Authentic
Szechuan and Hunan cuisine.

LYLE, WASHINGTON

Country Cafe, (509) 365-3883, WA 14. Burgers, omelettes, homemade pie.

BINGEN, WASHINGTON

Fidel's, (509) 493-1017, 120 E. Steuben. Mexican food.

Quigley's, (509) 493-3435, 201 W. Steuben. Steak, chicken, pizza.

CASCADE LOCKS, OREGON

Charburger Restaurant, (541) 374-8477, 714 S.W. Wa-Na-Pa. Breakfast specialties, chili, chicken.

STEVENSON, WASHINGTON

Betty's Silver Grill, (509) 427-5399, 2nd St.

The Crossing, (509) 427-8097, 127 Russell. Sandwiches, soups, salads, sweets.

Dee's Kich-Inn, (509) 427-4670, 10 N.W. 2nd St. Home-cooking three meals a day.

Skamania Lodge, (509) 427-2508, in the Skamania Lodge. Sunday brunch.

PORTLAND, OREGON

B. Moloch-Heathman Bakery and Pub, (503) 227-5700, 901 S.W. Salmon. Gourmet pizza, inventive breakfasts.

Celilo, (503) 224-3400, in the Governor Hotel. Northwest specialties, Sunday brunch.

Hamburger Mary's, (503) 223-0900, 850 S.W. Park. Omelettes and burgers at funky local favorite.

Jake's Famous Crawfish, (503) 226-1419, 901 S.W. 12th St. Wide seafood menu.

Macheesmo Mouse, (503) 228-3491, 723 S.W. Salmon and other locations. Heart-smart Mexican fare.

Tad's Chicken 'n Dumplins, (503) 666-5337, east on Crown Point Hwy. (Troutdale). Dining on Sandy River.

Zell's: An American Cafe, (503) 239-0196, 1300 S.E. Morrison. Breakfast and lunch.

VANCOUVER, WASHINGTON

The Crossing Restaurant, (360) 695-3374, 900 W. 7th. Railroad-themed eatery.

Juanita's Mexican Restaurant, (360) 834-5856, 231 3rd Ave. (Camas). Daily specials.

Krackle's Grill, (360) 573-3815, I-5 179th St. Exit. Hamburgers, seafood, steaks.

Pinot Ganache Restaurant, (360) 695-7786, in the Vancouver Marketplace. Northwest cuisine.

Tee Dee's Pie House & Restaurant, (360) 693-6736, 6600 N.E. Hwy. 99. Family dining.

HAZEL DELL, WASHINGTON

Brubaker's Restaurant, (360) 574-2270, 605 N.E. 78th. Fresh fish, pasta, Cajun meals.

KALAMA, WASHINGTON

Columbia Inn Restaurant, (360) 673-2800, 698 N.E. Frontage.

KELSO/LONGVIEW, WASHINGTON

Charlie's, (360) 636-5661, 1826 1st Ave. (Longview). Family dining, wide menu.

Hart C's, (360) 425-6292, 3171 Ocean Beach Hwy. (Longview). Thai and American cuisine.

The Masthead, (360) 577-7972, 1210 Ocean Beach Hwy. (Longview). Seafood, burgers, chicken.

CATHLAMET, WASHINGTON

Birnie's Retreat, (360) 795-3432, 83 Main. Seafood, steaks, Cajun food.

Ranch House Restaurant, (360) 795-8015, 3rd & Una.

SKAMOKAWA, WASHINGTON

The Duck Inn, (360) 795-3655, WA 4.

CHINOOK, WASHINGTON

Sanctuary Restaurant, (360) 777-8380, US 101. Seafood and more in turn-of-the-century church.

SEAVIEW, WASHINGTON

42nd Street Cafe, (360) 642-2323, 42nd St. and Pacific Hwy. Chicken, pot roast, seafood, steaks.

Michael's Lamplighter Inn, (360) 642-2375. Steak, seafood, big salad bar.

Shoalwater Restaurant, (360) 642-4142, WA 103 at 45th St. Regional specialties.

LONG BEACH, WASHINGTON

Chuck's Restaurant, (360) 642-2721, WA 103. Chicken-fried steak, seafood, prime rib.

Cottage Bakery & Delicatessen, (360) 642-4441, downtown Long Beach. Famous pastries and espresso.

The Lightship Restaurant & Lounge (360) 642-2311, 409 S.W. 10th St. in the Nendels Inn. Ocean-view family dining.

Long Beach Barbecue, (360) 642-3600, 604 S. Pacific. Ribs and barbecue sandwiches.

CLATSKANIE, OREGON

Northwoods Inn Restaurant, (503) 728-4311, 945 E. Columbia River Hwy.

ASTORIA, OREGON

Andrew & Steve's Restaurant, (503) 325-5762, 12th & Marine Dr. Three meals daily, homemade pies.

Cafe Uniontown, (503) 325-8708, 218 W. Marine Dr. Steaks, seafood, pasta.

Dutch Cup Restaurant, (503) 325-5286, 12 W. Marine Dr. American food with view of river.

Pig 'n Pancake, (503) 325-3144, 146 W. Bond. Breakfast anytime. Also in Seaside.

Red Lion Seafare Restaurant, (503) 325-7373, 400 Industry St. in Red Lion Inn. Seafood and steak with Columbia River view.

Ship Inn, (503) 325-0033, 2nd St. at Marine Dr. Fish and chips, other pub fare.

SEASIDE, OREGON

Dooger's Seafood Grill, (503) 738-3773, 505 Broadway. Clam chowder, steak, salads. Also in Cannon Beach.

Mazatlan, (503) 738-9678, 1455 S. Holladay. Mexican food.

The Oceanside Restaurant, (503) 738-7789, 1200 N. Marion Dr. (Gearhart). Casual gourmet dining with Pacific view.

Pudgy's, (503) 738-8330, 227 Broadway. Seafood and steaks with outdoor dining.

Weaver's Coffee Mug Cafe, (503) 738-8608, 20 N. Holladay. Breakfast and lunch.

CANNON BEACH, OREGON

Lemon Tree Inn, (503) 436-2918, 140 N. Hemlock. Breakfast and lunch.

The Loft Restaurant, (503) 436-9338, 123 S. Hemlock. Seafood, steaks, pasta.

The Whaler, (503) 436-2821, 200 N. Hemlock. Wide menu featuring seafood.

Oregon Coast at Ecola State Park near Cannon Beach, Oregon.

EPILOGUE

It took Lewis and Clark eighteen months to reach the Pacific Ocean on their outbound trip. But like any travelers eager to return home, they made much better time on the return journey, arriving in St. Louis September 23, 1806, six months to the day after leaving Fort Clatsop. A newspaper account reporting the occasion read thus: "Mssrs. Lewis and Clark arrived here about one hour ago. Three cheers were fired. They really have the appearance of Robinson Crusoes, dressed entirely in buckskins."

In the years following the expedition, many of its members went on to fame and fortune. George Shannon, the enlisted party's youngest man, became a congressman from Kentucky. John Colter returned to the West, exploring the Yellowstone Valley. York was freed by Clark, who helped get him started in a freight-hauling business. Patrick Gass, the first corps member to publish his journals, was a bit slower to establish his personal life. At age sixty, he finally married Maria Hamilton, a woman one-third his age. He died shortly before his ninety-ninth birthday, outliving his young wife by more than a decade.

As for Clark, he enjoyed a stellar post-expedition career. He was appointed Superintendent of Indian Affairs in 1807 and served in that role until his death in 1838. In 1813, he was also appointed governor of the newly established Missouri Territory and was reappointed three times, holding the office until Missouri became a state in 1821 (although he failed to win the post in the first state election). But it was in his position as Indian Superintendent that he won his greatest acclaim. "In this role, he broadened the base of goodwill the Lewis and Clark Expedition had established, and probably did more to help the Indians than any of his successors," wrote Roy E. Appleman in his National Park Service survey. "Their friend, protector, and advocate, who always tried to obtain as much justice as possible for them, he was fondly known as the 'Red-Headed Chief.'" Clark also had a happy personal life, marrying his sweetheart Julia Hancock in 1808. They had five children, naming the firstborn Meriwether Lewis Clark. Julia died in 1821, but Clark remarried Harriet Kennerly Radford, a widow with three children. Together, they went on to have two more sons.

And what of Lewis? Sadly, fate was not as kind. Despite his keen intellect and bright record of service, Lewis had difficulty establishing himself after the expedition, either professionally or personally. Things started well enough: Lewis was appointed governor of the Louisiana Territory and made plans for publication of the expedition's journals. But long given to brooding and mood swings, Lewis was not an especially adept politician. He also suffered financial problems, particularly after the U.S. War Department refused to honor drafts Lewis had signed to provide for the safe return of an Indian party that had accompanied the corps back east at Jefferson's request. Lewis was held personally responsible for the debt, and it appeared he would have to sell title to the 1,600 acres of land he was rewarded for his part in the expedition.

In the fall of 1809, Lewis set off for Washington to plead his case in person. On the night of October 9, two of his party's pack horses escaped, and Lewis dispatched his companion, Maj. James Neelly, to search for them. On October 11, Neelly found Lewis dead of two gunshot wounds. He was just thirty-five years old. To this day, no one has proven conclusively whether the captain's death was murder or suicide, but his memory is honored at a park along Tennessee's Natchez Trace. The park's centerpiece is a broken column that stands in mute testimony to Lewis's untimely death.

Actors at the Lewis and Clark Pageant, Seaside, Oregon.

But even tragedy could not blunt the expedition's impact nor dull the sense something great had been accomplished. "The expedition of Mssrs. Lewis and Clark for exploring the River Missouri and the best communication from that to the Pacific Ocean has had all the success which could have been expected," Jefferson said in his report to Congress in December 1806. "They have traced the Missouri nearly to its source, descended the Columbia to the Pacific Ocean, ascertaining with accuracy the geography of that interesting communication across our continent, learned the character of the country, of its commerce and inhabitants, and it is but justice to say that Mssrs. Lewis and Clark and their brave companions have by this arduous service deserved well of their country." Long after their deaths, the legacy left by Lewis and Clark ensured the future of America as a world power and, even more important, as a nation that ever dares to dream—and to discover.

ABOUT THE AUTHOR

Julie Fanselow was born in Illinois and grew up in Bethel Park, Pennsylvania. She earned a bachelor's degree in journalism at Ohio University.

After ten years as a reporter and editor for daily newspapers in Ohio, Idaho, and Washington state, Fanselow turned to full-time free-lance writing in 1991. A lifelong history buff, Fanselow first wrote about the West's great trails in *Traveling the Oregon Trail*, also published by Falcon. She is also the author of *Idaho Off the Beaten Path* (Globe Pequot) and has contributed to travel guidebooks from Lonely Planet, APA/Insight, and Macmillan Travel.

A member of the American Society of Journalists and Authors, Fanselow's byline has appeared in many magazines including *American Heritage, Backpacker, Sunset, Parenting, Entertainment Weekly, and Independent Business.* She is the recipient of awards from the National Association for Interpretation, the Associated Press, and the Idaho Press Club.

Fanselow enjoys traveling, hiking, camping, reading, and the arts. She lives with her family in Twin Falls, Idaho.

Julie Fanselow at Castle Butte lookout on the Lewis and Clark Trail in Idaho. Photo by Bruce Whiting.

Lewis & Clark
EVENTS 1998

Third weekend in May – *Lewis and Clark Redezvous,* St. Charles, Missouri
(314) 947-3199

June – *Lewis and Clark Festival,* Lewis and Clark State Park, Onawa, Iowa
(712) 423-2829

June 5-7 – *Lewis and Clark Days,* Washburn, North Dakota (701) 462-8535

June 25-28 – *Tenth Annual Lewis and Clark Festival,* Great Falls, Montana
(406) 761-4434

June 29-July 2 – *Lewis and Clark Trail Heritage Foundation 30th Annual Meeting,*
Great Falls, Montana (509) 783-1207

July 4 – *Grand Opening of the Lewis and Clark National Historic Trail Interpretive
Center,* Great Falls, Montana (406) 791-7717

Third weekend of July – *Lewis and Clark Festival and White Catfish Camp,*
Council Bluffs, Iowa (402) 444-4775

July – *Lewis and Clark Days Festival,* Chamberlain, South Dakota
(605) 734-6542

July 25 – *Clark's Day at Pompey's Pillar,* east of Billings, Montana
(406) 238-1540

August 1-2 – *Re-Enactment of the Council with the Missouri and Oto Indians,*
Fort Atkinson State Historic Park, Fort Calhoun, Nebraska
(402) 468-5611

get **FALCON** GUIDED

HIKING GUIDES

Hiking Alaska
Hiking Alberta
Hiking Arizona
Hiking Arizona's Cactus Country
Hiking the Beartooths
Hiking Big Bend National Park
Hiking Bob Marshall Country
Hiking California
Hiking California's Desert Parks
Hiking Carlsbad Caverns
    and Guadalupe Mtns. National Parks
Hiking Colorado
Hiking the Columbia River Gorge
Hiking Florida
Hiking Georgia
Hiking Glacier & Waterton Lakes National Parks
Hiking Grand Canyon National Park
Hiking Great Basin National Park
Hiking Hot Springs
    in the Pacific Northwest
Hiking Idaho
Hiking Maine
Hiking Michigan
Hiking Minnesota
Hiking Montana
Hiker's Guide to Nevada
Hiking New Hampshire
Hiking New Mexico
Hiking New York
Hiking North Cascades

Hiking North Carolina
Hiking Northern Arizona
Hiking Olympic National Park
Hiking Oregon
Hiking Oregon's Eagle Cap Wilderness
Hiking Oregon's Three Sisters Country
Hiking Pennsylvania
Hiking South Carolina
Hiking South Dakota's Black Hills Country
Hiking Southern New England
Hiking Tennessee
Hiking Texas
Hiking Utah
Hiking Utah's Summits
Hiking Vermont
Hiking Virginia
Hiking Washington
Hiking Wyoming
Hiking Wyoming's Wind River Range
Hiking Yellowstone National Park
Hiking Zion & Bryce Canyon National Parks
The Trail Guide to Bob Marshall Country

BEST EASY DAY HIKES

Beartooths
Canyonlands & Arches
Best Hikes on the Continental Divide
Glacier & Wateron Lakes
Glen Canyon
North Cascades
Yellowstone

FALCON®

■ *To order any of these books, check with your local bookseller*
*or call FALCON® at **1-800-582-2665**.*

Visit us on the world wide web at
www.falconguide.com

get
FALCON GUIDED

Mountain Biking Guides

Mountain Biking Arizona
Mountain Biking Colorado
Mountain Biking New Mexico
Mountain Biking New York
Mountain Biking Northern New England
Mountain Biking Southern New England
Mountain Biking Utah

Local Cycling Series

Fat Trax Bozeman
Fat Trax Colorado Springs
Mountain Biking Bend
Mountain Biking Boise
Mountain Biking Chequamegon
Mountain Biking Denver/Boulder
Mountain Biking Durango
Mountain Biking Helena
Mountain Biking Moab

FALCON®

■ *To order any of these books, check with your local bookseller*
or call FALCON ® *at **1-800-582-2665**.*

Visit us on the world wide web at
www.falconguide.com

get
FALCON GUIDED

BIRDING GUIDES

Birding Arizona
Birding Minnesota
Birder's Guide to Montana
Birding Texas
Birding Utah

FIELD GUIDES

Bitterroot: Montana State Flower
Canyon Country Wildflowers
Great Lakes Berry Book
New England Berry Book
Plants of Arizona
Rare Plants of Colorado
Rocky Mountain Berry Book
Southern Rocky Mtn. Wildflowers
Tallgrass Prairie Wildflowers
Western Tree
Wildflowers of Southwestern Utah
Willow Bark and Rosehips

FISHING GUIDES

Fishing Alaska
Fishing the Beartooths
Fishing Florida
Fishing Maine
Fishing Michigan
Fishing Montana

PADDLING GUIDES

Floater's Guide to Colorado
Paddling Montana
Paddling Oregon

HOW-TO GUIDES

Bear Aware
Leave No Trace
Mountain Lion Alert
Wilderness First Aid
Wilderness Survival

ROCK CLIMBING GUIDES

Rock Climbing Colorado
Rock Climbing Montana
Rock Climbing New Mexico
   & Texas
Rock Climbing Utah

ROCKHOUNDING GUIDES

Rockhounding Arizona
Rockhound's Guide to California
Rockhound's Guide to Colorado
Rockhounding Montana
Rockhounding Nevada
Rockhound's Guide to New Mexico
Rockhounding Texas
Rockhounding Utah
Rockhounding Wyoming

WALKING

Walking Colorado Springs
Walking Portland
Walking St. Louis

MORE GUIDEBOOKS

Backcountry Horseman's
   Guide to Washington
Camping California's
   National Forests
Exploring Canyonlands &
   Arches National Parks
Exploring Mount Helena
Recreation Guide to WA
   National Forests
Touring California & Nevada
   Hot Springs
Trail Riding Western
   Montana
Wild Country Companion
Wild Montana
Wild Utah

FALCON®

■ *To order any of these books, check with your local bookseller*
*or call FALCON ® at **1-800-582-2665**.*

Visit us on the world wide web at
www.falconguide.com

FALCON GUIDES® are available for where-to-go hiking, mountain biking, rock climbing, walking, scenic driving, fishing, rockhounding, paddling, birding, wildlife viewing, and camping. We also have FalconGuides on essential outdoor skills and subjects and field identification. The following titles are currently available, but this list grows every year. For a free catalog with a complete list of titles, call FALCON toll-free at 1-800-582-2665.

SCENIC DRIVING GUIDES

Scenic Driving Alaska and the Yukon
Scenic Driving Arizona
Scenic Driving the Beartooth Highway
Scenic Driving California
Scenic Driving Colorado
Scenic Driving Florida
Scenic Driving Georgia
Scenic Driving Hawaii
Scenic Driving Idaho
Scenic Driving Michigan
Scenic Driving Minnesota
Scenic Driving Montana
Scenic Driving New England
Scenic Driving New Mexico
Scenic Driving North Carolina
Scenic Driving Oregon
Scenic Driving the Ozarks including the
   Ouchita Mountains
Scenic Driving Texas
Scenic Driving Utah
Scenic Driving Washington
Scenic Driving Wisconsin
Scenic Driving Wyoming
Back Country Byways
National Forest Scenic Byways
National Forest Scenic Byways II

HISTORIC TRAIL GUIDES

Traveling California's Gold Rush Country
Traveler's Guide to the Lewis & Clark Trail
Traveling the Oregon Trail
Traveler's Guide to the Pony Express Trail

WILDLIFE VIEWING GUIDES

Alaska Wildlife Viewing Guide
Arizona Wildlife Viewing Guide
California Wildlife Viewing Guide
Colorado Wildlife Viewing Guide
Florida Wildlife Viewing Guide
Idaho Wildlife Viewing Guide
Indiana Wildlife Vewing Guide
Iowa Wildlife Viewing Guide
Kentucky Wildlife Viewing Guide
Massachusetts Wildlife Viewing Guide
Montana Wildlife Viewing Guide
Nebraska Wildlife Viewing Guide
Nevada Wildlife Viewing Guide
New Hampshire Wildlife Viewing Guide
New Jersey Wildlife Viewing Guide
New Mexico Wildlife Viewing Guide
New York Wildlife Viewing Guide
North Carolina Wildlife Viewing Guide
North Dakota Wildlife Viewing Guide
Ohio Wildlife Viewing Guide
Oregon Wildlife Viewing Guide
Tennessee Wildlife Viewing Guide
Texas Wildlife Viewing Guide
Utah Wildlife Viewing Guide
Vermont Wildlife Viewing Guide
Virginia Wildlife Viewing Guide
Washington Wildlife Viewing Guide
Wisconsin Wildlife Viewing Guide

■ *To order any of these books, check with your local bookseller or call FALCON* ® *at* **1-800-582-2665**.

Visit us on the world wide web at
www.falconguide.com

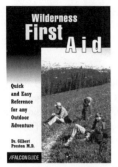

WILDERNESS FIRST AID

By Dr. Gilbert Preston M.D.

Enjoy the outdoors and face the inherent risks with confidence. By reading this easy-to-follow first-aid text, all outdoor enthusiasts can pack a little extra peace of mind on their next adventure. *Wilderness First Aid* offers expert medical advice for dealing with outdoor emergencies beyond the reach of 911. It easily fits in most backcountry first-aid kits.

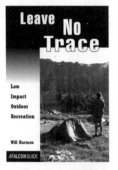

LEAVE NO TRACE

By Will Harmon

The concept of "leave no trace" seems simple, but it actually gets fairly complicated. This handy quick-reference guidebook includes all the newest information on this growing and all-important subject. This book is written to help the outdoor enthusiast make the hundreds of decisions necessary to protect the natural landscape and still have an enjoyable wilderness experience. Part of the proceeds from the sale of this book go to continue leave-no-trace education efforts. The Official Manual of American Hiking Society.

BEAR AWARE

By Bill Schneider

Hiking in bear country can be very safe if hikers follow the guidelines summarized in this small, "packable" book. Extensively reviewed by bear experts, the book contains the latest information on the intriguing science of bear-human interactions. *Bear Aware* can not only make your hike safer, but it can help you avoid the fear of bears that can take the edge off your trip.

MOUNTAIN LION ALERT

By Steve Torres

Recent mountain lion attacks have received national attention. Although infrequent, lion attacks raise concern for public safety. *Mountain Lion Alert* contains helpful advice for mountain bikers, trail runners, horse riders, pet owners, and suburban landowners on how to reduce the chances of mountain lion-human conflicts.

To order these titles or to find out more about this new series of books, call FALCON® at **1-800-582-2665.**